365 DAYS OF FREELANCE WRITING

The Practical Guide to Surviving Your First Year as a Self-Employed Writer

CARTER KILMANN

Copyright © 2021 Carter Kilmann.

All Rights Reserved. This book contains material protected under International and Federal Copyright Laws and Treaties. Any unauthorized reprint or use of this material is prohibited. No part of this book may be reproduced or transmitted in any form or by any means, electronic or mechanical, including photocopying, recording, or by any information storage and retrieval system without express written permission from the author/publisher.

Paperback ISBN: 978-1-951503-55-0
Ebook ISBN: 978-1-951503-56-7

AUTHORSUNITE
Authorsunite.com

CONTENTS

Acknowledgments v
Prologue vii

January 1
February 35
March 65
April 96
May 134
June 176
July 220
August 260
September 304
October 338
November 373
December 406

Afterword 441
Citations 443
Index 451

ACKNOWLEDGMENTS

Kaileigh Ducharme, I've always told you that we make a great team. Without you by my side, I doubt I'd have the mental and emotional fortitude to navigate self-employment. You make life more meaningful and fulfilling. I love you and thank you with all of my heart.

Dad, thank you for teaching me independence and instilling in me the drive to aspire to bigger and better things. Without those personality traits, I wouldn't have been able to pursue my calling and start my own business.

Mom, thank you for serving as a constant reminder of how fragile life can be and to live life fully while I can. Although you never had a chance to read this book, your spirit has guided me through life's rocky waters.

Max Falcon and Tracy Dye, thank you for providing invaluable feedback that helped this book become a reality.

Lastly, I want to thank my future self. You motivate me to dream bigger and push harder. That often means sacrificing my free time and living well within my means now so that you can reap the benefits later. Wherever you are at this moment, I hope my efforts paid off and that you look back on this with pride.

PROLOGUE

Who are you?

Carter Kilmann.

A self-employed freelance writer with a story.

What's your story?

In July 2016, I entered the workforce as a financial analyst in the wonderful world of corporate banking.

It took one month to realize banking wasn't for me. One month into my first big boy job, as a contributing citizen and full-time adult.

One month. That's all it took.

I wound up working in banking for three years and two weeks. I was so soured by the experience that I couldn't imagine working in another corporate job again. I quickly learned what I *don't* like and what I *don't* want to do.

But it was my first job. I wasn't ready to jump ship and hit the restart button. I worked my hindquarters off, learned a lot, and developed transferable skills that would help me down the road.

Around September 2017, I started exploring other career paths. I don't remember how I found his work, but I came across James Altucher, a zany businessman with an up-and-down career as an entrepreneur. In one of his articles, Altucher shared a list of unconventional entrepreneurial jobs — which included freelance writing.

I wondered, "What on earth is freelance writing?"

When I googled "freelance writing," I discovered Elna Cain and Jorden Roper (now Makelle), two prominent freelance writers who built successful businesses and then developed courses to help new freelancers follow in their footsteps. They opened my eyes to this career. I consumed their content and teachings like a starved wolf.

I was hooked.

Why freelance writing?

I consider myself to be a pretty observant person, but I had no clue how prevalent writing is in our day-to-day lives. When I heard the word "writer," my mind jumped to authors and columnists. I connected the occupation with books, newspapers, magazines, and publishers.

But that's only scratching the surface.

Every word you see in public or online had to be written. Whether it's a billboard, a menu, an instruction manual, a case study, an email, a website's "about" page, or the disclaimer on the back of a ticket stub. Those words didn't appear out of thin air. Someone had to write them.

I figured, why not let that someone be me?

Freelance writing was the perfect creative outlet for someone who'd been grinding in a six-by-six cubicle within a regulated bureaucratic organization.

Before we go any further, I need to admit something: **writing isn't my passion**. It wasn't the "writing" aspect of freelance writing that sold me — it was the idea of running my own business.

I'm a good writer, not a great one. Prose doesn't sing from my fingertips. I can't effortlessly write thousands and thousands of words every day. I'm far from mastering the English language.

Being relatively good at writing was good enough for me. Writing was my way out of the corporate world and into the entrepreneurial jungle.

The transition from corporate to entrepreneurship

Balancing 60-80 hour work weeks and starting a business was a brutal challenge. Learning a new industry, experimenting with different creative processes, building a portfolio, taking courses to accelerate my growth — oh, and working full-time — it all takes so much longer than you'd expect. I had to sacrifice most of my free hours.

Even though I had my eyes fixated on freelancing, I wasn't ready to ditch my stable salary yet. Not until I felt totally prepared.

I had a list of conditions that needed to be met before I'd even consider quitting my job:

1. A year of runway for financial stability and peace of mind
2. A portfolio of ten posts, including samples on my website and guest posts on others
3. A website to house my portfolio and promote my services
4. A semi-decent writing process (i.e. idea generation, outlining, etc.)
5. A steady client

Fast forward two years — it's July 2019. After dedicating many weekends to freelance writing, I'd met four out of five conditions. All I needed was a steady client. I'm on the brink of leaving my banking job.

Thanks to a timely referral, I connected with the owner of a small consumer products company. Although I had zero experience writing product descriptions and feature bullets (not to mention I'm not exactly a connoisseur of skincare products), I managed to secure a trial assignment.

I spent hours studying face washes and body creams. I compiled multiple drafts highlighting the salient details of herbal moisturizers and lip balms. I deliberated over every word as if the fate of my writing career hung in the balance. After reviewing my work countless times, I finally shared it with the company.

The owner liked it. She wanted to continue working together.

My last condition was met.

The only thing left to do was quit…

The day I quit my job

Looking back, I was so fearful and anxious about my decision. I knew I was going to do it, but there was this massive emotional buildup that grew every day (more like every hour). By this point, I had wanted to quit for months; I was actually on the cusp of quitting in April 2019, but I didn't have a client yet, so I convinced myself to postpone my departure.

So, once July rolled around and I secured my copywriting client, I was *beyond* ready. No more conditions. No more excuses. No more waffling.

When it came time to do the deed — to inform my boss I was quitting — I had to step outside and gather myself. I rehearsed what I was going to say 30 times, and that's not hyperbole. Of course, my boss's calendar was packed, so the meeting wasn't until 2:00 pm. For six hours, I had to pretend like everything was business as usual.

I was a nervous wreck. It was the single biggest decision I've ever made. Honestly, rehearsing my speech didn't really help soothe the anxiety. Nothing did. Well, except reminding myself that I was ready to quit. That kept me determined, at least.

It was like a bandage — I just needed to rip it off and be done with it.

I gathered myself and made my way back inside. With the aplomb of a triumphant gladiator entering the arena (more like the anxiety of a mouse in a lion's den), I stormed into my boss's office and took a seat. And then I had an out-of-body experience. I just watched myself fly through my big speech, touching on all the reasons I was fed up with my job.

We were short-staffed. The hours were grueling. I felt undervalued. (I didn't even mention the fact that my social life had dwindled to practically nothing — or that I barely slept anymore, at least not without experiencing spreadsheet-based nightmares.)

As I uttered my last words, I reentered my body and met my boss's stoic gaze.

He said, "Alright, no problem. I'll start the offboarding process with HR."

And that was it.

No heated discussion. No backlash. No fireworks.

Just a mundane and seemingly automated response. As if I had been unknowingly speaking to his voicemail the entire time.

It was so anticlimactic. I'm sitting there like, "Why did I make this such a big deal?"

I mean, don't get me wrong, it was a big deal. I quit a well-paying job to start mostly from scratch. But my emotions leading up to it did not match the actual "theatrics" of what played out. I expected at least some pushback, some fight to retain me. I put countless hours into that job. I sacrificed sleep, social activities, and my general well-being to outperform expectations. Instead, the departure was nonchalant and transactional, which was frustrating.

But as soon as I walked out of my office for the last time, my excitement outweighed my frustration.

It was time to begin my journey as a self-employed freelance writer.

My first five months as a freelance writer

The first few months of freelancing are empowering. Each day, I woke up with an inexplicable zeal for life. This is the "honeymoon" phase of freelance writing. Don't get me wrong, I haven't lost my enthusiasm — not at all, I still love my job. Those first few months are just different. I felt invincible. I couldn't be deterred. I'd attribute rejections and mistakes to being new or inexperienced.

Although it's impossible to pinpoint the day when this forcefield subsides, it does eventually wear off. (I'd estimate between one and three months.)

The initial stage of freelancing is also different because you get your first taste of running a business. I was decently prepared, but there's still a steep learning curve. My first "business" steps were as follows:

1. Establish an LLC
2. Open business bank accounts
3. Revise my monthly budget
4. Set S.M.A.R.T. goals
5. Figure out rates
6. Land more clients

Since these activities were vital to getting my business off the ground, I want to quickly go over them so that you're fully informed and caught up before we explore my yearlong journey.

Establishing an LLC and opening business bank accounts

These are dull but important steps when starting a business. First things first: I'm not a lawyer, and I don't want this to be misconstrued as legal advice. If you want to work without a formal business structure, be my guest. But there are several reasons why it's smart to establish a Limited Liability Company (LLC) and open business bank accounts.

First, you aren't just a writer — you're a business owner. If you want clients to take you seriously, you need to operate like a business. Officially establishing a company is about as businessy as it gets. Instead of working with some guy named Carter, my clients rely on the professional services of Kilmann Media LLC.

Second, the LLC structure helps you separate your personal finances from your business's operations. You don't want commingled funds — that'll be a headache come tax season.

With an LLC, you can open business bank accounts to help you keep track of business income and expenses (which are tax deductible). You'll have to select a bank, which is mostly a personal preference. However, pay attention to the following characteristics.

- **Interest rates**: It's not uncommon for rates to be between 0.01% and 0.10% for checking accounts. Savings accounts are usually higher, but it depends on the Fed Funds rate at the time. These accounts won't move mountains financially, but some passive income is better than nothing.
- **Fees**: Look out for annual fees or monthly maintenance fees. Many providers will waive your fees if your balance is above a certain threshold.
- **Transaction volume limits**: Some accounts limit the number of transfers you can make. This isn't a dealbreaker

necessarily, but it's important to be aware of your account's limits.
- **Bonus offers:** You should be able to find a bank that provides introductory rewards like upfront cash offers. Make sure to shop around to find the best deals.

I opened a business checking account and a business savings account. My business income flows into my checking, and my tax allocation transfers into my savings (as a freelancer, you pay quarterly estimated taxes). Since my accounts are separate from my personal finances, it's easy to monitor my cash flow.

The cost to create an LLC varies by state, but it's usually between $50 and $100. Nolo.com is a helpful website for learning more about corporate structures and other legal matters — here's a resource for forming a single-member LLC.[1]

Revising your monthly budget

Budgeting is important, whether you become an entrepreneur or not. That importance exponentially grows once you lose the luxury of stable and predictable biweekly paychecks.

If you transition to freelance writing and expect a major income dip, you need to adjust your lifestyle expenses accordingly — which means creating or updating your budget. (Funny enough, I wrote a Medium article about this that wound up doing very well; you'll read about it later on Day 70.)

You'll also have business expenses (like your website or accounting services), but 90% of your total monthly expenses will relate to general lifestyle choices. Regularly budgeting will help you stay in control and avoid financial stress. Running a business is stressful enough — don't operate blindly.

Think about budgeting another way: the better you manage your monthly expenses, the higher your chances of succeeding as a freelancer.

Setting S.M.A.R.T. goals

Goals give you meaningful direction. Otherwise, you're aimlessly grinding, and then you'll look up one day and realize you're way off track. Trust me, it happens.

A vague goal doesn't help you accomplish anything. If I said, "Be successful." What are you supposed to do with that? That's why I recommend setting S.M.A.R.T. goals.

S.M.A.R.T. stands for Specific, Measurable, Attainable, Relevant, and Time-Based. I won't bore you by digging into each of these generic words — you can google S.M.A.R.T. goals and see the pertinent definitions. But I will say this: if you want to make real progress, use number-based goals that are bound to timelines. This lets you divide your goals into smaller, more palatable pieces.

For example, let's assume you set a goal to gain 1,200 email subscribers in one year. You can break that down into 100 new emails per month — or roughly 23 every week. That means you need to devise a weekly strategy for reaching 23 new people.

Your goals are unique because your experience as a writer is unique. Still, I recommend some sort of financial goal, such as "I want to make $3,000 per month by my sixth month of freelancing." That's an arbitrary number, but setting a value lets you reverse-engineer the process.

You'll see later, but I often struggled to stay aligned to my goals, mainly because I set a bunch and then stopped monitoring my progress.

Figuring out rates

Rates aren't permanent. They can change and adapt to different situations and services. That said, you have to start somewhere. And, like most writers, I wasn't sure what to charge at first.

That was partially because there are several rate structures and multiple writing services. For instance, you might charge a different rate for editing than you would for writing a blog post — and you might charge hourly for one and a fixed rate for the other.

The three most common rate structures are hourly (e.g. $50 per hour), per word (e.g. $0.20 per word), and fixed (e.g. $200 per project). *Again, those are arbitrary figures.*

Several variables impact rates:

- Experience
- Niche (i.e. the field/topics you write about)
- Research requirements
- Company budgets
- Bylines (i.e. whether you'll get credit for the work or it's "ghostwritten")

You can reverse-engineer this process too. Let's assume you want to make $3,000 per month. At $0.10 per word, you'd need to write thirty 1,000-word articles to meet that goal. That's one post **per day**, including weekends.

From what I've noticed, charging per word is the most common approach for new writers, and any assignment below $0.10 per word is not worth your time. But you can charge more if you can position yourself as an expert in your field. High-quality samples are the best way to do this. These are examples of your work, whether they're guest posts on relevant websites or self-published articles on platforms like Medium.

From the get-go, I was determined to charge well above industry standards for an amateur writer, so I set my rate at $0.30 per word for blog posts. I was confident that my skills and work experience compensated for my lack of client history. Plus, I had several samples to prove my ability.

Landing clients when you're new

My tactical approach to immediately landing clients: **announcement posts**. As in, social media posts that announced my transition from corporate America to the freelance jungle.

In the months leading up to my banking departure, I came across similar posts that expressed frustration with the corporate grind and announced newfound startups and entrepreneurial pursuits. These announcements garnered thousands of likes and comments. I figured I could try something similar on Facebook and LinkedIn to hopefully attract writing opportunities.

Carter Kilmann
Personal Finance Writer | Financial Copywriter | LinkedIn Ghostwriter | Editor
1yr

This past Friday, I made the biggest decision of my life: leaving my comfy, secure corporate job to become a solopreneur.

My three years of banking have been an irreplaceable experience. But it wasn't the lifestyle I wanted. It wasn't meant to be my ultimate path.

In October 2017, I began moonlighting as a freelance writer – at least when my workload and schedule permitted. So this career shift is almost two years in the making. A lot of preparation went into it: working on the weekends, researching the field, studying those who've had success, and saving up to build enough runway to make it happen.

Three days later, I know I made the right call. Although this journey is just beginning, I couldn't be happier. I've always loved taking on big projects and challenging myself, and I view this as the ultimate opportunity to do so.

Even though I've been doing this off-and-on since 2017, I consider today (7/22/2019) to be the true first day of my self-employed journey. For those of you who are interested in following my progress along the way, I'll be sure to update my LinkedIn page and website – carterkilmann.com

#solopreneur #freelancewriter

And it worked.

My LinkedIn post amassed 36,000 views. More importantly, my announcements led to three new clients.

Thanks to that tactic, I established a stable income floor early on. I was stunned. I didn't expect to make more than a few hundred dollars for at least a few months. Much to my surprise (and to my wallet's delight), I actually made $1,341 in my first month of freelance writing. That was August.

By October, I cracked $2,000 and turned a profit. It wasn't much, but it was something.

That's when I realized that documenting my process could be invaluable to other writers.

Why write about your journey?

The "free" in "freelancing" can be misleading.

When I looked into freelance writing as a creative outlet and potential career, I read article after article about "how great freelancing is." Most people highlighted the benefits — like total autonomy and a flexible work schedule — while glossing over the downsides, such as constant rejection and spontaneous feelings of self-doubt. They painted a rosy picture of rainbows and butterflies.

That's not only unrealistic but also an outright lie. Anyone that's sold on that pipedream is in for a rude awakening.

So, I want to provide a resource to potential and new freelance writers that's honest, transparent, educational, and reliable. I want to pull back the curtain on the world of freelance writing and shed light on both the ups and downs.

Because let's face it: freelance writing isn't for everyone.

It's not the fix-all solution to life's problems. You might not make a livable wage right away. You'll be stressed. You'll be overwhelmed with doubt and fear. You'll learn the true definition of imposter syndrome. You'll feel the constant need to do more with finite time. It's not all bad, but it's deceiving to say it's all good.

After reading through my 365-day journey*, you'll see what it takes to write full-time and run a business. Strategy, finance, marketing, networking, client acquisition — you name it. It's a lot for one person to handle, which is why I wrote this book. I want you to be as prepared as possible to take on this challenge.

By spotlighting the day-to-day life of a freelance writer, I hope to provide insights that you can use to:

1. Determine if freelance writing is for you
2. Inspire new ideas and approaches for you to incorporate into your freelancing journey
3. Avoid mistakes that would otherwise set your business back and delay your success

Before we board my year-long rollercoaster, I want to share one last thought.

A lot of knowledge you gain in life isn't laid out for you on a silver platter. No shiny plates or linen napkins. Life makes you sift through the minutiae and pick out the relevant, valuable information that you can leverage on your journey. Take this into account when you read through my story — or any other for that matter.

I've done my best to provide a literal year's worth of value. But, I'll admit, sometimes I ramble. Sometimes I talk about my personal life — like when ants invaded my apartment or when an unprovoked duck attacked me in public. While these things aren't pertinent to freelance writing, this is a quasi-journal after all.

Now, buckle up. It's gonna be a wild ride.

*Of course, I picked a leap year. So it's actually 366 days.

Editor's note: To stay in touch, you're welcome to join the Facebook community: 365 Days of Freelance Writing. If you're having trouble finding it, feel free to email me at carter@carterkilmann.com.

JANUARY

Day 1: January 1, 2020 - 4:09 pm (Wednesday)

Happy New Year! Well, I doubt it's New Year's Day for you, so it's just me celebrating here. But you can pretend.

Anyway, we're here to observe what it's like to live as a freelancer — more specifically, a freelance writer.

A lot of successful freelancers will sell you on the idea of total independence. They'll shove their flexibility and work-life balance in your face. They'll tell tales of days spent with feet propped up on a lounge chair, laptop in hand, an icy cocktail within reach, and the gentle waves of the ocean brushing the cool sand. They'll make it seem easier than it is.

The point of this book/journal/guide isn't to sell you this dreamlike lifestyle.

However…

My feet are buried in the sand as we speak. The ocean's intermittent drumming of the shell-covered shore is soothing. So, yes, I'm living that fantasy life at the moment.

But this is pure coincidence, I swear. I'd be here regardless of my occupation. I've spent New Year's at the beach with my beautiful girlfriend (Kaileigh) and her family each of the last four years — three of which while working in banking. So this isn't new. It's not some unlocked freedom. In fact, if I were at my corporate job, I probably wouldn't be working at all.

The beauty lies in the fact that I *can* work (mostly) stress-free — wherever and whenever I please. On a whim. At the drop of a hat. (Insert some other adage about doing things freely.) I'm typing this initial page from my phone while listening to the ocean, drinking a Corona, and waiting for sunset.

So, what did my day look like? Considering the holiday and vacay setting, it was pretty laid back. Answered a couple of emails. Did a little bit of goal setting. Typed this. Nothing too crazy.

Well, actually, one of those emails was a potential lead.

If I've learned anything from freelancing, it's that every job opportunity is unique. You can't apply some template to client acquisition — not every lead is going to respond to the same sort of pitch, not every lead will have the same needs and goals, not every lead will become a client (quite the opposite).

Anyway, I'm in early discussions with the CEO of a FinTech startup. The company's platform looks promising, and the people seem experienced.

The issue with startups is they usually can't pay you what you want — at least not right away. It usually entails "free" work to an extent. And there's a high risk of never earning anything for your contributions.

So, I'm contemplating what I'm going to do. I can pursue this opportunity with the potential of earning equity in a FinTech startup (which just sounds cool, right?) — but also risk it being a worthless investment. It sounds like it'll be a hefty time commitment too. I'm still ironing out the details.

Overall, it was a relaxed day, and there's potential for excitement. Time to sip champagne while watching the sun dip over the horizon.

Day 2: January 2, 2020 - 11:52 am (Thursday)

Day number two of the new year.

I'm exhausted. It was an active morning. Went to the gym for an hour, then spent another two hours playing pickleball.

But moving on to the good stuff. I recently launched a publication on a writing platform called Medium. It's arguably the best writing platform out there because (a) it's free to write for, (b) it pays you based on viewership, and (c) it has millions of active readers/members. That's hard to beat.

Before I share the details behind my publication, let's walk through Medium.com and how the platform operates.[2]

Medium is a free platform — whether you participate as a reader or a writer. As a reader, you can pay for a subscription to unlock unlimited content; otherwise, the free version only allows you to view a handful of stories each month. As a writer, you can enroll in Medium's Partner Program (free to join), which lets you make your stories eligible to earn money.

Although the algorithm changes now and then, Medium pays you each month based on reading time by Medium members (i.e. Medium's paying subscribers). Non-members don't contribute to earnings. According to Medium's guidelines, "Each member's subscription fee is distributed proportionally to the stories that the individual member engaged with that month."[3]

I pay for Medium. So, if I only read one story this month, that story's author will split my monthly subscription fee with Medium. (Medium doesn't disclose what portion they retain.)

Just as anyone can write for Medium, anyone can start a publication — which is a collection of stories, sort of like a magazine.

Phew, okay, there's your high-level overview of Medium. Moving on...

My Medium publication, Bacon Bits, is positioned to be a go-to resource for personal finance advice.[4] I give ~extra crispy~ tips for people's hard-earned bacon. (I know, it's silly — but the idea is to have an affable brand and tone.)

I think I'm also going to experiment with giving personal finance advice that specifically targets freelancers as well. My background is in finance, so it felt like a natural transition to have personal finance be my niche. But I'm also planning to churn out posts on self-employment and freelance writing.

It's funny, these are topics I read a lot about when I was preparing to make the career-shift. The people I aspire to emulate wrote about freelancing, digital marketing, entrepreneurship, etc. Now that I'm in the fray and writing on a regular basis, I'm drawn to writing about these fields too.

My Medium content serves two purposes: (1) build a portfolio and (2) eventually generate a reliable revenue stream.

So, weekly output goals:

1. Client work
2. Bacon Bits post
3. Medium post on a non-financial topic
4. Daily 365 Days of Freelance Writing entries

The tricky element is client work. It's more variable. I've had weeks where I focus on pumping out client work every day, all day. I've also had weeks with zero client work.

Nada. Zilch. Bupkis.

During those weeks, I usually focus on "personal" work. Medium posts, tweaking my website, pitching, and so on.

With this FinTech opportunity sitting in my periphery, I might have even less personal work time going forward. But time will tell.

Day 3: January 3, 2020 - 1:37 pm (Friday)

It's been a productive day already. I had an exhilarating workout this morning (a Tabata-based weight session followed by some interval running). I was sweating like a pig...which is an expression I've never quite been able to piece together.

Do pigs sweat with an unrivaled profuseness?

Are pigs in a constant state of stress?

They seem pretty lazy to me. But what do I know? I haven't studied the intricacies of porcine perspiration.

Anyway, I'm a big advocate for health and fitness. Exercise clears the mind and provides a natural energy boost. It puts your head in a good place going into the workday. It's also a remedy for writer's block.

Speaking of writing, today's been more of a workday than a leisure-day. I updated and reviewed my December budget, had a 2020 strategy call with a client, sent that same company an invoice for December deliverables, followed up on some cold pitches, and emailed back-and-forth with the CEO of that FinTech startup.

They're looking to grow and grow quickly. They said they can't pay much since they're just getting started and haven't received their initial seed funding yet. The CEO offered $500 a month for a nondescript amount of writing (a bit of a red flag) and 0.25% equity in the company with the promise of more income and equity down the road — again, nondescript amounts.

I've never negotiated for equity or worked with a brand new startup, so this is uncharted territory for yours truly.

Could they be screwing me over? Should I push for more?

Maybe. Probably. I don't know.

He also challenged me to come up with unconventional ways to get people to write about their company and, ultimately, grow the waitlist for their financial platform. Well, I'm not some startup wizard or marketing veteran. I'm a writer. This feels a bit out of my scope (and league).

That said, I have a background as a problem solver, and I don't balk at a challenge. So, we're going to give this a try. As of this moment, we're commencing a one-month trial period, during which I'll provide blog content in return for $500.

And as I type this, I realize I need to nail down an expected work output...and a service contract that specifies this information...

Day 4: January 4, 2020 - 11:51 am (Saturday)

I could get used to working from my phone with the breeze at my back and sand between my toes.

It's rare for me to work on a Saturday, but the "365 Days of Freelancing" moniker would be misleading if I didn't at least write my daily entry.

Since I began freelancing full-time, I've maintained the standard workweek of Monday through Friday — and 9:00 to 5:00/6:00 on average (give or take an hour or so). As flexible as freelancing is, it's important to maintain some sort of structure. You won't get enough done otherwise.

That was one positive of working in the corporate world. The parameters of my work were defined. I knew, for the most part, when I'd be working. Brutal hours? Yes. Soul sucking? Big time. I wanted to drive a hammer through my desktop…frequently.

But it was predictable, and I operated within a defined box. *Literally, remember that six-by-six cubicle?*

Now, that doesn't mean I'm against taking a random midweek day off (which I've done) or working some on the weekends (done that too). It's just good practice to keep your schedule consistent.

I'm also going to spend time today compiling blog post ideas and outlines. I try to segment my content creation process into four components:

1. Brainstorming and researching
2. Outlining
3. Writing
4. Editing

I might spend one day coming up with ideas and outlining, and then I'll spend the next day writing. If I'm pressed for time, I'll spend a morning doing one step, and the afternoon/evening doing another. By breaking up this process, it simplifies one big task into four smaller ones. It's not as overwhelming and reduces the pressure of cranking out a full post at any given time.

So, today is "brainstorming" day.

Day 5: January 5, 2020 - 8:21 am (Sunday)

If you're a freelance writer or you plan to be one, get ready for these questions:

"Do you, like, make any money?"

"So, what, you're writing books or something?"

I liken it to banking or any industry that the average person either (a) knows little about or (b) relies on misconceptions to form an opinion.

I can't tell you how many times people thought I worked as a bank teller. They heard banking and that's what they assumed. "So you handle the money, right?"

Sigh...

Writing is no different. The typical person doesn't realize there's a vast grid of avenues for writing. That millions of corporations, small businesses, websites, publications, agencies, etc. all need content.

If you see words written somewhere, online or in-person, someone had to write them.

The typical person might list books, blog posts, and newspapers/magazines.

But there are also white papers, case studies, websites, advertisements, grant applications, and even instruction manuals.

Content is king. Period.

Week 1 Lessons & Takeaways

#1: Freelancing isn't stress-free, but you don't have to worry about getting to and working from an office.

#2: Every gig is different. Every client has different needs. You might be expected to come up with an editorial calendar (schedule of posts). You might have to clear ideas with an editor first. One client may pay more than another. It all depends.

#3: Medium is a powerhouse platform for writers to both (a) earn money and (b) build a portfolio. It's not world-changing money, but it's something. And every bit of something counts.

#4: Pigs sweat. Maybe due to stress (unconfirmed).

#5: It's important to give yourself a break — just like you would take a vacation from a corporate job. Without some quality you-time, you'll burn out. It's hard to relight a burnt match.

#6: Structure matters. Creativity might not be confined to a box, but that doesn't mean a schedule will stifle it. Productivity is important, and having a set schedule will boost productivity.

#7: Break up your creative process into stages, such as (1) researching/brainstorming (2) outlining, (3) writing, and (4) editing. This is less taxing and more organized.

#8: Be prepared to answer awkward questions about your job as a freelancer. Don't worry, they get easier to answer with repetition.

Day 6: January 6, 2020 - 2:06 pm (Monday)

I'm on my post-lunch walk. Back home (in Atlanta), my usual view is my apartment pool, while I walk in place on a treadmill. Today, I'm strolling in the sand along the coast's edge. I have to take advantage of my last few beach days.

It feels like my first official day "back" in business. I'm juggling emails, calls, client work, personal work, bookkeeping, taxes (tax season looms ahead), and more emails.

To keep track of everything, I've experimented with several approaches to stay on top of my to-do list.

I built a snazzy task calendar with goals/tasks for each business day. I tried pairing that with an hourly calendar for each day. I also tested the opposite approach — no calendar whatsoever. I don't recommend that strategy.

I think time management is 100% dependent on your personality. I'm organized, but I'm not anal. I like order, but I'm not going to panic at the sight of having 10 tabs open on my computer. I can feel some of you shuddering from here.

For me, I like a basic task list:

Monday - 1/6/2020

- X
- Y
- Z

I've found this to be the best setup for me. It's not too time-consuming to create, it's simple, and I still get that sweet little drop of dopamine when I check off a task.

I also don't like being handcuffed to a schedule. When I worked in banking, I jumped between tasks at random to survive. I think this habit carried over into my business because I tend to switch between writing tasks too.

It may not be the most efficient approach, but I can't help but be me.

6:17 pm

I've decided to pursue this FinTech opportunity. At first, my skepticism grew with each interaction. A wimpy 0.25% equity and $500 for running point on a startup's content strategy just didn't sound enticing enough.

But we had a call today regarding expectations and responsibilities. I asserted that 0.25% of equity would not cut it for what I would provide in exchange. The CEO was more than understanding and adamant about his willingness to bring me in if I can prove value.

Now, this still means I'll work a lot for a little for the time being, but the trial period benefits me as well. If it's not worth the effort, I can move on and learn from the experience.

So long as I do my job, he'll get to allocate his time elsewhere. As a result, he'll grow accustomed to not stressing about content. That alone increases my value.

Day 7: January 7, 2020 - 8:20 pm (Tuesday)

Money is an awkward subject.

That awkwardness amplifies when setting or raising rates. It's this weird conundrum. On one side, I want to get paid for my hard work, and I want to be paid well. But, on the other side, there's a tendency to feel like I'm overcharging or overselling my worth.

From what I've heard from other freelancers, this is a common dilemma.

You might be wondering why this is the subject of the day. Well, don't you worry — I'm going to tell you.

But here's a little context around rates first.

There are several rate structures in the freelance writing world:

1. Per word — such as 40 cents per word
2. Fixed — such as $200 for a blog post or $500 for a case study
3. Hourly — such as $50 an hour

Freelancers can also charge ancillary fees like retainers, research fees, editing fees, etc.

I had a quick strategy call with one of my clients (a digital marketing agency) last week. Let's refer to this client as "Client A." For this particular client, I charge $0.30 per word for ghost-written blog posts. As an agency, Client A has multiple clients (which, ultimately, are the businesses I'm writing for).

One of their clients wants to change their content approach, requesting that blog posts be much shorter and from the viewpoint of the company's CEO. Going forward, each blog post will be half the length — so my income halves too.

At first glance, that might not seem like a huge issue. I mean, it's a one-for-one decline, right? Less pay, but less work.

Not exactly.

The problem is my upfront work loses value. Idea generation, research, outlining, etc. Regardless of post length, I have to perform these tasks. A writer's rate should capture this work. It might be "revenue per word," but that payment covers everything from the first idea to the final edit — not just the written words.

This is the risk you take when you charge per word. If a client ever alters their content strategy to have shorter posts, your income will take a hit.

That's why I recommend using a fixed rate. Your initial reaction might be, "Well, wait a second. What if a client goes the other way and wants long-form content?"

A reasonable question. In that case, you let them know your rate was based on the word count/length of the existing strategy and that you'll have to adjust your new rate accordingly.

Getting back to the situation with my client, I had a somewhat awkward conversation about raising rates. In case you're curious, here's how I phrased it:

"I was running the numbers for the content strategy we discussed on Friday. Considering that we're shortening the posts (which I know is the client's doing), I'm proposing a higher rate of 40 cents per word. I'm losing out on the time I spend on the upfront research/idea generation - which takes the same amount of time regardless of post length.

Happy to talk it over if that's not clear!"

My client was receptive to the idea, and we landed on a fixed rate for blog posts. It doesn't recover the entire hit from the word count reduction, but I'm no longer tied to a word count, which is a plus in my opinion.

Day 8: January 8, 2020 - 3:44 pm (Wednesday)

One downside to having ultimate, unrivaled flexibility: you get the short end of the stick when it comes to running errands or doing chores.

It's a workday for me, Kaileigh, and her parents. But lunch must be made, laundry must be done. Guess who controls their schedule? This guy. Guess who's sitting by the communal laundry machines waiting to switch loads? This guy.

I'm a team player, ya know?

On to business: guest posts are instrumental in promoting your brand, building your portfolio, and establishing yourself as a subject matter expert.

Plenty of sites — big and small — accept guest posts. Larger sites have the benefit of bigger audiences, while smaller sites are usually more niche and targeted.

Today, I'm scouting some possible guest post sites for this FinTech startup. But here's the problem: when you have the intention to promote a company/product/service, you're now contributing a sponsored post. Sites aren't as warm in their welcome for sponsored posts.

Why? Because they're salesy, like advertisements. Readers of genuine content aren't guaranteed to appreciate a sales pitch in the form of a blog post.

When I'm trying to land guest posts for myself, it's not an issue. I'm not trying to sell anything.

In this case, I'm faced with the challenge of selling this startup's platform without being salesy.

Wish me luck.

Day 9: January 9, 2020 - 11:31 am (Thursday)

If you don't have a productivity playlist, find one.

There will be times when you'll need to buckle down and knock out assignments. There will be times when noisy neighbors, lawn care workers, and emergency vehicles will synchronize in a cacophony of sounds that will plague your ears and disrupt your concentration.

For whatever reason, I can't listen to music while writing. I don't know if it's lyrics, song changes, or something else, but it's harder for me to focus.

I was fortunate to come across a playlist on Spotify titled Thunder & Rain Sounds, which I think is intended to help people sleep rather than be productive, but whatever. It helps me not only block out external distractions but also find my writing stride.

For whatever reason, I'm in the zone when I listen to the rumblings of thunder and the soft patter of rain. *Plus, it helps when there's a leaf blower whining outside your window.*

Day 10: January 10, 2020 - 2:15 pm (Friday)

Working for a startup is all about perspective.

If your glass is half-full, you get the unparalleled experience of managing a wide range of responsibilities and trying all sorts of new tactics. For instance, I've been tasked with running an ad campaign on Reddit. This is new to me.

If your glass is half-empty, you have to field spontaneous and disassociated tasks that may or may not be relevant to your services or areas of expertise. Regardless, it's your job to figure it out.

In reality, it's a mix of full emptiness.

Studying Reddit marketing strategies might not sound like too tall of a task, but, alas, it's starting to tower over me.

First off, I'm not very familiar with Reddit. I've read threads before, but my presence on the platform would be best described as...infrequent. Rare, even.

Yep, rare would be more accurate.

On top of that, it's a different ballgame when you're approaching it as a business trying to advertise. There are different levels of accounts (according to the FinTech CEO), different types of ads with varying costs, and you have to be masterful with your posts and responses because the folks on Reddit will tear you to shreds.

I might have bitten off more than I can chew.

Day 11: January 11, 2020 - 9:41 am (Saturday)

Sometimes...you just don't know what to write.

You'll have days when your creativity machine struggles to get the gears moving.

Words...just...don't come.

But that's okay, those days are inevitable.

You can repurpose your day and focus on less writing-intensive work, such as reading, pitching, budgeting, goal setting, and topic research. This can even jumpstart your creativity.

Or, if you're ahead of schedule, you can even take the day off.

I'll shut my workday down on a Wednesday and have a me-day. Sometimes it's just not clicking, and there's nothing wrong with taking a day off to recharge.

That's the beauty of being your own boss.

Day 12: January 12, 2020 - 4:21 am (Sunday)

Sometimes I have random ideas in the middle of the night, and I have to pull myself from bed to write them down.

On more than one occasion, I've managed to convince my semi-conscious self that I would remember my ideas the next morning.

Nope, empty slate upon waking up.

Keeping a pen and notepad by your bed (or even just your phone) is helpful.

1:57 pm

I've only dabbled with writing fiction (wrote like 250 words about a man in a room once — sounds super thrilling, right?), but, for whatever reason, my late-night ideas are usually novel premises.

4:09 pm

Some old grumpy guy just got fussy with me at the airport (called me "Hoss"). I feel that it's good practice to not be an angry human being.

But the gatekeeper checking tickets permeates cheerfulness, compensating for ole grumpy Gus. We need more people like him in this world.

5:16 pm

I think I've made this clear by now, but freelancing offers unrivaled flexibility. Today, I got the opportunity to flex my flexibility muscles.

That sounds weird, ignore that.

My flight was offering a $500 gift card to anyone willing to take a later flight. Delta just can't help itself, always overbooking. I faced the same decision on my flight to Florida two weeks ago, but I elected not to take the free digital dough. I was ready to be on the beach.

Now, I don't care too much about my arrival time in Atlanta. I can take tomorrow off — if I so desire.

At the very last minute, I took the gift card and forfeited my seat. My new flight isn't for another two hours, so I'm enjoying an overpriced Bud Light.

Screw it, I deserve it.

Week 2 Lessons & Takeaways

#1: Keep some form of a task list so that you stay on track. It doesn't have to be complicated or flashy. Mine sure isn't.

#2: Money is an awkward subject, but be firm with your rates. Don't be afraid to have a difficult conversation to ensure you receive fair pay.

#3: Productivity playlists are a must. Find yours.

#4: There's nothing wrong with taking a day to recharge. You can't always force creativity.

#5: Keep your phone or a notepad by your bed. You never know what time inspiration will strike. Be prepared.

Day 13: January 13, 2020 - 4:10 pm (Monday)

Alright, now it's officially official. I'm back in the office (my living room).

Aside from my random life ponderings and tidbits of freelance advice, I also want this guide to capture the emotional journey of working for yourself.

Maybe it'd be a little too descriptive to start my entries with my current emotion, maybe that'd be useful. Eh, screw it, let's try it.

Today, I am cheerful.

I think that saint of a man running the show at my flight's gate rubbed off on me. Or my vacation did wonders to reset my system.

Will it persist? I hope so. But self-employed or not, emotions can swing. I'm not impervious to human nature. I'm as fallible as the next guy.

What did my Monday look like? I worked out and thoroughly cleaned my apartment in between a few phone calls. I thought it'd be good to ease back into work, so I made sure my writing environment was spotless.

After all that, I got back to writing. It's about time for me to publish another post on my Medium publication (Bacon Bits). I've had 1,200 or so views in the last 30 days, so I want to ride that momentum while I can.

Day 14: January 14, 2020 - 3:42 pm (Tuesday)

Today, I am tired.

I stayed up watching LSU whoop Clemson, so my late-night dose of football led to a less productive Tuesday.

You know that Snickers slogan? "You're not you when you're hungry."

Well, I'm not me when I'm tired.

I've also been on a weird eating schedule these last two days. Breakfast around noon and lunch around 2:30/3:00 pm.

Since I control my schedule, it's easy for other non-writing responsibilities to slip past me if I'm too focused on my business. That includes basic necessities like — ya know — eating.

Oh, on another note, I highly recommend post-lunch walks. Great for avoiding that sluggish mid-day feeling, while also clearing your head.

9:28 pm

Networking is like gardening. You plant seeds with the hope of growth.

Business relationships can take a lot of time before they become fruitful — at least monetarily. The more seeds you spread, and the more you tend to them, the higher the chance of a successful harvest.

Day 15: January 15, 2020 - 3:35 pm (Wednesday)

Today, I'm a little less tired.

Last night, I had a great conversation with a friend of mine, Brandon Mackie, who's a financial advisor here in Atlanta. As you might piece together, my talk with him spurred my networking-gardening analogy.

He's an amazing human being and an invaluable resource for me — considering his wealth of financial knowledge. During our call, he gave me an in-depth analysis of his approach to advising clients. This was invaluable insight, as I now have several ideas to write about. You can't put a price on relationships like that.

It's so important to connect with industry experts. Cultivating relationships across your niche can lead to countless opportunities.

Day 16: January 16, 2020 - 2:27 pm (Thursday)

Today, I'm not tired (woohoo)! I'm pretty neutral, to be honest.

What's your Thursday look like, Carter? Ah, I'm glad you asked, friend.

It's been one of those days where I'm working but I don't feel like I'm accomplishing anything. I tried to come up with unconventional ways to get this FinTech company's name out there. That's led to a lot of dancing around and running in mental circles.

As the name states, you'd assume being a freelance writer is all about writing. Not quite. Aside from all the administrative tasks required of a business owner, writing demands plenty of non-writing creativity (like coming up with fresh perspectives, post ideas, etc.).

You'll have days where you don't feel like you're accomplishing a lot, yet you're working hard. Like today, for me.

To combat this, I shifted gears and focused on more clear cut tasks. I'm still writing and editing, but what I need to do is more defined. I'm editing a client's website copy.

Since it's copywriting, it still requires a level of creativity. But the base content is there already, so it's not as strenuous.

Day 17: January 17, 2020 - 6:46 am (Friday)

Today, I am in rough shape. Well, my eye is.

I woke up with a significantly swollen right eye. I knew something was off when I couldn't open it...

What a start to the day.

But hey, I'm watching a golden retriever pup this morning. So things are looking up. *See what I did there?*

11:49 am

Oh, no. Oh, no. I'm on hold with poison control. No no no no no.

I picked up an eye drops prescription this morning. The bottle was on the counter (which is pretty high), but it was no match for a determined golden retriever puppy. She managed to jump up and snag it without me noticing, then proceeded to chew it open and drink it.

Panic.

11:53 am

Well, thankfully that was an overreaction. Eye medicine is for eyes. Eyes are sensitive. Sensitive things require low doses of antibiotics. The dog will be totally fine.

I'm furious with her but she's so freaking adorable.

It's been a day.

11:59 am

Prescription refills are $105…

…or 265 words at $0.30 per word…

…*ugh*.

Day 18: January 18, 2020 - 4:50 pm (Saturday)

Today, my eye is annoying the bananas out of me.

I know that doesn't make sense. I'm grumpy, leave me be.

In positive news, I had a pitch accepted to a big credit card website (The Points Guy). That's always a good feeling.

I generally don't work too much on the weekends, but I have a client that asked for some editing work by tomorrow.

Editing is a solid ancillary service by the way.

Day 19: January 19, 2020 - 8:11 pm (Sunday)

My editing client has been so pleased with my work that she not only asserted I should be paid more, she'll also set me up with additional clients as she uncovers opportunities.

Lesson of the day: It's important to always deliver great work. Exceed expectations. Meet deadlines.

You never know what kind of opportunities will open up if you do.

Week 3 Lessons & Takeaways

#1: A clean, organized environment can boost your mood and productivity.

#2: Since you control your schedule, sometimes it'll get away from you. That's okay.

#3: Build your business network. Relationships are integral to success.

#4: Some days, you just won't feel like you're getting anything done. That's okay.

#5: Puppies will find your antibiotics and consume them if you don't take extra precautions to protect them. Also, pharmaceuticals are way overpriced.

#6: Editing is a solid secondary service to copywriting.

#7: Exceeding expectations will unlock additional opportunities.

Day 20: January 20, 2020 - 2:33 pm (Monday)

Today, I'm pretty cheerful again.

I've never really tracked my day-to-day life experiences. Since this is like a semi-diary, it's unearthing insights I wouldn't have realized otherwise.

Dear Diary, are Mondays my cheeriest day of the week?

That's a wild thought. I used to dread Mondays.

I guess that's a pretty blatant sign that I was in the wrong profession. I don't miss my banking days at all.

Today's a big writing/editing day. Lots of post ideas and assignments to crank out.

I know I've mentioned this before, but it's worth noting again: segment your creative process. Even if you have multiple posts in your pipeline. Work on one, let the creative juices flow, and when you're plateauing a bit, switch gears to another post.

It's hard to come up with an idea, research it, outline a post, write it, and edit it all in one sitting. That's a taxing mental exercise.

Day 21: January 21, 2020 - 3:40 pm (Tuesday)

Today, I'm in a pretty decent mood.

I took a longer lunch break than I probably needed to. I'm rewatching The Walking Dead (I got through seven or so seasons back in its prime but never finished), so I'm kinda hooked on it right now.

Anyway, I'm human. I couldn't pull myself from watching it. No shame in taking a longer break now and then.

While we're somewhat on the topic of productivity, one of the biggest reasons I chose freelancing in lieu of corporate life is the ability to step away and decompress. During my stint in banking, my free time was nonexistent. Vacations were just work-deferrals. Work didn't go away. It kept coming and coming, piling on top of itself.

It was suffocating.

I experienced burnout. For that reason, I run my business with a balanced approach. I don't work late into the evenings (unless I need to, but that hasn't happened much). I don't stress out about client work and tasks — most of the time.

And I get it, there are good and bad consequences to that. The good: I have work-life balance. The bad: my business will take longer to grow. And that's okay.

There's a direct correlation between work ethic and work results. The more work you put in, the more results you'll see. But at some point along that curve, there's a sharp cliff representing burnout from working too hard.

Day 22: January 22, 2020 - 8:28 pm (Wednesday)

Today, I am spent.

I had a three-hour lunch with a couple of friends. They're business connections, but they're friends nonetheless. Great guys. But that's a long time for me to be engaged, especially when I work in solitude most of the time.

I'm an introvert at heart. To clarify though, I don't think you're either an introvert or an extrovert. I think people can share the qualities of both. I know how to be outgoing, social, personable, and so on.

I think you can gauge which side you trend toward by answering the following: does socializing energize or drain you?

For me, it depletes my energy. That doesn't mean I don't like being around people — I'm not a misanthrope. It's just tiring for extended amounts of time.

But it's worth mentioning with respect to freelance writing because your personality type will determine your ideal work environment. If you're an introvert like me, the comfort and quiet of your home will do just fine — with the occasional relocation to a coffee shop or wherever. We introverts need a little human presence too.

If you're an extrovert, you might need to find a co-working space or a fellow freelancer.

Day 23: January 23, 2020 - 3:05 pm (Thursday)

Today is a big editing day, which is a nice change of pace. It sounds so nerdy to say, but I like editing. Making sentences flow, formatting for emphasis, touching up language to make it more natural.

Yep, I'm a nerd.

Day 24: January 24, 2020 - 9:10 am (Friday)

While a personal website is an excellent place to house your portfolio, another option is ClearVoice — a content marketing platform.[5] Based on your portfolio (and portfolio tags), ClearVoice will send opportunities to you. You can choose to apply to these assignments or ignore them. (In exchange, ClearVoice keeps 25% of your writing fee.)

Why am I mentioning this today? Well, I realized I missed a major opportunity to land a big-named client in my niche.

Back in November, a member of the ClearVoice team reached out to me about a large-scale project for their biggest client. The pay was okay ($0.125 per word), but a third of my usual rate (~$0.30). Regardless, I should've looked more into the client, who owns a large portfolio of digital companies. Some of which are big brands in my personal finance niche.

In short, I should have taken the gig anyway. The lesson of the day is to do your research. *Sigh.*

Day 25: January 25, 2020 - 10:28 am (Saturday)

Back when I worked in banking, the days blurred together. Even so, I managed to keep track of what day it was. (I guess I constantly counted down to the weekend, which was a big red flag.)

I don't operate within a strict, regimented schedule anymore but it's still rare for me to forget the day of the week. Writing deadlines keep me oriented to the calendar, I suppose.

Day 26: January 26, 2020 - 5:16 pm (Sunday)

As a freelancer, you have to juggle a variety of projects. I imagine my client list will expand as my career unfolds, but, as of right now, I work regularly with three or four companies. Each of these companies requires vastly different services.

I've written product descriptions and feature bullets. I've ghost-written for corporate blogs. I've compiled technical whitepapers. I've contributed to digital publications. I've provided editing services. The list goes on.

Every project has a different scope, rate, deadline, and revision process.

In short, it's a lot to learn and adjust to.

Week 4 Lessons & Takeaways

#1: Mondays aren't so bad.

#2: Working hard is critical to success, but burnout has a long recovery time. I needed a balanced work approach during my transition to full-time self-employment. Maybe you will too.

#3: Think about how your personality type (introvert or extrovert) will impact your work environment. You may need to relocate to a coffee shop or co-working space if you need more social contact.

#4: Editing is a nice change of pace, and I'm a nerd for enjoying it. I accept that.

#5: Sometimes the brand name makes up for a less than stellar paycheck. Do your research and know who (and how big) a potential client is.

Day 27: January 27, 2020 - 7:44 am (Monday)

There are a ton of writing job newsletters out there. They provide curated lists of open gigs and calls for submissions. Here's an example from the Freedom With Writing newsletter:

> **Tom's Guide** covers all things consumer tech including smartphones, cameras, wearables, video games, TVs, and drones. They are looking for 2 to 3 freelancers to cover the EV space (news, hubs, and features). They encourage women and POC to apply. They pay "$50 for quick news hits to $400+ for reviews and other major features." For details, refer to their news editor's Tweet. To learn more about them, refer to this page.

The editor's tweet states "DM me for email. Include cover, resume & clips." The request for a DM is a little unorthodox (usually they just include an email address); otherwise, the request for a cover letter, resume, and clips (writing samples) vary. Some requests for proposals want all three, others just want a couple of previously published samples.

I'd estimate about 75% of writing newsletter gigs are irrelevant (just because they're about other niches), but that 25% is invaluable. These types of newsletters provide easy leads — no digging needed. But the obvious trade-off is you'll be competing with other newsletter subscribers.

Here are a few I subscriber to:

- Write Jobs Plus+ (one-time $30 fee)*[6]
- Freelance Writing (free)[7]
- Freedom With Writing (free)[8]

I highly recommend signing up for Write Jobs, it paid for itself (and then some) within a week. It informed me of a blog opportunity with one of the biggest names in my niche — to the tune of $350 for about 700 words.

Edit: Write Jobs moved to Patreon and a monthly subscription payment model ($3 per month). Their website still has free listings though.

Day 28: January 28, 2020 - 3:24 pm (Tuesday)

I found an awesome writing tool for overcoming writer's block or jumpstarting your creativity: Squibler.[9]

On this platform, if you stop writing, you lose all your progress. It's a thrilling (and risky) twist. But it forces you to pour out your thoughts, keeps you writing, and eliminates the threat of distractions.

If you stop writing for five seconds, poof. Gone.

But it's not some endless torture device, you can set time limits or word counts (default is five minutes). Once you hit your goal, you can stop without the risk of losing everything.

It's also not ideal for anything research-based, for obvious reasons. Still, I recommend giving it a try. If anything, it's a fun challenge.

Day 29: January 29, 2020 - 8:56 am (Wednesday)

Another tip of the cap to networking and maintaining connections. You plant seeds, they grow (without you even knowing), and you get a luscious plant (opportunity).

That metaphor is here to stay, get used to it.

Now, I might be jumping the gun here, but I connected with another freelance writer last year. Exchanged a few emails, nothing too extensive. But he reached out last night to see if I was interested in some client work that he didn't have the capacity for. I don't know if it's a good fit yet, but it's an opportunity nonetheless.

This is how a business grows!

In my writing world, I'm juggling a few things right now: client work, sporadic assignments from this FinTech startup, one-off guest posts on bigger sites, Bacon Bits posts, and Medium posts related to freelancing.

Day 30: January 30, 2020 - 7:12 am (Thursday)

You know what I really don't miss? That dreadful feeling of having to pull yourself up out of bed in the morning to go to work.

I HATED that sensation of reluctance. I mean, *ding ding ding*, a big red flag that I wasn't doing something I enjoyed.

Nowadays, I wake up content. Cool, calm, and collected. They call me cucumber Carter, I'm so cool.

I'm...I'm sorry...

When I first started freelancing, I woke up excited. Not to say I'm not excited about what I do anymore — I'm thrilled to be running my own business — but the proverbial honeymoon phase wears off at some point. My self-employed status sank in; I'm used to it.

But waking up satisfied is so much nicer than waking up wishing for Friday.

4:53 pm

How did "fiddlesticks" become a substitute for "nonsense"? Why are fiddlesticks nonsensical?

Day 31: January 31, 2020 - 9:24 am (Friday)

We did it. We made it through a month of my babbling.

Maybe you're inspired to start down this path too. Maybe I've scared you away altogether. Maybe you're still unsure.

Regardless, I'm glad you're here, and I hope you're enjoying my quasi-diary entries.

JANUARY STATS

To give you more quantitative insight into the world of freelance writing, I'm providing a statistical overview of each month in 2020.

Since this is the first month, I'll define each category. I'm calculating **income** based on work delivered (from an accounting standpoint, income should be tied to payments received, not work delivered, but this is just for illustrative purposes).

For confidentiality, I've labeled each of my **clients** with letters.

Blog posts represent the number of posts I deliver/publish. Note: this doesn't consider incomplete drafts or unaccepted pitches. I've separated paid posts from unpaid posts. "Unpaid" essentially means "not guaranteed" because Medium posts can make money — but not always.

I've also separated **copywriting assignments** from blog posts. As of right now, Client C (the FinTech startup) is the only client I provide copywriting services for.

Lastly, I've laid out **follower** statistics for Medium and LinkedIn (the two platforms I focus on).

In case you're curious, I've categorized my clients below:

- Client A — Digital marketing agency
- Client B — Digital marketing agency
- Client C — FinTech startup
- Client D — Digital publication

365 Days of Freelancing - Monthly Stats	Jan
Income	
Client A	960
Client B	329
Client C	500
Client D	350
Medium	32
Total Income	**$2,171**
Growth (%)	-
Blog Posts (Paid)	
Client A	6
Client B	3
Client C	1
Client D	1
Total Paid Posts	**11**
Blog Posts (Unpaid)	
Medium	1
Bacon Bits	1
Total Unpaid Posts	**2**
Total Blog Posts	**13**
Copywriting Assignments	
Client A	-
Client B	-
Client C	5
Client D	-
Total Copywriting Asgns.	**5**
Total Assignments	**18**
Medium	
Views	1,151
Reads	439
Existing Followers	54
New Followers	9
Total Followers	**63**
LinkedIn	
Existing Followers	458
New Followers	7
Total Followers	**465**

Highlights

- As the first month, January serves as a benchmark. It sets a status-quo, so to speak. $2,171 isn't much, but it's a stable floor.
- Since I started writing full-time, I've averaged about two Medium posts per month, so January was on par. Last October (zero posts) and December (five posts) were outliers, but they offset each other.
- Client B receives my editing services, but it seems simpler to just include it under "blog posts."

FEBRUARY

Day 32: February 1, 2020 - 10:45 am (Saturday)

I love coffee. It's integral to my operation. Should I start counting the number of cups I have each month? That seems like an important freelancer stat.

Day 33: February 2, 2020 - 10:12 am (Sunday)

Happy Super Bowl Sunday! Oh, and happy anniversary to me and Kaileigh — my favorite person on this planet. I won't overload you with sappy cliches, but she's the best thing that's ever happened to me, hands down. Four years of unrivaled happiness.

In writing news, I decided to reach back out to ClearVoice (on Wednesday) and see if they still need content help. Turns out they do, so I've got a couple of assignments due tomorrow. I don't get the Sunday Scaries anymore (one of the magical things about self-employment), but I'm feeling the pressure a little bit today.

On top of these assignments, the FinTech startup (Client C) wants a higher volume of content. But there's a circular problem: I'm not going to push my business aside unless he's willing to pay me or document my equity share, which would also need to be a reasonable percentage.

9:01 pm

Every now and then, when you least expect it, doubt will overwhelm you. You'll experience full-blown imposter syndrome. You'll feel lost and question everything you're doing.

It's a common phenomenon that's, well, not very fun.

Around halftime of the Super Bowl (great timing, right?), I started having one of these moments. Oh, and by moments, I mean it's been going on for the last hour.

I was reading a post in a Facebook group for writers that asked the following question:

"Has anyone hit the $5,000 a month mark?"

A normal question. Especially for aspiring writers who want to know if writing can provide enough income to live.

Now, to shed some light on my perspective, I've gotten close to $5,000. I hit the $4,500 mark in November. A figure I was and am still proud of.

But the comments on this post just got to me. Tons of "yeps" and "yups" that felt so...so...nonchalant. They might as well have said, "Uhhh yeah, duh — you haven't?" Realistically, this group is full of giving, friendly people, so I doubt anyone intended to sound condescending.

And then there were a few kind and sage writers willing to give detailed analyses of how to offer more value and charge more. And then there were a few people who shared staggering monthly cash inflows.

"$10,000"

"$20,000"

Those numbers should be encouraging. They're flashy figures that puff out their zeros and state, "I'm achievable."

But, for whatever reason, I got discouraged that I wasn't there. My guard was down, my emotions invaded while my logic was sleeping.

Oh, and a flurry of emails from the FinTech CEO hit my inbox at the same time. Which added a layer of frustration to the discouragement.

You will have days when you find yourself going down the rabbit hole of doubt. It's a helpless feeling. When it happens, raise the alarm and wake your logic soldiers up. Remember it's a process. Reassess your goals and make sure you're going in the right direction.

It happens, you get back up, you regroup, and you go after it again.

I'm speaking to myself as much as I'm speaking to you, my dear reader.

Week 5 Lessons & Takeaways

#1: There are plenty of cheap (or even free) freelance writing newsletters out there. You're missing out if you don't subscribe.

#2: Give Squibler a try if you want to jumpstart your writing brain.

#3: Networking. Networking. Networking. Make connections, cultivate relationships, repeat. It's not necessarily a short-term investment, but it'll pay off at some point.

#4: If you dread waking up every workday, chances are you're not doing what you want to do.

#5: The honeymoon phase of entrepreneurship wears off eventually.

#6: Hey, we made it through a month of freelancing!

#7: Coffee is the magical nectar of the productivity gods.

#8: You might not have a traditional boss, per se, but you still have deadlines. It's best not to get in the habit of turning work in at the last moment. It's better than missing the deadline, but it doesn't leave the best impression.

#9: Imposter syndrome will find you. Doubt will sneak past your defenses. Your ambition will waver some, maybe a lot. But you must regain control of the wheel and refocus your sights on the road ahead.

Day 34: February 3, 2020 - 8:57 am (Monday)

I woke up at 4:20 am ready. To. Go.

Alright, maybe I was forced awake by a zombie apocalypse dream. All that Walking Dead I've been watching must've slipped into my subconscious. Alas, I still got to work when I awoke.

Silver linings of doubt: the resurgence is even more powerful. Once you stand back up, you'll be even more driven than before.

I'm not about to start waking up at 4 am every day — no, thank you. But you better believe I'm attacking each day.

Day 35: February 4, 2020 - 6:48 am (Tuesday)

Sometimes, you need to part ways with certain clients.

My trial period with the FinTech startup concluded this past weekend. It just never felt like the best fit, to be honest. They wanted a slew of content — and weren't willing to pay their fair share for it.

That's a huge red flag, but I was aware of it.

So, last night, I decided to email the CEO to get the ball rolling on discussing future payment terms. Here's what I said:

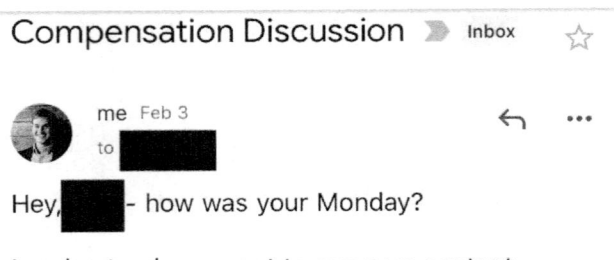

Compensation Discussion → Inbox ☆

me Feb 3
to ▇

Hey, ▇ - how was your Monday?

I understand you want to ramp up content output. You want to drive relevant traffic to the ▇ site and grow your wait list. Totally get it.

The right content and copywriting can do that.

I know we didn't get time today to discuss how we're going to structure compensation, so I wanted to get your initial thoughts before it slips through the cracks. What's your budget for content/copy? What are you willing to spend in exchange?

My usual process is to provide a bundle of services. Examples:

(1) a set number of blog posts
(2) running # email marketing campaigns
(3) writing website copy for #pages

And so on...

I think structuring pricing around this would be more efficient and incentivizing.

What do you think? Happy to talk further, I can send over how I usually price this work.

And his response:

> **Feb 3**
> to me
>
> Hey Carter,
>
> Sorry been flat out - will give you a call tomorrow.
>
> Quick thoughts - I think we need a content strategy that is more dynamic, higher volume and real time. A voice on Twitter, Reddit, rapid development of copy and then sharing it across multiple channels in part and full. A true social media strategy not just a few blogs now and again.
>
> I don't consider the $500 for the last month good value to be honest and won't do that again.
>
> Not sure if your aspiration is as a writer or a social media strategist - if its the second we can talk if its the first I don't see the need. I can churn out blogs posts myself at a far higher rate.
>
> Lets chat tomorrow

Now, don't get me wrong, I didn't like reading his response, but I understand what he's saying. I wasn't solving his problems or fulfilling his business's needs. His business has **a lot** of content, copy, and social media needs — and he'll need a couple of full-time employees to handle those if he wants it done right (in my opinion).

Over the trial period (a month), I completed nine writing assignments (blog posts and copywriting projects), had six unfinished drafts (I was told, verbatim, to "prioritize everything"), and ran their Reddit account.

From my point of view, I was hella undercharging. He didn't think he was getting value for his $500, and I didn't think I was getting value for my work. A flashy sign that this wasn't meant to be.

It was a worthwhile experience, I learned what not to do and what kind of writing arrangement I don't like. Maybe the startup dynamic — all over the place all the time — isn't for me.

I hope he figures it out because I think his company has potential.

Day 36: February 5, 2020 - 9:26 am (Wednesday)

The communal coffee machine in my apartment's leasing office…

…is…*broken*.

gasp

11:26 am

Coffee secured. Crisis averted. Thankfully, Dunkin Donuts is within walking distance.

Day 37: February 6, 2020 - 8:41 am (Thursday)

My network seeds are starting to sprout.

I've gotten two inbound leads via recommendations — a financial advisory firm and a consulting company. I have introductory calls with them to make sure they're good fits, but it's reassuring to be in this position.

Day 38: February 7, 2020 - 9:03 am (Friday)

One expensive downside to freelancing: health insurance rates.

I turn 26 in about a month, and then it's sayonara to my dad's insurance plan — which I've been fortunate to be on. It's not like I've been getting a free ride, I pay my dad every month. But his plan has great coverage at an affordable rate, so I'm going to ride it out until the last possible day (no shame).

Unfortunately, health insurance on the open marketplace is much more expensive. Like anywhere from three to five times as expensive. So, I've been doing some research and exploring my options. Here's what I've found (keep in mind your rates will vary):

- **COBRA**: $550 monthly premiums. No thanks.
- **Healthcare.gov**: $270 to $427. Better, but still ridiculous.
- **Oscar**: $328 to $501. Worse. These are the plans you can get through the freelancers union. I was kinda disappointed these were so high.

That said, you can get government subsidies in the form of tax credits, which you can apply to your monthly premiums to lessen the financial burden. In simpler words, depending on your estimated income, you might qualify to get financial assistance with your health insurance from the government. The less your income, the higher your tax credit.

Keep in mind, this is based on your **estimated** income for the year. And freelancing is not the most predictable venture. So, you should be conservative (i.e. don't underestimate).

Health insurance is very subjective and should be considered on a case-by-case basis. If you tend to require more medical attention, the higher premium and lower deductible are probably worth it. You'll save money in the long run. If you're young and healthy, then you can roll the dice a little more and get cheaper insurance with worse coverage/deductibles. Either way, it's a cost you need to factor in and budget for.

Day 39: February 8, 2020 - 11:03 am (Saturday)

So, I took a course recently...well, it's more like an hour-long video...anyway, I watched this video lecture on inbound sales calls.

In his lecture, Joel Klettke shares his process for nailing calls with prospective clients. Not cold calls, but calls with leads that have been referred to you or found you through an ad, google search, or whatever. He has very simple, straightforward lessons — yet it somehow feels like a revolutionary solution that clarifies the whole process (and he's Canadian, so he says process like prOHcess).

I'm not unfamiliar with having business conversations over the phone. But, before starting my business, I never had to sell myself and my services. So, I've approached calls with prospective clients without a proven, concrete plan. I usually wind up talking more than I should.

Joel's teachings changed that for me.

From a high-level perspective, he helped me adopt a different mindset going into a call. Instead of selling a service, sell a problem — and the only way to do that is by letting the client do the talking and listening to their issues. With the right mindset (and a little preparation), it's so much easier to convert inbound leads into clients.

The principles of Joel's lecture make the course worthwhile if you're new to freelancing or you're uncomfortable on sales calls. Check it out for yourself.[10]

Day 40: February 9, 2020 - 9:30 am (Sunday)

Man, I don't want to jinx anything, but I have four potential new gigs knocking on my door.

The client acquisition process can be so frustrating — you can go weeks without anyone responding to your cold pitches or post submissions. So It's nice when there's a bunch of work coming down the pipeline. That pretty much sums up the early stages of freelance writing though. Back and forth swings of the workload pendulum.

Hard work pays off though. You won't see it coming, but it's around the corner, I promise.

Keep plowing ahead.

Week 6 Lessons & Takeaways

#1: If you fall, get back up. If you dig yourself into a pit of doubt, climb out. Doubt, anxiety, and fear are normal emotions. We all experience them. But it's how you respond to them that determines if you'll be successful or not.

#2: Sometimes you need to break up with a client. Not every working relationship is going to be a good fit. It could be the right niche, the right type of writing, and a promising opportunity overall. But sometimes it just doesn't work out. Be professional, don't burn the bridge, and move on.

#3: I'm addicted to coffee.

#4: Big buzzkill statement incoming: health insurance is super expensive for freelancers. But, depending on your income (under $52k this year), you can qualify for federal tax credits that'll lessen your insurance premium cost burden.

#5: If you want to be the master of inbound sales calls and exponentially increase your odds of converting leads to clients, check out Joel's course.

#6: Looking for and finding the **right** clients is up there with the "biggest challenges of freelancing." At least top three.

#7: Work rarely flows in at a steady state, it's more like a clogged faucet. Periods when you're twiddling your thumbs, waiting for anything. Just a few drops would be nice. Then, without warning, it's discharging way more than you can handle.

Day 41: February 10, 2020 - 4:27 pm (Monday)

So, one potential gig looks like a bust, while two others look promising. I won't know about the fourth (editing gig priced at $100 an hour) until next month.

For the bust, I sent an email detailing my process and rates...

> No problem at all! I know the feeling.
>
> All of my clients have different needs and preferences, so it's a bit of a case-by-case scenario. But this is a general overview of my blog content process:
>
> I'll come up with a list of post ideas (40 - 50), so that you'll have a big pool to work with for months ($250 one-time). No time required on your end whatsoever, but obviously you can always send me some ideas you want to see or if you prefer to handle the idea generation that's totally fine too.
>
> Then I'll take care of writing posts every month. For any topics that require quotes from you guys or any other sort of feedback/opinions, we can either hop on a quick call or I'll send some questions over via email. It'll take less than an hour of your time every month, and as a bonus, I'll round up some social media images with each post so sharing it is quick and easy (unless you have a graphic designer or prefer to do that yourself).
>
> A blog post every other week will only cost you $900 a month (I see that you guys generally post once or twice a month - but let me know if you're looking to ramp up output).
>
> But if you'd like, I could also repurpose those posts into a checklist or downloadable worksheet so that you have a lead magnet for clients to engage with. That would add just $200 per month, or $1,100.
>
> In terms of turnaround time, I can usually knock out a post in two to three days. But I can also provide an editorial calendar with deadlines and upcoming post topics so you guys have a transparent view of our content pipeline.
>
> Let me know if you have any other questions! A few questions for you guys:
>
> 1. What are you looking to get out of your blog? What problem/need of your business will blog content address?
> 2. What have you found works best for your blog? What hasn't worked?

...swift (but polite) rejection. They didn't like my rates.

> ▓▓▓▓▓▓▓▓▓ Feb 10, 2020, 12:05 AM
> to Carter, ▓▓▓
>
> We appreciate you taking the time to provide us a proposal on writing blogs for ▓▓▓▓▓▓▓▓. We are going to pass as the cost is much higher than we anticipated.

> Carter Kilmann <carter@carterkilmann.com> Feb 10, 2020, 6:30 AM
> to ▓▓▓▓▓▓
>
> No problem at all, ▓▓▓. Could you give me an idea of what you were looking to spend? I'll see what I can offer within your budget.
>
> Like I said, every client's situation is different!

If you can get a prospect to provide their budget without offering your rate, you're in a much better negotiation position. You avoid lowballing yourself, and you figure out if the relationship will be a profitable fit.

I'm going to see if it's still salvageable — as you can see, I asked what they expect to spend for blog posts. Let's see what they come back with, maybe I can work with them. I've wanted to work with a financial advisory firm.

Honestly, I didn't think $450 per blog post would be ridiculous for a financial advisory firm. I've seen higher.

For one of the promising gigs, I had a great intro call with the marketing guy for a SaaS company. Not my usual industry, but it qualifies as technical subject matter, which I like to cover. Technical writing = more complicated and specialized = better pay.

For the other promising gig, I signed a non-disclosure agreement (NDA) and will be assigned a trial post sometime this week. Guess how much that one pays?

$450.

See, that's not a ridiculous price.

Day 42: February 11, 2020 - 8:41 am (Tuesday)

Somewhat out of the blue, a close friend of mine texted me and applauded my bold decision to quit my cushy corporate job and start a business. Here's the actual text:

> Hopefully you know this but it's so awesome that you found something you really enjoy and had the balls to just go for it and do it and make it happen. It's seriously shows how badass you are and is amazing that you're already starting to get rolling and be successful with this so fast. Proud of you man

Of course, I appreciated the kind words. Who doesn't like being called a badass? That kind of feedback is always validating. But I also told him that the divide between doing something ordinary and doing something unconventional isn't as wide as one would think. I didn't mean to take away from the compliment or get all philosophical on him, but I had a bit of an epiphany when he sent that.

For most of life's challenges, the hardest part is just getting started — deciding to **do** rather than **dream**.

I know, I know...things are always simpler in retrospect. But it gets easier to handle big decisions when you practice making big decisions. Your grip on life gets a little firmer each time.

It gets easier.

Day 43: February 12, 2020 - 8:30 am (Wednesday)

I've been going through a mental transformation the last few days (maybe weeks, who knows).

I'm starting to grasp the concept of being open to creativity and writing at any point in the day. I don't mean waiting for inspiration to strike. I mean going on the offensive and making an effort to write during the little moments of the day (when I'm just lounging around, between sets at the gym, on the toilet, you feel me?).

You might be thinking, "Isn't that overkill?" No, and I'll explain why.

One of the hardest challenges of being a writer is tuning your brain for maximum creativity and content output. It comes naturally for some people, but not for me. As much as I enjoy being a writer, I do not naturally spout 1,000-word blog posts in a couple of hours. You have to work to achieve that kind of output. You have to develop your flow state (which is intense focus and clarity).

I'm not saying spend a half-hour in the bathroom to knock out a blog post. But little thoughts here and there go a long way.

Day 44: February 13, 2020 - 8:30 am (Thursday)

Update on the health insurance search: a representative from USHealth Advisors contacted me through LinkedIn, offering his services.

I had a call with him and talked through my insurance situation. He asked a few basic questions (height, weight, whether I smoke) and then compiled a quote for me.

It was ridiculously cheaper than all the other insurance options I've researched ($185 a month), which has me skeptical.

After reading reviews and a benefits summary, it doesn't qualify as essential insurance (I think that's the term?) — it's supplemental insurance. The sales pitch was that this plan is for healthy individuals who don't expect to need medical services. About 90% of reviews are negative, with a small caveat — they're all from 2016 to early 2019.

And I looked across a host of platforms: Trustpilot, Glassdoor, Bogleheads (whatever that is), and even Reddit. The positive reviews were a little sketchy too, as they were often posted by people with no post history (i.e. that was their first post).

I've reached out to a few people who might know better, but, for now, I'm going to avoid USHealth Advisors. Their reputation is questionable at best.

10:02 am

Aaaaaand the coffee machine is down again.

Looks like we're going cold turkey today.

12:20 am

I caved and got Dunkin. I'm addicted.

Day 45: February 14, 2020 - 9:47 am (Friday)

I have this frustrating habit of straying from my daily task list. I go rogue and do whatever my mind gets caught up in. It doesn't happen every day, but enough to realize it's a tendency. Like yesterday, instead of working on a couple of blog posts, I was looking for other freelancers to connect with on LinkedIn. It wasn't unproductive, but it wasn't what I had planned.

To combat this, I'm beginning a new strategy of working in intervals of 90-minutes with 20-minute breaks in between. When I'm up against a timer, I feel less inclined to stray from my designated tasks.

Day 46: February 15, 2020 - 9:23 am (Saturday)

I reread some of my earlier entries this morning. On Day 3, I mentioned service contracts, which I should expand on. As you can probably guess, these are legal documents that detail your relationship with a client. They'll outline everything from project scope to payments and termination clauses.

To be honest, I've only executed a service contract with Client C and Client D. Otherwise, I've operated on a trust system. Maybe that's the risky approach, but I haven't been stiffed by any clients yet. *Knocks on wood*

You can google "freelance writing contract" and find a basic but suitable template.

Day 47: February 16, 2020 - 9:57 am (Sunday)

I enjoy writing from my phone. I'm still trying to nail down why that is. Maybe I've just gotten used to it? I write these daily entries on my phone, so it's become a habit. It's a change of pace and can be done from anywhere at any time.

On my laptop, I'm a psycho that opens a bazillion tabs and leaves them open as reminders. On my phone, there's no tab distraction.

Side note: if you're like me and keep a bunch of tabs open, it may be impacting your ability to focus. At any given time, I might have potential clients' websites, publication sites, insightful articles for later, a Google Doc for each of my writing projects — all open at once.

I noticed I'm more likely to jump around from task to task when I have a bunch of tabs open, which isn't good for productivity.

My solution: I started adding items to my task list (even if they were super small tasks) and created a doc with the links to whatever my tabs were. And when I start working on a post, I open the document and associated research in a new window, so the tabs I'm looking at are for only one project.

I've also started bookmarking pages, saving them to designated folders like "leads" and "post ideas."

Just food for thought if you're a tab psycho like me.

Week 7 Lessons & Takeaways

#1: Just because you get a good lead, doesn't mean it'll be a good fit.

#2: There isn't some massive canyon between doing nothing and doing something. Taking control of my present and my future by quitting corporate and becoming self-employed wasn't some revolutionary epiphany or movement. Yes, it took calculated preparation. But what I thought was the hardest part (deciding to quit), turned out to be pretty anticlimactic. Anyone can decide to redirect their life and carve their own path.

#3: I've been trying to write in the little moments throughout the day. They might not last long, but they add up.

#4: Health insurance update: proceed with caution if you're speaking with a rep from USHealth Advisors. They have a lot of bad reviews online.

#5: My coffee machine broke. Again.

#6: I've started working in timed intervals. Being up against a running clock keeps me focused.

#7: Working from your phone is surprisingly nice. It's convenient and allows you to work with your feet propped up on the couch.

#8: Tabs are productivity inhibitors. If you're a tab psycho like me, try saving the links in a Google Doc so you can close them.

Day 48: February 17, 2020 - 9:31 am (Monday)

You know what goes great with a food-stocked pantry?

Ants! Lots of em.

After clearing my pantry, fumigating the bottom shelves, removing the casualties from the battlefield, and cleaning the rest of my apartment for good measure, I'm ready to begin my Monday.

:)

Day 49: February 18, 2020 8:42 am (Tuesday)

I've been called Corey, Connor, Christian, even Mark once.

But I think Kelly is the new winner.

Especially since, you know, my email is carter@carterkilmann.com…

> **R** ▮▮▮▮▮▮▮ 3:08 PM
> to me ⌄
>
> Hi Kelly,
>
> We are working on a new personal finance app and looking for content
> writers. Would you be interested in chatting? If yes, please email me.
>
> Thanks!

This should go without saying, but if you're going to cold email someone, get their name right.

Sigh.

Day 50: February 19, 2020 - 2:38 pm (Wednesday)

Let's dig a little deeper into that cold email from yesterday.

First, they got my name wrong. That's a tough start, but there are a couple more insights to point out, outside of that blatant red flag.

#1: They're looking for content writers. Plural. That could mean they're looking to roll out a TON of content in a short amount of time. That's not necessarily a bad thing, per se, but I'm wary.

It also implies they're reaching out to multiple writers, which was also apparent when they addressed me as "Kelly." I'm sure he just copied and pasted this email to a bunch of writers.

#2: It looks like it was typed up quickly without much review since there's an erroneous line break right in the middle of a sentence. Hopefully, this wasn't a mass copy and paste job because he would have made the same error multiple times.

If there's a glass-half-full perspective here, it's that he needs a writer or editor based on his mistakes. But it also suggests he's not very attentive.

Day 51: February 20, 2020 - 3:21 pm (Thursday)

The cold email wound up being legit.

After signing an NDA, the cold email sender (let's call him Ricky) sent me a list of 13 blog post ideas with varying levels of detail.

The initial stages of a business relationship can be tricky, especially when you're navigating how much a service is going to cost. I tried to be upfront about the matter to establish some leverage. It's a delicate game though, you don't want to scare someone off or rub them the wrong way.

I asked for a rough, non-binding budget estimate to give me an idea of what we're working with and how I can maximize their spendings. Here's my exchange with Ricky:

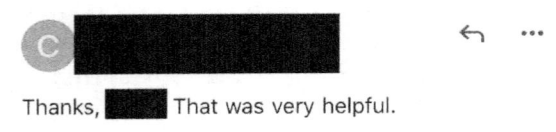

Thanks, ▇ That was very helpful.

The framework for the content is a fit for me. I appreciate the personal story you laid out too, Do you have a rough budget in mind? I won't hold you to this - we can define it together! But it's useful to get a sense of how I might help maximize the ROI of the spend you have.

We are flexible with the budget. Here are some more thoughts to help you decide pricing.

- No Byline
- We need the first dozen "product articles" (from my doc) within 4 weeks.
- We would then need "traffic generating articles" at a constant clip - say 2-4 per week.
- long-form high quality content of around 1500-2000 words, we are building a niche luxury brand

"Flexible" budget doesn't mean anything. It's better than getting a "we're bootstrapping" response. Those people are just looking for high volume at a low price. Pardon my language, but fuck that.

"Flexible" doesn't establish any sort of range, it just indicates an unquantifiable willingness to work with you. They might negotiate with you or they might scoff and bolt at the first number you throw out.

Ricky's proposed workload demands a high premium. That's a lot of content in a short amount of time. But there are two important words to focus on: high quality.

Here's the thing about quality and quantity. People can get away with underpaying for a lot of low quality work, and they can *usually* get away with underpaying for a little high-quality work.

They'll never get away with underpaying for a lot of high-quality work — or at least they shouldn't.

That's theft.

Based on our correspondence so far, my gut tells me Ricky isn't willing to pay for high volume and high quality.

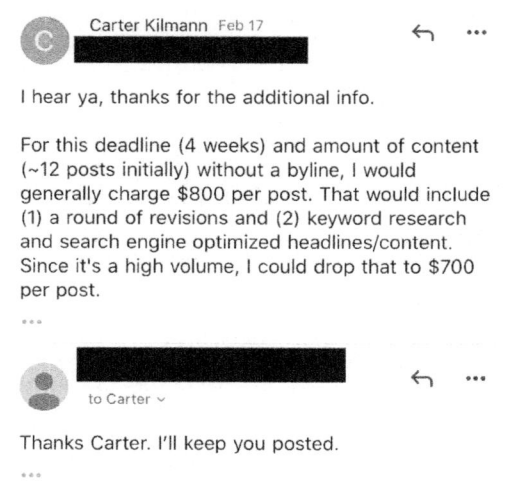

> **Carter Kilmann** Feb 17
>
> I hear ya, thanks for the additional info.
>
> For this deadline (4 weeks) and amount of content (~12 posts initially) without a byline, I would generally charge $800 per post. That would include (1) a round of revisions and (2) keyword research and search engine optimized headlines/content. Since it's a high volume, I could drop that to $700 per post.

> to Carter
>
> Thanks Carter. I'll keep you posted.

I don't expect to be kept posted.

Editor's note: I was right.

Day 52: February 21, 2020 - 2:35 pm (Friday)

It's been a hectic writing week, to say the least. Several deadlines happened to hit at the same time. Thankfully, they were spaced out just enough to be achievable without any all-nighters.

My pipeline is starting to take shape. Since parting ways with Client C, I've picked up a few clients with promising workloads. I'm waiting to start a trial period with one, and I just submitted a trial piece for another. If everything goes according to plan, I'll have a healthy $5,000 monthly income spread across five clients.

Fingers crossed.

Day 53: February 22, 2020 - 2:11 pm (Saturday)

I'm going to share a passage with you about prune juice. Pay close attention to the last sentence.

"Like the dried plums it's made from, prune juice is an excellent source of sorbitol, a naturally occurring sugar alcohol that can't be digested. Four ounces of prune juice — or the equivalent of a 1/2-cup serving — supplies about 14.5 grams of sorbitol. While this amount of sorbitol will probably get your bowels moving, it isn't likely to cause loose, watery stools. Drinking a full 8-ounce glass of prune juice, however, could easily lead to diarrhea."[11]

Guess who drank 16 ounces of prune juice. Guess who's having a rough day.

This guy!

Day 54: February 23, 2020 - 6:36 pm (Sunday)

I've noticed something.

Working just a little bit on Sunday eases the transition from weekend leisure to a weekday grind. Even if it's just checking a few emails and setting your task list for the next day/week.

Of course, it's healthy and important to get away from your work — to clear your mind and recharge. All work, all the time just leads to burnout. But a little prep work on Sunday gets a little momentum on your side.

Unless you wake up to an ant invasion. That'll derail your Monday morning.

Week 8 Lessons & Takeaways

#1: Ants suck.

#2: Be wary of cold emails that don't even get your name right. Be wary of grammar mistakes too. You can learn a lot from dissecting the sender's word choices. Demanding high quality, high volume content with a quick turnaround is a big red flag — make sure to price that into your rate.

#3: Negotiating rates can be tricky, but be direct upfront. When potential clients reach out to you, try to get a rough estimate of their budget. People don't like committing to anything without discussion, so ease their comfort by saying you won't hold them to any number.

#4: Sometimes all of your clients will have deadlines landing in the same week. Time management becomes critical. But don't forget, being busy is a good problem to have.

#5: Don't drink 16 ounces of prune juice.

#6: A little prep work on Sunday for the week ahead is smart. You're on track from the get-go.

#7: No, seriously. Don't drink 16 ounces of prune juice. Ever. It's not worth it.

Day 55: February 24, 2020 - 3:36 pm (Monday)

If I knock out my weekly task list by the end of Thursday, I'm taking Friday off.

Or at least half of it.

When you don't have guaranteed income and that reliable biweekly paycheck, it's hard to give yourself a break. Since I started freelancing full-time, I've only taken a handful of days off, including holidays like Thanksgiving and Christmas.

It's just hard to justify it at this stage. There's always something that I can work on. My workload is perpetual. *But that's freelance life baby!*

In all seriousness, it's good to take time off. You can use it as an extra incentive or reward for clearing a hefty task list.

The good news: I don't even notice because I enjoy what I'm doing (for the most part). Sure, some topics can be dry and some tasks are tedious, but the trade-offs are worth it. What's that saying? If you love what you do, you'll never work a day in your life? That expression is hyperbolic, but it's mostly true.

Work doesn't feel as much like *work* when you enjoy it.

Day 56: February 25, 2020 - 8:48 am (Tuesday)

I still get a little anxious when I accept assignments about an industry and topic I'm not familiar with. Doubt creeps into my mind. If I don't pull on the reins and apply logic, it can spread.

"I don't know anything about this, what if it shows in my writing?"

"What if I look like I have no idea what I'm doing?"

Imposter syndrome in full swing.

If I had to guess, I imagine this is a common obstacle for writers.

Instead of panicking, my best solution is to dig into the prompt or material a little. The neurons start firing, connections are made, the unknown takes shape, and the uncertainty fades. It's not immediate, but it doesn't take long to shoo the doubt away.

The latest example: I'm starting a trial period with a software as a service (SaaS) company. They're in the business of accounts payable automation. I haven't worked with SaaS before, but I understand accounts payable.

Still, it's technical writing, so I'll need to dig deep into the material. Thankfully, they provided explanatory white papers, but it's still pretty dense stuff. Whenever I don't understand a concept, I use Google and YouTube to find helpful guides — which I'll probably have to do for this assignment.

Day 57: February 26, 2020 - 9:10 am (Wednesday)

Hmmm...I need to figure out and create a freebie to entice readers to join my list. Ever since I started freelancing, writers I follow have stressed the importance of growing your email list. Those people become your go-to readers and possible customers (if you sell a course, book, etc.).

I plan to have a newsletter to accompany this book. But first, I'll be launching a personal finance newsletter to pair with my Medium publication.

So...what's that freebie gonna be...

Day 58: February 27, 2020 - 10:13 am (Thursday)

What is up with this friggin coffee machine?

It breaks down like every other week now. This is madness...

...and such a first world problem. Ugh. I can't be that upset.

#fortunate #blessed #DunkinSavesLives

Day 59: February 28, 2020 - 6:55 am (Friday)

Yesterday was tough. It was frustrating. And no, I'm not referring to the coffee machine breaking. *Although that was annoying.*

For context, I need to explain my writing style. I'm a perfectionist writer (which may or may not be a real term but I'm rolling with it). I'll edit as I write. It's counterproductive since it takes longer to write this way.

It's like being in traffic — start, stop, start, stop. Write, edit, write, edit.

Let me rephrase that, I *can* be a perfectionist writer. When I write about topics I'm comfortable with, the words flow without care. It's much faster.

I relapse to perfectionism when I don't know the material, especially when it's technical writing. I second guess every sentence. "Does this make sense? Is this correct? Is it obvious I don't know what I'm talking about?"

Major imposter syndrome.

This inefficient writing style is amplified when it's for a new client. First (writing) impressions are important, ya know? Well, yesterday, I spent the entire day focused on my first post for that SaaS client. I rewrote the same three or four sentences in nine thousand different ways.

I wanted to pull my hair out.

As the evening hours ticked by, I wound up with a rough, rough draft. But it was a painfully inefficient day. That's all I worked on. And I'm not even pleased with the result.

I know the solution — hell, I *knew* the solution — I was just too stubborn to do it the proper way. I should have spent an hour or two just reading about the topic. Then I would've felt more comfortable. Instead, I skimmed a few resources and then wrote as I researched.

Curse my stubbornness.

10:40 am

Also, so much for taking a half-day. I was making great progress through Wednesday, but yesterday set me back. *Ugh.*

Day 60: February 29, 2020 - 11:45 am (Saturday)

I would pick a leap year to write a "365 Days of Freelancing" book…

That makes today my day off, right?

FEBRUARY STATS

February was a good month. A couple of business relationships started to blossom. I landed a couple of assignments on ClearVoice ("Client F"). I made quality LinkedIn connections and grew my Medium following.

In January, I defined each of the below categories. As a reminder, here's each client's category:

- Client A — Digital marketing agency
- Client B — Digital marketing agency
- Client C — FinTech startup (no longer a client)
- Client D — Online finance publication
- Client E — Auto finance company
- Client F — ClearVoice assignments
- Client G — SaaS company

365 Days of Freelancing - Monthly Stats	Jan	Feb
Income		
Client A	960	960
Client B	329	119
Client C	500	-
Client D	350	350
Client E	-	450
Client F	-	225
Client G	-	200
Medium	32	21
Total Income	**$2,171**	**$2,325**
Growth (%)	-	*7.1%*
Blog Posts (Paid)		
Client A	6	6
Client B	3	2
Client C	1	1
Client D	1	1
Client E	-	1
Client F	-	2
Client G	-	1
Total Paid Posts	**11**	**14**
Blog Posts (Unpaid)		
Medium	1	-
Bacon Bits	1	2
Total Unpaid Posts	**2**	**2**
Total Blog Posts	**13**	**16**
Copywriting Assignments		
Client A	-	-
Client B	-	-
Client C	5	-
Client D	-	-
Total Copywriting Asgns.	**5**	**-**
Total Assignments	**18**	**16**
Medium		
Views	1,151	1,352
Reads	439	468
Existing Followers	54	63
New Followers	9	17
Total Followers	**63**	**80**
LinkedIn		
Existing Followers	458	465
New Followers	7	28
Total Followers	**465**	**493**

Highlights

- I stopped working with the FinTech startup ("Client C") but picked up three new gigs, which more than offset the loss.
- The editing work for Client B in January was a bit of an anomaly. I edited their entire website, so I got paid more than usual. February's payment ($119) is on par.
- Three more blog posts than usual resulted in a 7.1% increase in income — woohoo!
- Consistency is paying off — I gained 17 more followers on Medium (a 27% growth rate).
- My LinkedIn connections made a sizable jump too, growing by 6%. I've focused on expanding my audience there, so that's good to see.

MARCH

Day 61: March 1, 2020 - 3:20 pm (Sunday)

I read a powerful message today that aligns with the purpose of this book — here's the tweet by Work Notes:[12]

"Freelancing can be a brilliant option, but it's not the right choice for everyone.

Unfortunately, it's sold as a solution for lots of problems:

Hate your boss? Go freelance.
Starting a family? Go freelance.
Want to earn more + work less? Go freelance.

It's not that simple."

Freelancing is an exciting opportunity made possible by the advancement of technology, but it's not the solution to *everyone's* work/life struggles.

The objective of this book is to sidestep the usual rainbows and butterflies facade by pulling back the curtains to provide genuine insight into an unconventional career path. Yes, there can be unfathomable highs that'll hurt your face from smiling so hard. But there can also be uncomfortable, doubt-filled lows that'll leave you questioning every decision you've ever made.

That leads to the all-important questions. Is it worth it? Are you willing to make a hard, unwavering commitment for an indefinite amount of time? Are you willing to make sacrifices?

If you answered yes to all three of these questions, you've come to the right place, comrade.

Week 9 Lessons & Takeaways

#1: I didn't get to take Friday off. I was crushing my task list, but a challenging post derailed my productivity. Taking time off is important, but it's honestly such a challenge. It's hard to convince yourself that you deserve it — *even when you really do deserve it.*

#2: If you have doubts about a topic and begin to second guess yourself, start working on it. Read about the material. Just get started, the doubt will pass.

#3: The coffee machine continues to mock me by breaking.

#4: Do yourself a favor and don't be stubborn when it comes to doing upfront research and required reading. I drove myself insane trying to write the perfect post on an unfamiliar technical topic. I should've done more reading before diving in. Taking the time to read about your topic before getting started will save you time in the long run.

#5: If you're going to be a writer, you're going to experience imposter syndrome. But that's okay. What matters is how you respond to it. Don't beat yourself up, keep plugging along.

#6: Freelancing isn't a fix-all solution to life's problems.

Day 62: March 2, 2020 - 8:59 am (Monday)

Freelance writing can be a pretty sedentary lifestyle. Even with a flexible schedule, the time can get away from you.

I've mentioned that I like working on my phone as a change of pace. Most gym days, I walk or run on the dread mill (that was an autocorrect but I'm keeping it, that's hysterical). I've found that writing while walking at a 4 mph speed is doable even on an incline, so I'm going to start walking farther distances. Since I'm simultaneously working, it doesn't feel like I'm burning precious work time.

Editor's note: don't do this all the time, it's good to use exercise to escape work and clear your mind too.

Day 63: March 3, 2020 - 5:47 pm (Tuesday)

Oof. I've spent the majority of my day on one Bacon Bits post.

It's roughly 2,000 words, so I guess that's somewhat excusable. It just hurts to look back on a day and see that I only accomplished a few tasks.

I don't think I'll ever be the guy that can produce thousands of words every day. I'm a meticulous writer, it takes me longer.

I don't want to try to be something I'm not. But, on the other hand, the more I produce the more I can make (so long as I maintain quality).

Who knows? Maybe one day. It's a work in progress.

Day 64: March 4, 2020 - 9:06 am (Wednesday)

So I think it'll be helpful if I outline how I come up with blog post ideas.

As a reminder, I separate my creative process into three stages:

1. Idea generation and outlining
2. Writing
3. Editing

When I'm coming up with posts, all I'm doing is looking for ideas and putting together a rough outline. No significant writing. The outline usually consists of two parts: (1) a brief intro to summarize the post and my angle and (2) section headers and a summary sentence or two below each header.

In my experience, there are two types of ideas: unassisted ideas and assisted ideas. Unassisted ideas are spontaneous — they strike you out of the blue or without any research. On the other hand, assisted ideas take a little bit of digging; I'll have to look into a topic first. From there, I'll either narrow down my scope or pivot to another one based on my reading. Soon enough, an "assisted idea" will pop into my head.

Here's an example. Last night, I was looking up possible financial topics for Money.com. I didn't have any archived ideas that I wanted to use for a pitch, so I had to brainstorm new ones.

Step #1: Browse the website you want to post on. This not only jumpstarts your creativity machine but also syncs your thought process with the site's usual content. Look through different sections to get a feel for the kind of content they publish.

I scanned Money.com and found that they have the following sections: Investing, Banking, Career, Travel, Shopping, Retirement, Insurance, Mortgages, and Credit Cards. From here, I whittled down to three sections to look into.

Step #2: Choose two or three posts that catch your eye — or address topics you're familiar with. Read them. There's a reason these were published. Analyze the tone, message, and format. Ask yourself, what is the purpose of this post? What problem is it solving?

In the Careers section, I looked at recent featured posts. One was titled "Hey, Stop Being Weird on LinkedIn." This let me know that they're open to a more human perspective and touch.

While looking into the Investing section, I noticed there was a lot of content about the Coronavirus — what to do, how to react, and so on. The underlying theme was how to respond to bad news in the market.

That's when an idea hit me. People tend to act on emotions in the stock market. But a human advisor serves as a safeguard against this. I decided one of my pitch ideas would be about robo-advisory and the loss of a personal touch.

Step #3: Google the topics you looked into. Look into other site's opinions. See what experts think about your topic. Keep track of any relevant information or sources you can reference later on.

I googled robo-advisory and assessed what kind of content is already published. There's a lot of "pros and cons" types of posts. For my pitch, I want to see if "loss of personal touch" is one of those cons — or if there are other angles to consider.

Step #4: Begin your outline. By now, you should have a general idea of what you want to write about and the perspective you're going to take. Format those thoughts.

When I start a post, I create three sections:

1. Title ideas
2. Research
3. Outline

When you start this process, come up with a couple of title ideas. It'll put some high-level structure to your outline. When you finish your post, you'll have more context to base your title decision on. Reassess these ideas and brainstorm a few more.

And that's pretty much it. Pretty straightforward, right?

Day 65: March 5, 2020 - 8:52 am (Thursday)

Man, this week has flown by.

I've decided I need to be more active on my professional Twitter account. I'm on Twitter more than any other social media platform, except 99% of my time is spent on my personal account. Not anymore. If I'm going to mindlessly open up Twitter, I might as well make the most of it.

Well, timing has a funny way of working out.

As you know, I'm a personal finance guy. It just so happens that Jorden Makelle (founder of Writing Revolters) tweeted the following request:

> **JORDEN ⚡ MAKELLE**
> @JordenMakelle
>
> can anyone recommend an amazing personal finance advisor who specializes in helping self-employed people?
>
> would really appreciate it!
>
> 3:09 PM · 3/4/20 · Twitter Web App

Ahaaaa right up my alley. For context, Jorden was one of the freelance writers I studied way back in the day. She was one of my inspirations.

Now, I don't know a financial advisor that specializes in helping self-employed people — but based on my knowledge of the process (through discussions with FAs), I don't think it'd be that different for a freelancer versus anyone else.

So, I tagged my friend and FA, Brandon.

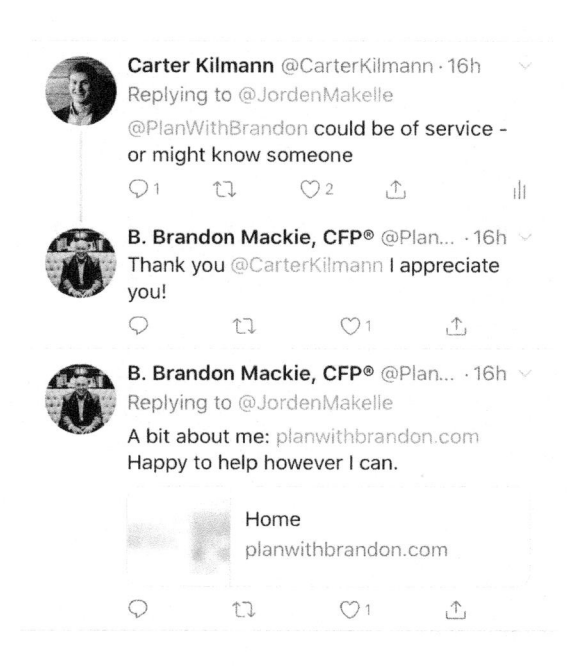

> **Carter Kilmann** @CarterKilmann · 16h
> Replying to @JordenMakelle
> @PlanWithBrandon **could be of service - or might know someone**

> **B. Brandon Mackie, CFP®** @Plan... · 16h
> Thank you @CarterKilmann **I appreciate you!**

> **B. Brandon Mackie, CFP®** @Plan... · 16h
> Replying to @JordenMakelle
> A bit about me: planwithbrandon.com
> Happy to help however I can.
>
> Home
> planwithbrandon.com

I'm not looking for anything from Jorden, but it's cool I get to help someone who's helped me in a lot of ways. Plus, maybe Brandon gets a client! That's how business gets done, son.

Day 66: March 5, 2020 - 8:59 am (Friday)

Where do people find the time to post on Medium every single day?

Well…I guess if I wasn't writing this, working on a newsletter, pitching publications for guest posts, and managing client work….then I probably could.

I'm not trying to sound like a smartass or like "look at everything I'm doing." In all honesty, that realization hit me after I wrote the first sentence.

There's only so much time in the day. I'm the kind of person that tries to do and succeed at everything. It's just not possible. Time, energy, and sanity are finite. No, seriously — sanity.

You'll burn out before you accomplish anything if you try to do it all.

And when I say "you," I mean me too.

Day 67: March 7, 2020 - 10:41 am (Saturday)

Medium should have a feature that allows you to sort the posts on your profile by category or something.

Every now and then, I stumble across a writer with enjoyable and relevant content. But a Medium profile isn't set up to efficiently sift through people's content.

You have to scroll…and scroll…and scroll…

Whether it's a filter based on tags or a profile editor function that lets writers organize their posts, something needs to change.

Get to it, Medium.

Day 68: March 8, 2020 - 11:04 pm (Sunday)

Not a fan of daylight savings. I feel robbed. I want my hour back.

But, in other news, my latest post was curated in the "Money" section of Medium. In other words, Medium distributed my story under this term, so whoever follows or searches the word "Money" on Medium will see my story. I've accomplished this a few times, so I'm wondering how often that needs to happen to be a "Top Writer" on a certain topic.

I'll get back to you.

12:15 pm

Alright, so it's pretty straightforward. I just read a quality post about obtaining "top writer" status; here are the top two recommendations.[13]

1. Focus on less popular tags (unless you're willing to pump a TON of content out). For instance, instead of "Money," I could focus on "Budgeting."
2. Start a publication with your desired tag and write about it frequently.

Week 10 Lessons & Takeaways

#1: Don't forget to exercise and get outside every day. It's easy to let this life responsibility slip through the cracks when you're a writer. Go to the gym, take periodic walks — it's good for your body and mind.

#2: I'm a meticulous writer, and I own that. It's rare for me to pump out 1,000 words in an hour. That's just not how I write. And that's okay. It's also okay if you pump out 1,000 words an hour and spend the rest of the day editing them. Whatever your style is, it can work.

#3: I had a sizable entry about my idea generation process. Go ahead and flip back to it, I separated my approach into four easy steps.

#4: If you're like me and spend too much time mindlessly scrolling through social media, shift this social media attention to your business profiles and feeds. It's way more productive and can lead to work and connections.

#5: Don't lose your sanity trying to do everything. I imagine this is a constant theme across entrepreneurship, but I often think I can do way more in a day than is possible. Be realistic when it comes to self-expectations. There's nothing wrong with a high bar, but don't beat yourself up if you can't reach it.

#6: Medium needs more profile organization functionality. I want to be able to sort by types of posts on someone's profile.

#7: I've always thought Benjamin Franklin would be a cool historical figure to meet if I could go back in time. But what the hell, Ben? What did we pose to gain from daylight savings?

Day 69: March 9, 2020 - 9:50 am (Monday)

I've been on a steady rise since experiencing a big-time case of imposter syndrome a couple of weeks ago. I feel good about my pipeline and process.

During my first week of freelancing full-time, I compiled a list of 28 serial goals, spaced out over the next few years. One of the categories is "Publications" — which are websites I want to be featured on.

Examples include Forbes, the Wall Street Journal, the New York Times, Money.com, and The Simple Dollar.

Over the last week or so, I've started to brainstorm ideas for these sites. I think I've got a worthy Op-ed piece for the NYT. It's about the unheralded heroes of sports: referees.

The piece highlights the negativity that referees receive by the nature of their role. They're the scapegoat of sports. Is your team sucking? I bet the refs made some unfavorable calls, right? But organized sports couldn't exist without them.

The body of this Op-ed would highlight the admirable characteristics of referees and how we can learn a thing or two from them.

I'm feeling good about it. Fingers crossed.

Day 70: March 10, 2020 - 7:01 am (Tuesday)

Last week, I published a blog post on Bacon Bits titled "How I Cut My Monthly Expenses by 32%."[14] Whenever I post to Medium, I advertise it on LinkedIn.

My LinkedIn post for this piece received a fair amount of attention (3,103 views), which translated to 176 article views on Medium (a 5.6% conversion rate). My latest post was trending under the #personalfinance hashtag, which helped boost these numbers.

I know, 5.6% doesn't seem like a high conversion rate, but it's solid compared to some of my past posts:

Post	LinkedIn Views	Link Clicks	Conversion Rate
Tell Me About a Time You Failed	1,462	43	2.9%
5 Lame Excuses You're Making to Avoid Managing Your Money	808	48	5.9%

A Mistake New Freelancers Need to Avoid	621	12	1.9%
5 simple finance principles you need to know	897	44	4.9%
Finding Your (Writing) Voice	904	16	1.8%
3 critical lessons from my first month of freelancing	914	48	5.3%
Quitting Corporate: Why I Chose Happiness Over Money	2,324	97	4.2%

As you can see, 5.6% is the second-best rate I've had.

What I'm more excited about is that my expense-cutting post received 319 views on Medium yesterday.

Day 71: March 11, 2020 - 7:15 am (Wednesday)

I haven't slept well this week.

I want to blame daylight savings, but it's never affected me in such a way before. I don't think it's stress — I've felt quite relaxed lately.

So, my body must not like the new hours?

I'm having trouble falling asleep, and then I'm suddenly waking up throughout the night. I wake up semi-alert and restless. It's that sensation where your mind feels like it's been straining when it should be rebooting.

Bad sleep = foggy mind = bad productivity

Plus, I'm grumpy.

Day 72: March 12, 2020 - 9:57 am (Thursday)

Today's a big day.

I'm celebrating 26 years of life, and I'm on the way to Nashville to celebrate my friend's bachelor weekend.

What a time to be alive.

I'm trying to let myself take a vacation while also managing personal and client expectations. Wish me (and my liver) luck this weekend.

Day 73: March 13, 2020 - 8:23 am (Friday)

Oh, man. I've felt better.

It feels weird telling clients I'm on vacation — or that I'll get back to them next week. That's not something I've had to do before because I haven't taken a true vacation.

Ugh, I need to go for a run or something. My body feels gross.

Day 74: March 14, 2020 - 12:49 pm (Saturday)

Hot damn — my latest Bacon Bits post is killing it.

I've almost gotten 2,000 views on Medium and it's made over $75. My previous best was $55. My follower count is up as well; I started the month at 80, now I'm up to 107.

I know these aren't world-breaking numbers, but it's a real confidence boost when my Medium posts get a lot of attention.

It's one of my goals to make consistent, respectable money from Medium. I enjoy writing that type of content more than any other. It's where I feel that I'm truest to my writing voice.

Day 75: March 15, 2020 - 7:47 pm (Sunday)

I survived the bachelor weekend (barely). I'm making detox soup to try to replenish my system.

I think this is the first time I've experienced the Sunday Scaries as a writer. I feel like I have a ton to do tomorrow, and I'm so physically drained from this weekend that I'm not looking forward to it.

Week 11 Lessons & Takeaways

#1: Don't forget about your publication goals — the big-name sites you want your work to be featured on. I'm in the process of writing a few drafts for mine (Money.com, the New York Times).

#2: Only 2-6% of the people who view my LinkedIn post advertisements follow the link to my Medium blog posts. So don't be dissuaded by low view rates.

#3: Bad sleep = bad productivity. I've tried to prioritize sleep during my time as a freelancer. I used to sacrifice sleep to be able to work more. Now, I make sure I get eight hours a night.

#4: My Medium post ("How I Cut My Monthly Expenses by 32%") is doing well. I know I'm far from "making it" on Medium, but stay committed to creating content on this platform. It can help you build a following and make money in the process. I'm only able to produce 2-4 posts on there a month, but I'm already seeing my follower count increase at a high rate.

#5: I am not immune to the Sunday Scaries, but they are rare. Back in the corporate world, they were weekly occurrences. So, it's better now.

Day 76: March 16, 2020 - 2:50 pm (Monday)

I suppose you could say my business has officially been impacted by the Coronavirus — albeit in a pretty minor way.

One of my clients emailed me and let me know that she may take longer to provide feedback on in-process posts while her company prioritizes content topics. It doesn't sound like there won't be consistent work, just that it may take my client a little longer to edit and publish content.

I'm fortunate to have a job that is naturally secluded.

Day 77: March 17, 2020 - 7:32 am (Tuesday)

It's sort of ridiculous. Aside from going to the gym, my day-to-day routine is pretty much identical to what it was before self-quarantining.

Working from home? *Check*

Limited human interaction for days at a time? *Check*

Cooking all of your meals? *Check*

I suppose you could say being a freelancer prepares you for global pandemics. So, there's another selling point.

Day 78: March 18, 2020 1:14 pm (Wednesday)

A few updates:

#1: Making your own workout routine at home is a challenge — but not impossible. It would help if I had even just a couple of free weights though.

#2: My budget post on Medium is still getting a lot of attention. For the "Money" tag, it's #16 under top stories. It's been huge for picking up followers. I entered the month at 80 followers, and Bacon Bits had about 30-35 (I think).

Those are now at 121(!!!) and 70, respectively.

As of yesterday, the post has earned $112. According to the last Medium monthly newsletter, only 8% of writers make over $100 a month from Medium.

#3: My business has been minimally impacted by the coronavirus quarantine. In fact, my most consistent client (Client A) requested estimates for a white paper and three or four in-depth blog posts.

My response: $2,000 for the white paper and $450 per blog post.

Day 79: March 19, 2020 - 10:51 am (Thursday)

Good thing I budget for coffee each month because I've relied on Dunkin to get my fix (walking there right meow).

It just dawned on me: I wish my Bacon Bits newsletter was farther along (i.e. up and running). I've planned to include email list CTAs at the end of my posts, but I haven't gotten around to it, which is my own fault.

I imagine my latest budgeting post would have attracted a few signups. It's up to 4.5k views.

Squandered opportunity.

BUT — I did have the idea this morning to name the newsletter "Bits" (I had been thinking "Sizzle") and to do shorter emails with a more narrative-based approach on specific topics.

Day 80: March 20, 2020 - 8:30 am (Friday)

Last week, I started noticing that it's easier to reach a writing flow while walking. So, I've started to walk three times a day (after each meal) for 20-30 minutes.

This keeps me active too since I'm inside on my computer most of the day.

For each session, I aim to accomplish one of my daily tasks — like "outline a Bacon Bits post" or "write 500 words of a guest post."

Day 81: March 21, 2020 - 9:03 am (Saturday)

You know what? I think this whole quarantine situation might be good for freelance writers.

There's a higher demand for content since more people are on their phones and computers at home. How can I tell? ClearVoice notifications.

In any given month, I'll receive one or two writing opportunities from ClearVoice. Well, in 20 minutes last night, I received (I kid you not) 14 opportunities.

Well-paying opportunities. Like $300 for 800 words.

I'm not guaranteed to land any of them, I have to apply (it's just a one-click "I'm interested" application). But it's a positive sign nonetheless.

Day 82: March 22, 2020 - 9:49 am (Sunday)

What're the odds that the grocery store restocked its meat section?

I went on Thursday to grab a couple of things, including meats to grill for the weekend. Kroger posted signs saying, "Limit 3 packs of chicken or beef to one cart."

Except these packaged meats disappeared. No chicken or beef in sight. Slim pickings of pork products. A weird amount of sausage though — it was untouched. I guess Atlanta doesn't like sausage.

I understand why it happens, but the hoarding mentality frustrates me. It's so selfish. Not that I'm the patron saint of sharing or generosity, but c'mon. Who needs a grocery cart full of milk?

On another note, I'm very much looking forward to my sausage dinner tonight.

2:02 pm

Quick Medium update, since I'm still pumped about how well this post is doing:

- Views: 7.3k
- Reads: 2.6k
- Claps: 1.3k
- Earnings: $240.51
- Follower count: 161 (started March at 80)

It's been a confidence booster, too. I've been more motivated to produce Medium content — since then, I've added two more posts to Bacon Bits.

Week 12 Lessons & Takeaways

#1: The pandemic hasn't interfered with my business. If anything, content is in more demand than ever. *Freelancers were more prepared for quarantine than anybody.*

#2: To promote my personal finance newsletter ("Bits"), I've added a sign-up link at the bottom of my skyrocketing Medium post. It's only led to a handful of subscribers — but hey, it's something.

#3: I've upped the frequency and duration of my walks. I use this time to knock out daily writing tasks. I'll walk three times a day (after each meal) for 20 to 30 minutes. The time depends on how long it takes me to finish a task (like writing 500 words of a post).

#4: ClearVoice is a solid platform for organizing and presenting your portfolio. Once you establish a decent portfolio (~15-20 pieces, although that's a guess), you'll start receiving push notifications to apply for semi-curated assignments.

#5: Hey, you can earn decent money on Medium without a legion of followers. Who knew?

Day 83: March 23, 2020 - 2:01 pm (Monday)

If you're not on LinkedIn, I urge you to change that fact. I'm a big believer in LinkedIn. It's a must-have for freelance writers.

Over the last few months, I've focused on improving my LinkedIn profile, optimizing it for lead generation. It's been a reliable source for opportunities — I've landed a few gigs and clients through LinkedIn.

Here are a few LinkedIn profile tips:

- Once you've written for a client for a few months, add them to your experience section. The same goes for publications once you've written two or three pieces. If it's a client, make sure to ask them if they're okay with this first (especially if you provide ghostwritten work). If it's a publication, that's not necessary. For example, I added The Startup (a Medium publication) to my profile after a couple of my posts were published. I also had a client agree to let me include them in my work experience section.
- Make sure your experiences have at least one to two sentence descriptions. It adds more depth to your profile and helps viewers see the specifics behind what you've done in the past — not just who you've worked with. If you can include tangible results (i.e. increased interaction by 50%) in these descriptions, that's a huge plus.

- Be efficient and precise with your headline. Viewers should immediately know your role, services, and specialty after reading your headline. For example, my headline is "Personal Finance | B2B Technical Writer | Editor."
- LinkedIn also gives you the option to list "services provided." This lets viewers know you're open for business.
- Your "About" section should (a) provide your background and (b) demonstrate the value you can provide to potential clients.
- Recommendations can be the difference between a prospect passing on your profile or sending you a message.

While reading a Medium post a couple of weeks ago, I discovered LinkedIn Profinder, which connects businesses with freelancers of all types. I applied to be a "pro" and received the following feedback:

LinkedIn

View this case on our Help Center

Subject: ProFinder Writing and Editing Application [200301-002875]

Response (03/02/2020 11:22 CST)

Hi Carter,

My name is Lathan and I'll be helping you out today. thank you for reaching out!

Your ProFinder profile highlights your career, education, and other relevant content that showcases your skills as a freelance professional. Your profile strength is a weighted factor in how we deliver you leads and the first thing potential clients will see so it's important to stand out and make a good impression.

Here are some things that will help to make sure you're putting your best foot forward:

• Experience - Add a few sentences to the Experience section of your profile to highlight the type of work you do in your own words. You can receive up to 8x more profile views if your experience is up-to-date!

Also, having at least 2 to 3 recent recommendations in your chosen field are encouraged, as they help build you credibility and validate your skills. Here are the steps for requesting a Recommendation: http://help.linkedin.com/app/answers/global/a_id/96. We suggest following the steps under "Requesting a recommendation from a connections profile".

To learn more about creating a professional LinkedIn profile, please check out this FREE LinkedIn Learning course, "Rock Your LinkedIn Profile" to bring your personal career story to life: https://www.linkedin.com/learning/rock-your-linkedin-profile/connect-to-opportunity-with-linkedin?u=0

Let me know once you've had a chance to apply these tips and I'll be happy to revisit your application.

Lathan
Member Engagement Consultant

As you can see, per the LinkedIn staff, detailing your experiences and landing recommendations help solidify your profile.

Day 84: March 24, 2020 - 9:30 am (Tuesday)

Man, the days are blurring together. I know I said the pandemic hasn't impacted my business, but it's messed with my weekends, that's for sure.

Since I treated my Saturday and Sunday like quasi-work days, it feels like I'm living in Bill Murray's Groundhog Day universe.

5:11 pm

Update: I'm giddy with excitement. My budget post is THE top post under the "money" tag.

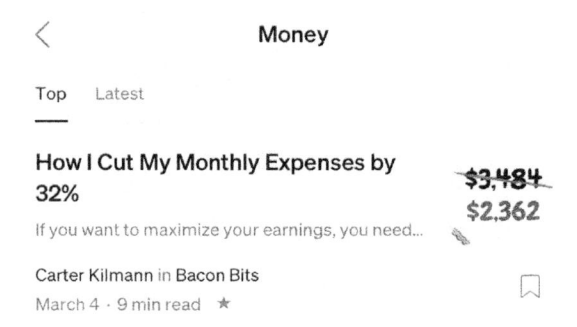

> Money
>
> Top   Latest
>
> **How I Cut My Monthly Expenses by 32%**   ~~$3,484~~ $2,362
> If you want to maximize your earnings, you need...
>
> Carter Kilmann in Bacon Bits
> March 4 · 9 min read ★

Day 85: March 25, 2020 - 9:51 am (Wednesday)

I have no idea what I did to appease the Medium algorithm, but I'm at least certain of one thing: the title appeals to a broad audience.

Your title/headline works like a carnival barker, drumming up business for your article. You want that carnival barker to be loud, attractive, and intriguing. *Maybe even a little mysterious.*

So, don't overlook or rush your titles. That would be a costly mistake. You can write the world's greatest story, but if your title sucks, people won't read it.

Effective headlines tend to have one or more of the following features:

1. Result-oriented numbers. My budget headline tied a result (reduced monthly expenses) to a number (32%).
2. Relevant questions. For example, my audience here consists of aspiring writers. So, a headline like "How much money do freelance writers make?" would be appealing.
3. X-to-Y explanations. In other words, "How X did Y." My budget headline accomplished this too.
4. Bold statements. "You're not cut out for writing."

Coschedule.com has an incredible (and free) headline analysis tool.[15] Once you submit a headline, it provides a general score — based on factors like length, sentiment, and clarity — and a search engine optimization (SEO) score, which compares your submission to the top Google headlines that relate to your topic.

Day 86: March 26, 2020 - 10:41 am (Thursday)

Woaaah, my creativity is uncontainable today. I'm having idea after idea. It's a mind explosion.

I'm loving every second, but my hands can only move so fast.

I'm not sure *why*, but I read a couple of Medium posts this morning and a fire sparked in my brain.

- I started with this one: "How I Got 30,000 Views in My First Year on Medium" by Matthew Enubuje[16]
- Which led me to this one: "The Strategy I Used to Write My First $6,000 Story" by Richie Crowley[17]

It all just clicked. The gears started turning, and the words flowed. The feeling is surreal — as if today was my first day of full-time freelancing all over again.

Day 87: March 27, 2020 - 8:20 am (Friday)

I've come down from my creativity high. The culprit? An editor from Client D.

In the Write Jobs newsletter, I came across a request for pitches from Client D — which is a big name in the personal finance space. I sent the editor a post idea back in January and received a response two days later.

They loved the idea. Through a few email exchanges, we established a deadline and payment. I submitted on time, set up my profile on their billing platform, and filed my invoice. *No problem.*

Email responses from the editor were a bit slow — but nothing more than three or four days.

I followed up on February 10 with a few pitch ideas. Three days later, they responded and selected one. We agreed to another deadline, and I operated under the assumption of the same payment as before ($350).

Lesson learned: ask for the purchase order to be filed upfront, especially for slow communicators.

Again, I sent my post on time (February 21). **One week later** (February 28), the editor responded with a thank you, saying they would review shortly.

On March 2, following my usual pattern, I sent the editor a few pitch ideas. *Nothing.*

On March 18, I followed up on (a) my post submission and (b) my pitch ideas in one polite email. *Nothing.*

On March 25, while updating my ClearVoice portfolio, I noticed my second post was published (on March 22). So, I followed up again — stating that I saw the post was published and then asking for the editor to submit a PO. *Cause I wanna get paid.*

The email was read, but no response.

Lack of communication agitates me. Couple that with lack of payment, and it's not a pretty picture. But I don't want to sour the relationship because I want to keep contributing to the site.

So, my plan? Keep following up (in a polite but forward fashion) until I get an answer. Not much else I can do.

I want my money.

Day 88: March 28, 2020 - 8:32 am (Saturday)

It doesn't feel like a Saturday. I still feel like I should be working. Honestly, without these daily entries, I'd forget what day it is. They're blurring together.

I'm certain I'd lose my sanity if I didn't take a few walks every day.

Anyway, enough about my cabin fever.

I'm trying to grow my social media presence, starting with LinkedIn. Why? To widen my reach, increase the likelihood of landing clients, and attract more readers to my content.

If you haven't read those Medium posts I mentioned on Thursday, Richie's post outlines an effective process for gaining LinkedIn connections and post views. For every story he writes, Richie sends 500 connection requests to people that would fit into his target audience.

He uses the following example:

"If I write about meditation, my audience is meditation teachers, employees of meditation app brands, and authors of meditation books."

Once people accept his request, he messages them, complimenting their profile and asking for their opinion on his post. In his email, he'll include a link to his post and a link to his newsletter's landing page.

It's genius.

Day 89: March 29, 2020 - 1:47 pm (Sunday)

I'm on my way to Florida to quarantine with Kaileigh and her family — including this fuzzy guy (Brewster).

The change of scenery is most welcome.

Week 13 Lessons & Takeaways

#1: I urge you to optimize your LinkedIn profile. LinkedIn has been pivotal to the growth of my brand. It introduced me to other freelancers and plenty of leads. It's also my largest social media audience, so I've generated a lot of traffic to my Medium posts via LinkedIn.

#2: My post on reducing monthly expenses claimed the title of top post under Medium's "money" tag. It's been an absolute shot in the arm — my follower count is up 294% and I've earned more than $600 from this post alone. It's bananas.

#3: As a freelancer, I'm more prepared than the average bear to endure quarantine — but 19 days of the same routine got old. Wake up, in-home workout, work, breakfast, walk, work, lunch, walk, work, dinner, walk, watch Netflix or play video games, sleep, repeat. For the sake of my sanity, I've escaped to Florida.

#4: Every now and then, without warning, you'll be swept up in a wave of creativity. This past Thursday, my creativity neurons were firing. Ideas flowed from my brain to my fingertips and onto my computer.

#5: UGH. I'm getting frustrated by the lack of communication from one particular editor. It's one thing to take weeks to answer emails — it's another level when it concerns getting paid. I want my $350.

#6: Medium has proven to be a legitimate source of income (for me and others). Well, before I get too far ahead of myself, I only tasted what it could be (I'm a one-hit-wonder at the moment). But it has potential. Plus, there are plenty of personal anecdotes that explain how people made $1,000+ on Medium in one month or with one article.

Day 90: March 30, 2020 - 10:44 am (Monday)

Today, I woke up rejuvenated. Something about being in a new locale renewed my work ethic.

I haven't written on Medium long enough to do a viable analysis, but I'm curious how posts perform in the months after their initial publication. There are plenty of variables to account for — curation, publication size, follower count growth, the success of other posts (collateral views) — but I think it's worth looking into.

12:12 pm

Alright, so I ran a quick statistical analysis. I don't shy away from working in excel if you can't tell, *or if you haven't seen the endorsements on my LinkedIn profile.*

So, here's a quick guide to reading this table. I've listed all of my posts, their publication dates, their monthly earnings since they were posted, and total earnings.

Post	Post Date	Month 1	2	3	4	5	6	7	8	Total
Quitting Corporate: Why I Chose Happiness Over Money	8/2/2019	$8.78	$0.11	$0.30	$1.86	$1.14	$0.37	$1.36	$4.66	$18.58
3 critical lessons from my first month of freelancing	8/20/2019	7.69	1.03	0.01	0.77	0.10	0.17	0.12	0.03	9.92
Finding Your (Writing) Voice	9/7/2019	1.09	2.55	0.36	0.01	-	-	-		4.01
5 simple financial principles you need to know	9/30/2019	-	-	1.34	0.80	0.68	0.20			3.02
A Mistake New Freelancers Need to Avoid	11/9/2019	8.56	2.24	1.28	0.47	0.01				12.56
Why You Need to Take Command of Your Money	12/20/2019	2.40	1.49	0.61	0.40					4.90
How to Take Command of Your Money	12/20/2019	1.24	1.11	0.39	0.41					3.15
Get Your Finances Organized	12/20/2019	18.39	21.86	12.83	6.98					60.06
The Sexiest 15-Minute Budget	12/20/2019	1.81	3.22	0.67	11.48					17.18
Get Comfortable with Credit	12/20/2019	1.29	1.06	0.16	1.31					3.82
5 Lame Excuses You're Making to Avoid Managing Your Money	1/14/2020	0.35	0.09	0.27						0.71
"Tell Me About a Time You Failed"	1/28/2020	2.30	0.65							2.95
Why Every Freelancer Needs to Organize Their Finances	2/13/2020	0.47	0.26							0.73
4 Financial Tasks You Need to Prioritize as a Freelancer	2/13/2020	2.13	3.47							5.60
How I Cut My Budget by 32%	3/4/2020	617.03								617.03
How to Save Money as a Freelancer Without a Steady Paycheck	3/17/2020	2.77								2.77
How My Emergency Fund Is Keeping Me Sane During the Pandemic	3/20/2020	5.14								5.14
5 Financial Lessons to Learn From the Pandemic	3/24/2020	8.79								8.79
										$780.92

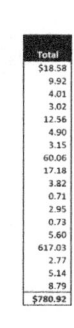

Now, there's an issue with my approach that I need to shed light on. If I wanted to be precise with this, I'd need to calculate earnings in 30-day increments rather than by month. In other words, if a post was published on 10/15, I should base calculate earnings through 11/14 (30 days).

In essence, I'm discounting each post's performance. Example: The first month for "Get Your Finances Organized" is December, but it was posted on the 20th — so that's only considering 11 days of earnings.

But I'd have to count each post's earnings day-by-day since their initial publication dates, which would take a long-ass time.

One interesting point: the success of "How I Cut My Monthly Expenses by 32%" resulted in a significant uptick in earnings of "The Sexiest 15-Minute Budget" (which I embedded at the end of the former post).[18]

Day 91: March 31, 2020 - 12:09 pm (Tuesday)

Well, damn — I can officially say I've lost business due to COVID-19.

"Lost" might not be the most accurate word. I've been furloughed? Or, at least, the freelance equivalent.

Remember that SaaS company I mentioned a little while ago (Client G)? Their business has stalled at the hands of the pandemic. As the domino effect prescribes, that means they're cutting back on contract work.

It's not the end of the world though — it's temporary (I hope). My contact at the company was adamant that he still wants to work with me once everything clears up. So, that's good news.

I need to land more gigs though.

MARCH STATS

March felt like a decade due to the COVID-19 pandemic and corresponding societal "shutdown." That led to a little bit of a slowdown for client work — but my Medium performance skyrocketed at the perfect time.

As a reminder, here's a brief description of each client:

- Client A — Digital marketing agency
- Client B — Digital marketing agency
- Client C — FinTech startup (no longer a client)
- Client D — Online finance publication
- Client E — Auto finance company
- Client F — ClearVoice assignments
- Client G — SaaS company (no longer a client, for now)

365 Days of Freelancing - Monthly Stats	Jan	Feb	Mar
Income			
Client A	960	960	960
Client B	329	119	153
Client C	500	-	-
Client D	350	350	-
Client E	-	450	450
Client F	-	225	-
Client G	-	200	-
Medium	32	21	719
Total Income	**$2,171**	**$2,325**	**$2,282**
Growth (%)	-	7.1%	(1.9%)
Blog Posts (Paid)			
Client A	6	6	6
Client B	3	2	2
Client C	1	1	-
Client D	1	1	-
Client E	-	1	1
Client F	-	2	-
Client G	-	1	-
Total Paid Posts	**11**	**14**	**9**
Blog Posts (Unpaid)			
Medium	1	-	-
Bacon Bits	1	2	4
Total Unpaid Posts	**2**	**2**	**4**
Total Blog Posts	**13**	**16**	**13**
Copywriting Assignments			
Client A	-	-	-
Client B	-	-	-
Client C	5	-	-
Client D	-	-	-
Total Copywriting Asgns.	**5**	**-**	**-**
Total Assignments	**18**	**16**	**13**
Medium			
Views	1,151	1,352	19,466
Reads	439	468	7,413
Existing Followers	54	63	80
New Followers	9	17	158
Total Followers	**63**	**80**	**238**
LinkedIn			
Existing Followers	458	465	493
New Followers	7	28	33
Total Followers	**465**	**493**	**526**

Highlights

- My income dropped a hair, but my big Medium month kept things afloat. Roughly $670 of that $719 figure is from one post.
- My post output appears down, but my total doesn't include several Medium post drafts.
- It feels ridiculous to even quantify it, but my Medium views and reads grew by **1340%** and **1484%**, respectively. That's going to be tough to duplicate.
- My Medium following was two followers away from **tripling**.
- My LinkedIn following grew by 6.7%, which was in line with last month's growth.

APRIL

Day 92: April 1, 2020 - 12:41 pm (Wednesday)

I think I'm going to give up writing this book, it's becoming too time-consuming.

I just can't do it anymore.

April Fools!

Probably not the best joke since you're reading this...

Anyway, I made it through what felt like 90 days of March and am ready to take on April! I'm used to semi-quarantine, but after three consecutive weeks of the exact same routine with very minimal socializing, I started to question my sanity.

That said, it was a positive and productive month (most of the time) from a business perspective. I need to land a couple more clients to compensate for losing Client D. Plus, I want to capitalize on March's Medium momentum (how's that for alliteration?). I'm aiming for four posts a month versus the historical two.

New month, new me. Here we go.

Day 93: April 2, 2020 - 10:41 am (Thursday)

Well, I have some potentially good news. The editor from Client D finally responded yesterday, apologizing for the delay. She said she just submitted the PO...but I haven't received anything yet.

It's a tough line to walk. On one side, it's been a while since I submitted my work, and I want my money. On the other, I want *more* work and money from this client. It's a big brand and they pay well.

As I mentioned last week, she hasn't responded to either of the pitches I sent her. She addressed the PO submission request — but ignored the pitches. So, I'm using subtle tricks to work her for a response.

> **Carter Kilmann** <carter@carterkilmann.com> 10:48 AM (19 minutes ago)
> to ▇
>
> Thanks, ▇! Do I need to fill out another work order form? Or does the first one carry over? I'll be on the lookout for the PO in workday - I haven't seen it yet.
>
> On another note, would you be interested in either of the below pitches?

I'm pretty positive I don't need to fill out another form, but it made for a sly way to say, "I still haven't been paid." Plus, I got to plug my post ideas again, which are the same ones I sent a while back. Maybe she'll notice them this time.

WAIT — I kid you not — the editor just responded. She liked both of them.

SUCCESS.

Day 94: April 3, 2020 - 10:03 am (Friday)

I've contemplated potential ways to exploit the Patreon platform. If you haven't heard of them, Patreon is a platform for creators (writers, songwriters, storytellers, artists, etc.) that enables them to provide subscription services to their fans ("patrons").

It provides total control to creators, who can use Patreon as a content-sharing platform and offer tiered subscriptions to followers. For example, if you're a musician, your entry-level tier might be early access to your songs for $2 per month. Your second tier could be a weekly Q&A in addition to the early access for $5 per month.

It's a great platform for establishing stable, recurring income. An entrepreneur's dream, right? Of course, it takes time to build a following, but that's the theme of freelance writing (or any startup for that matter).

4:26 pm

Oh, man...I am so freaking drained today. I sidestepped what I planned on doing (which, of course, I still need to do today) and created a Patreon page for 365 Days of Freelance Writing.

Day 95: April 4, 2020 - 8:42 am (Saturday)

There are two times during the day where my creative thoughts are most fluid. Right before I fall asleep each night and right when I wake up each morning. I've found that many writers (and people in general) share this ill-timed mental clarity.

Which is kind of frustrating, right?

We're awake approximately 16 hours each day, and the 15ish minutes you spend drifting to sleep or out of slumber is the peak of creative thoughts?

Far from optimal.

Now, that doesn't mean *zero* creativity takes place the other 15 hours and 30 minutes. And it's not uncommon to hit your stride during the day, producing fluid thoughts and well-designed content.

I just think it's baffling how easy it is to have abstract thoughts when the noises, stresses, and needs of daily life aren't top of mind or in the way.

Maybe I should meditate more. My walks have been creative triggers in the past. So have long drives.

This could be attributed to the therapeutic effect of taking your mind off everything.

Day 96: April 5, 2020 - 2:30 pm (Sunday)

Well, I begged for more communication from Client D's editor...

She's informed me that they're "putting a freeze on freelance content for the time being."

Ugh.

So, yeah, I'm feeling the impact of the pandemic. But my spirits are still high! There's more time to focus on Medium content, which I'm going to diversify. I'll still write regularly for Bacon Bits, but I want to start building up 365 Days of Freelance Writing's audience too. And I still want to get some posts on other Medium publications to expand my audience.

Most Medium subscribers aren't on Medium for a single topic; they have a broader range of interests. So, to provide the most value and reach the most people, I need to broaden my writing scope.

I was inspired to do this after reading every post on ijustrealizedsomething.com.[19] It's hilarious content. Cornelius Schmeckleman (not his real name) takes the most mundane situations and concepts and creates comedic gold.

How does this have anything to do with my Medium strategy? It made me realize I haven't been true to my writing interests and voice. I've been too business-oriented. As much as I believe sharing personal finance content is important, I also don't want to shy away from writing about things I enjoy.

And if that means writing about weird shit that bugs me, so be it.

Week 14 Lessons & Takeaways

#1: I compiled a quick analysis of my Medium posts' financial performances. It's a little messy, but there's one discernable pattern: the success of one post can amplify the earnings of others.

#2: Welp, Client G was hit hard by COVID-19. They lost a bunch of revenue, which means they're suspending work with freelancers. My contact at the company was adamant about still wanting to work with me once the world normalizes — but who knows when that'll be.

#3: March, the longest month in the history of time, came to a close. We're officially through one quarter of 2020! Woohoo!

#4: Sure enough, Client D finally got back to me. The editor submitted my purchase order (so I can finally get paid for work I finished in February) AND accepted two pitches. We're back in business. *(Or, so I thought.)*

#5: My Patreon platform is in the works. I did a little design work and filled out the "about" description. Figuring out the subscription tiers is a challenge. I want to provide as much value as possible, but how do you put a price on that?

#6: You know what's frustrating? The fact that my creative juices are gushing (is that an uncomfortable phrase?) right before bed and right when I wake up. That's when ideas take shape with minimal effort — when there aren't any distractions or things to worry about. But I suppose that's why I find it easier to write on walks. It's like meditation.

#7: Welp, Client D has asked me to hold off on the two accepted pitches. *Sigh.*

Day 97: April 6, 2020 - 10:09 am (Monday)

Wait...it's day 97 and I haven't mentioned Canva?[20]

I'm sorry, people. I can't believe it took me this long.

If graphic design is not your forte (it certainly isn't mine), don't worry — Canva is here to ease your worries.

Canva is a super simple design platform where you can create logos, headers, infographics, or whatever you please. I don't have constant graphic design needs, but I use Canva when they arise. That's how I designed the 365 Days of Freelance Writing logo.

And it's free.

There's also a subscription option that gives you access to more visual elements, pictures, and functionality, like the ability to resize a design. As of today, Canva Pro is $12.95 when you pay monthly or $119.4 if you pay annually (equates to $9.95 per month, so you're saving $36 if you pay one lump sum).

I don't pay for the subscription, but I could see the benefit.

Editor's note: Now I pay for the subscription. It's worth it.

Day 98: April 7, 2020 - 10:10 am (Tuesday)

Yesterday's entry made me realize something: I'm failing you.

I'm failing you because I haven't shared some of the resources I'm using (e.g. Canva).

I'LL DO BETTER, I PROMISE.

Today's highlight is Elna Cain's freelance writing course: Write Your Way to Your First $1k.[21] *(Disclaimer: this is an affiliate link.)*

When I first stumbled across freelance writing, I discovered one of Elna's blog posts. She opened my eyes to this career path. After devouring some of her content, I found her writing course for beginners. It's a detailed, step-by-step guide to starting a freelance writing business, including templates, resources, and video walkthroughs.

I highly recommend this course. It helped me build a foundation for my writing business.

Day 99: April 8, 2020 - 5:07 pm (Wednesday)

Next up, Jorden Makelle's Facebook group and courses.

But first...

I. Am. Exhausted.

I've spent my entire day editing, touching up, optimizing, and promoting my latest Bacon Bits post: "How to Invest When You Know Nothing About Investing."[22] It's my longest Medium post to date at approximately 3,500 words, which converts to a 15-minute reading time.

It's funny, it takes 15-minutes to read (which is decently long), but it took *days* to write.

On top of that, I feel like I've accomplished nothing today, even though I've been plugging away the entire time. But I know why.

It's because I tried to go the extra mile with this post. I created several graphics, tables, and even a freebie at the end that leads people to the Bits newsletter. THEN, I tweeted at the companies I mentioned and recommended. THEN, I sent LinkedIn connection requests to the social media managers of said companies.

Watch this post tank. That would be some serious irony and a true test of my mettle.

Anyway.

Jorden Makelle is a freelance writer, business owner, and certified badass. During my writing discovery phase, I couldn't get enough of Jorden's content. She has a very unique style. It's blunt, vulgar, and real.

She doesn't bullshit you. Plain and simple.

She's renowned for her cold emailing course, Killer Cold Emailing.[23] On top of that, she runs a YouTube page with 32,000+ subscribers and a Facebook group — Writing Revolters — with 12,000+ members.[24]

Editor's note: The Writing Revolters Facebook group is temporarily archived, meaning it isn't active; however, you can still search for relevant questions and answers.

If there are two things I've taken away from Jorden, it's the importance of (1) a business mindset and (2) a unique writing style/voice.

She'll be the first one to stress treating your freelance writing as a business. Why? Because that's what it is. It's a business — and you're a business owner.

You'll also quickly see the difference between traditional writing and writing with personality.

Day 100: April 9, 2020 - 7:29 am (Thursday)

Hey, look at that, we made it to the 100th day. I feel like I should get a cake or something.

In less exciting news, my "how-to" article on investing was *not* distributed, meaning Medium didn't share it across its various channels or include it under my article tags. Bummer.

Alas, it comes with the territory. Sometimes you pour your heart, soul, and time into your writing to no avail.

The question now: why wasn't it distributed?

There's no way to know for sure, but I'll have to study and compare it to my previous posts. Maybe I had too many external links to financial services companies. Maybe they didn't like my header image.

It's something to learn from, which is okay.

Plus, it's evergreen content. The fundamentals of investing haven't and won't change. I can link to it forever.

Day 101: April 10, 2020 - 10:57 am (Friday)

Continuing where I left off yesterday...

I published a follow-up to my investing piece, "How to Take Advantage of the Down Market Before It Rebounds."[25] This one goes into more detail around what to specifically invest in if you want to take advantage of bear market prices, assuming you're new to the investing game.

Guess what I linked to three times? *Yep.* Yesterday's post.

Of course, Medium curated today's post under "money." We'll see if either post has noteworthy success.

Quick aside: I'm still not certain this is factual, but I think posts that have the "coronavirus" tag are either automatically curated or have a much higher chance. I've referenced the pandemic in a few posts lately, tagging it in three of them.

All three were curated under "money."

It's still a small sample size, but it's worth mentioning.

Topic change: I reviewed Medium's distribution guidelines.[26] I think I figured out why my post, "How to Invest When You Know Nothing About Investing," was *not* curated. Here's why:

Reason #1: Third-party advertising. Medium promotes itself as "Ad-Free" — which includes the following provision:

- **Third-party advertising and sponsorships are not allowed.** You may not advertise or promote third-party products, services, or brands through Medium posts, publications, or letters. This includes images that indicate brand sponsorship in a post or letter, or as part of a publication name or logo.

I'm a little iffy about this one because I see curated posts that refer to third-party apps, services, tools, etc. all the time. I don't think I did anything outrageously against the norm. So, I'm not convinced I violated this particular stipulation.

Reason #2: Non-compliant CTAs or first-party promotion. While you're allowed to promote yourself and your products/services, Medium doesn't want you to oversell.

- Non-compliant CTAs or first-party promotion
  - Medium writers are welcome to promote themselves and their products/services in their writer bio. The story page is for the story. Any calls to action (CTAs) in the story should be simple, clear, and brief (under 40 words or so), including for publications. Embeds that collect user information must do it off-site only (collecting user info on Medium is a rules violation). Your CTA may include a limited number of hyperlinks to other content. Intrusive or deceptive CTAs or promotions may cause your story to be rejected.

You could make the argument that I had two CTAs (listed below). Individually, they're both under the word limit — but, together, they exceed the 40-word threshold. On top of that — and this may be the real kicker — my first CTA links to three other Bacon Bits posts, which are then embedded below. So, that's like...six links.

Medium doesn't specify a "limited number," but I imagine I exceeded it.

CTA #1:

> Our world is becoming more automated and user-friendly, so quit making excuses — <u>organize your finances</u>, <u>clean up your budget</u>, <u>build an emergency fund</u>, and **start investing**.

CTA #2:

> Want to calculate how much your portfolio could be worth in five years? Ten years? By retirement? **<u>Sign up</u>** for the Bits newsletter to receive a free Compound Interest Calculator in excel.

Further, you could argue that my second CTA, which encourages newsletter signups, violates another rule too:

- Disqualifying story types
    - No meta – no stories written *about* Medium
    - Sponsored content, content marketing, or stories whose sole purpose is to gather signups/traffic

This is a little subjective, but I think the keyword is **sole**. While one purpose was to gather signups/traffic, it was not the *sole* purpose.

As any successful Medium writer would attest, to be successful on this platform, you have to provide value to your audience. You have to engage, teach, or inspire them. That is purpose #1. The hope is that, by doing so, you generate traffic and broaden your audience, which is purpose #2.

Reason #3: Requests to read slowly or to the end.

I didn't know this was a policy, which is my fault. I can understand the reasoning behind it, considering Medium pays based on reading time.

If the other reasons weren't the causes, this did the trick. I mean, it was the post's fourth paragraph.

> If you're serious about investing (and you must be, because you're here), I urge you to read every step carefully.

If you're going to invest your money, it's critical to know the fundamentals and what you're getting yourself into (and I'll die on that hill). But I'll own it — I broke this curation rule.

So, learn from my mistakes. If you're trying to grow your Medium audience through curation, read the guidelines first.

Day 102: April 11, 2020 - 2:40 pm (Saturday)

In client news, I received a price request for a white paper. It should be around 2,000 words, and I was given a rough template/structure. I quoted $1,500.

That would be a nice shot in the arm after this past week.

Even though I've worked with clients for almost a year now, I still struggle with pricing. The last thing I want to do is undervalue my work — but it's tough to calculate a "fair" price.

I've written enough blog posts now that I have a decent feel for how much I'm willing to work for. I charge fixed rates for blog posts, but I benchmark it using "per word" rates. So, for example, Client E pays me $450 per blog post. They're between 1,500 and 2,000 words, which equates to a range of $0.225 to $0.30 per word.

I prefer closer to $0.35 to $0.40, but Client E is a good brand in my niche.

White papers are trickier because they demand a premium. They take a deeper dive into a concept or problem, so they're more technical and authoritative.

For reference, here's how I came up with $1,500. Using my first white paper as a base, I compared word count and time spent. For the first project, my rate came out to ~$0.74 per word — but only $57 per hour (there was a ton of research involved). This time, I don't expect nearly as much research time.

I rounded 74 cents to 75 cents and multiplied by my estimation of 2,000 words, which came out to a clean $1,500.

To see what this looked like in hours, I divided $1,500 by my preferred hourly rate of $75 — which came out to 20 hours. That feels right.

	Words	$/word	Hours	$/hour
White Paper #1	2700	$ 0.74	35	$ 57.14
White Paper #2	2000	$ 0.75	20	$ 75.00

	Price
White Paper #1	$ 2,000
White Paper #2	$ 1,500

While I'd prefer $100 per hour, that seemed like too large of a jump from the previous quote — so I want to ballpark around $75 per hour instead.

Day 103: April 12, 2020 - 8:00 am (Sunday)

Since it's Sunday, it's the most appropriate time to talk about Monday, right?

And by Monday, I mean Monday.com, of course.[27]

Alright, I'm sorry for that lame introduction. But, on Sundays, I plan for the week ahead, creating tasks for the week and assigning them to each day.

For the majority of my writing career, I've used a Google Doc to outline my weeks.

It looks like this:

Monday - 3/30/2020

1. ~~365 Days of Freelancing~~
2. ~~Pay accountant~~
3. ~~Write 200 words of Client A post~~
4. Finish writing Division post
5. ~~Write Gaming Nexus news post (x2)~~
6. Outline Digital Privacy News ideas

Tuesday - 3/31/2020

1. ~~365 Days of Freelancing~~
2. ~~Call with Client G~~
3. Edit Client G post
4. ~~Write / Edit Client A post~~
5. ~~Outline Client Client E post~~
6. ~~Write 250 words of Bits newsletter~~
7. ~~Send Divide post to Forge~~
8. ~~Outline Digital Privacy News ideas~~

As you can see, I separate my writing process across days. For example, on March 30, I wrote 200 words of a post for Client A; on March 31, I finished writing the post (another 200 words or so) and edited it too — since it's only 400 words in total.

Pretty straightforward.

Well, this past week, I decided to explore another platform for my task list: Monday.com

I discovered it while editing a client's blog post. She mentioned it as a helpful tool and recommended it for process management. *See, editing has other perks too.*

I'm still learning the ins and outs of the interface, but so far so good. It's a clean, intuitive platform. What's impressive is that it works for massive companies or solopreneurs.

Teetering on the fence, I wasn't sure I'd stick with it.

But I added a column that lets me count projected and actual words, so I can track productivity in another way. Plus, I figured out how to automate the process a little bit. I can just duplicate a board to create my next week.

And, I'll be honest, it feels nice to click "Done."

Editor's note: it's not free, which I realized at the end of my undisclosed trial. (See Day 110)

Week 15 Lessons & Takeaways

#1: If you're like me and graphic design is not your forte, Canva can be of assistance. Freelance writing requires some graphic design now and then — such as header images and logos. Canva is an intuitive design platform that anyone can use.

#2: Look up Elna Cain and her writing course. I was fortunate to stumble across her content, which drove me to pursue freelance writing.

#3: Don't underestimate the time it takes to edit, format, and promote your Medium posts. It'll suck up the majority of your day.

#4: Do yourself a favor, join the Writing Revolters Facebook group. It's full of diverse writers of varying niches, backgrounds, and levels of experience.

#5: If you want to be the best, you have to learn from the best. Jorden Makelle is one of them. Check out her posts and courses.

#6: We hit the 100-day mark — go us.

#7: If you're writing on Medium and want your work to be curated, read the guidelines for curation. While I've reviewed them before, I clearly didn't put forth a thorough effort. A few quick tips:

- Don't oversell third-party products and services. Medium doesn't like that.
- Don't oversell your products and services. Medium doesn't like that.
- Don't encourage your readers to read slowly or until the end. Medium doesn't like that either.

#8: Pricing is hard. The good news: once you price one service, you can use it as a baseline for pricing others. Plus, you can factor in expected hours and preferred rate per hour/word to calculate your ideal price. I did this recently for a white paper.

#9: If you need process improvements, check out Monday.com. It's a clean, easy-to-use platform for weekly planning.

Day 104: April 13, 2020 - 8:19 am (Monday)

My Medium strategy is paying off.

In early December, I had 32 followers. As of this morning, I'm up to **302** followers.

That's 944% growth over four months or about 68 new followers per month. It's been a real confidence booster. I'm feeling more and more inspired to focus my attention on Medium. After today, I'll already have three published posts in April — with more to come.

If you can't tell, I'm excited.

One of the reasons I'm excited is that I can analyze my approach and write about it. That's part of writing's beauty — whether you succeed or fail, you can write about your experience and takeaways. So long as you make an attempt, it becomes writing material.

You could even argue that you could still write about a topic without trying it.

"7 goals I wish I focused on last year"

You could be a couch potato and still write.

Day 105: April 14, 2020 - 10:23 am (Tuesday)

Towards the beginning of our yearlong trek, I mentioned a Spotify playlist, Thunder & Rain Sounds. I found a better genre and playlist for "focus music" that I've been listening to for the last couple of months.

"Binaural Beats: Focus"

It didn't take long to notice the positive effects, like increased concentration. Since then, it's been my go-to playlist for productivity. With the right headphones, it blocks out all external noise and distractions.

Day 106: April 15, 2020 - 11:38 am (Wednesday)

After living in Florida for the last two weeks, I have concluded that Floridians who brave the Summer heat are either cold-blooded or batshit insane.

It's so freaking hot here.

I went for a run this morning, and I was drenched in sweat after two miles.

I'm from Columbia, South Carolina — so I'm familiar with humidity and sweaty days. But Columbia isn't getting blasted by 90+ degree weather in April. I don't think I could embrace that level of heat for eight months of the year.

As we speak, it's a cool 57 degrees in Columbia.

Here? 90.

Day 107: April 16, 2020 - 7:05 am (Thursday)

Want to hear a little technique I've picked up that's led to more shares of my content?

Crediting the people and companies that have helped me during my freelancing journey.

For example, my most recent Medium post outlined the steps I took to ease the transition between the corporate grind and self-employment. One of those steps was studying successful writers — who I mentioned by name (Elna Cain and Jorden Makelle). They were instrumental in my development process, so it was only right to credit them. *You're probably recognizing that I recommended them a few pages ago in this book too.*

By promoting their brands, they're more inclined to share *my* content since it validates *their* content and courses.

It's a win-win.

Last month, this share/shoutout technique happened with a payment platform, Veem.[28] Except it was unintentional.

In my post, "4 Financial Tasks You Need to Prioritize as a Freelancer," I recommended Veem because the platform doesn't charge you transaction processing fees (unlike PayPal).[29] I didn't tag Veem on social media after posting, and I didn't expect them to find it.

But, they did — and they shared it.

One month later, I mentioned Veem in another post. Again, they shared it.

> ⟲ You Retweeted
>
> **Stay Home | Pay with Veem** @GoVeem · Mar 19
> Freelance writer @CarterKilmann shares his tips on how he saves money without a steady paycheck in this @Medium article.
>
> How to Save Money as a Freelancer Without a Steady Paycheck
> medium.com

Of course, this tactic only works if it's genuine. If you didn't gain anything from a person, product, or service, don't promote it. It'll come off as salesy. That's not the point.

The idea is to provide value by sharing the resources that helped you. The wider reach is just a lagniappe. *I never get to use that word, so I did.*

Editor's note: If you're reading the eBook version of 365 Days of Freelance Writing, that link to Veem's website is an affiliate link. I receive a commission if you sign up using that link.

Day 108: April 17, 2020 - 11:01 am (Friday)

I can't look at Tim Denning's content without getting a little down on myself.

The dude is a literal writing machine. He pumps out two, three, sometimes four posts a day. He's one of the most successful and followed Medium writers (82k followers as of today).

I don't read everything he posts, but I can't help but read his "how I'm a successful Medium writer" posts. He doesn't use that sort of self-inflated title, but often covers writing for Medium's Partner Program.

He delves into his approach, mindset, schedule, etc. from time to time. Although it provides a lot of value, I can't help but feel disappointed with my work ethic.

I'm pretty sure this dude has a full-time job, and he's still producing content left and right. He's an animal.

Writing is a long-term game. But, when you compare yourself to others' success, it's easy to forget that. All of a sudden, I start feeling insignificant. My goals feel much farther away.

It's not a productive sequence of thoughts.

Day 109: April 18, 2020 - 12:58 pm (Saturday)

I have trouble making time to read.

Not blog posts, articles, or newsletters — but actual books. That's been an issue ever since I started writing full-time.

I'm not sure why. You'd think it'd be easier since I have total control over my schedule. Could it be because writing, reading, and editing are primary features of my occupation now?

It's hard to say.

By telling you this, maybe I'll be more inclined to read going forward.

On another note, my Medium views/reads have begun to taper off. Yet, the budget-cutting post still earns $20-30 a day. Hopefully, my next post keeps the momentum going.

I noticed that several prominent writers write about how and why their posts succeed. My next Medium post will be my rendition of this type of analysis. I, for one, can't help but click headlines that state something along the lines of "how my post made $1,000."

We'll see if other readers feel the same…

Day 110: April 19, 2020 - 3:11 pm (Sunday)

Welp, Monday.com isn't free.

I opened up my dashboard to plan for the week ahead, and a banner notification stated that I had four days left on my trial.

What a downer. Didn't even realize I was in a trial period.

As of today, there are four tiers of access — Basic ($8 per month), Standard ($10), Pro ($16), and Enterprise (unlisted).

Eh, for what I'm using it for (weekly task lists), I don't think it's worth it right now. I'll give them credit though, I was tempted to subscribe now that I've gotten used to it.

Week 16 Lessons & Takeaways

#1: Since December, I've published more on Medium. It's paying off (literally). I've made a healthy chunk of change from Medium this year, and my following is up to 336.

#2: Look up binaural beats if you need focus music. These tones will ease you into a state of flow.

#3: Florida is a sauna.

#4: When applicable, tag the writers who inspire you or the brands whose tools you use. You never know, they might share your work with their followers.

#5: Tim Denning is a well-known, successful Medium writer. But, sometimes, reading his content causes me to doubt myself because he produces at such a high level. It's illogical and unnecessary to think this way though. I just have to bounce back.

#6: I don't spend enough time reading books, and I don't have a good reason as to why that is.

#7: My budget-cutting post is still racking up $20-30 a day.

#8: PSA: Monday.com is not free. I repeat, Monday.com is not free. If you only use it for task lists, it's probably not worth it.

Day 111: April 20, 2020 - 9:24 am (Monday)

Remember that white paper I mentioned last week? Bad news incoming:

White Paper — Inbox

9:06 AM

Unfortunately is a no go. Clients are clamping down on what they're willing to spend these days. Hope you're hanging in there?

Bummer.

Don't worry, Client A. I'm hanging in there.

Day 112: April 21, 2020 - 9:40 am (Tuesday)

I know I've mentioned a couple of sources for writing gigs, but I haven't talked much about pitching "random" companies. By random, I mean companies in your niche that may or may not need your services, but they haven't issued a request for proposals. These are companies you find through research and keyword searches. This is the process of cold pitching.

Why haven't I talked about cold pitching? Because I rarely do it anymore.

It's not a bad approach, per se, especially if you need clients (and money). Considering you have direct insight into my income, you might be thinking, "Well, Carter, couldn't you use more money?"

Yes, I'd like to make more. Of course. But I'd rather make more from my personal work (365 Days of Freelance Writing, Bacon Bits, my other Medium posts), which takes time to turn into reliable income streams.

Time is finite. Pitching takes time. More clients take time.

In an ideal world, my personal projects sustain me, and I don't need to do client work anymore. Until that day, I still need client work to pay bills and live.

Day 113: April 22, 2020 - 7:01 am (Wednesday)

I've been thinking, it could be helpful to share my old cold pitches — especially if you're unfamiliar with the process.

I never tracked my cold pitch success rate (opens, responses, wins), which might come as a surprise, considering my previous job was all about analyzing numbers.

In my first three-ish months of self-employment, I sent about 40 cold pitches to digital marketing agencies, digital banking platforms, and other businesses that seemed to fit within my scope of services. Of those, I think only five or six yielded responses. Of those five or six, only three led to meaningful conversations.

One was a FinTech startup that was open to a trial period but wasn't willing to pay (and no, that wasn't the same FinTech from earlier this year). *Seems like a pattern.*

Two were local digital marketing agencies. At first, one of them was really interested in working together. We emailed back and forth several times — we even talked on the phone once. Then he dropped off the face of the earth.

The other agency, Bearpaw Partners, didn't need a freelancer, but they did invite me in for an interview for a full-time position. (I wasn't ready to work for someone again.) Here's the pitch I sent Dee, the contact I reached out to at the company.

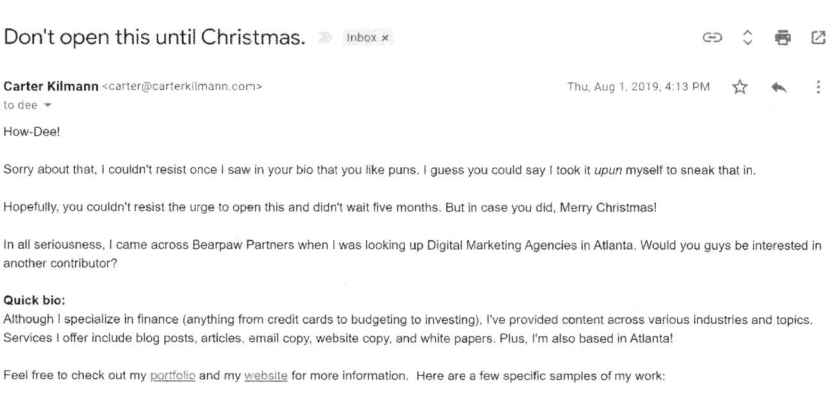

Don't open this until Christmas. Inbox ×

Carter Kilmann <carter@carterkilmann.com>   Thu, Aug 1, 2019, 4:13 PM
to dee

How-Dee!

Sorry about that, I couldn't resist once I saw in your bio that you like puns. I guess you could say I took it *upun* myself to sneak that in.

Hopefully, you couldn't resist the urge to open this and didn't wait five months. But in case you did, Merry Christmas!

In all seriousness, I came across Bearpaw Partners when I was looking up Digital Marketing Agencies in Atlanta. Would you guys be interested in another contributor?

Quick bio:
Although I specialize in finance (anything from credit cards to budgeting to investing), I've provided content across various industries and topics. Services I offer include blog posts, articles, email copy, website copy, and white papers. Plus, I'm also based in Atlanta!

Feel free to check out my portfolio and my website for more information. Here are a few specific samples of my work:

1. 7 Signs You're on Your Way to Financial Freedom
2. What is a REIT and How Can It Make You Money?
3. Why financial literacy will improve your life

Let me know if you guys would be interested. Have a dee-lightful day!

Alright, yeah. I cringed with that one.

Best,

Carter Kilmann
Personal Finance | Freelance Writer
Carter@carterkilmann.com

Out of all the companies I contacted, this was the most personalized in the sense that I targeted Dee's appreciation of puns, which her company bio mentioned. It's those little connections that trigger someone to respond rather than ignore.

...

Depending on your experience with cold pitching, 40 pitches either sounds like a lot or nothing. Which is it? Well, the answer to that question depends on your cold pitching strategy. From my perspective, cold pitching boils down to two schools of thought: quantity and quality.

Quantity advocates focus on high volumes of pitches. These pitches will be pretty cookie-cutter (i.e. practically identical with minimal personalization).

Quality advocates focus on substance and personalization. It should be apparent that these pitches don't follow a simple "lather, rinse, repeat" formula (i.e. addressing everyone you pitch to as "Kelly").

I think quality is more effective, but that's just me. Ten super personalized, hyper-targeted, well-researched pitches are going to outperform 100 general emails. The more time and substance you put into a cold email, the higher chance it'll receive a response.

My pitches trended more towards quality, but I'll admit that I could have put way more time into exploring the company's needs.

11:46 am

Welp, I spoke too soon. More bad news incoming: Client A is reducing my monthly content output.

Quick refresher: Client A is a digital marketing agency; therefore, Client A has multiple clients. My writing work for Client A is spread across several clients. It's been stable, reliable work.

Unfortunately, one of Client A's clients paused blog content. Not the end of the world, but $320 of my monthly income disappeared.

So, guess what I just did? Sent a cold email to a digital marketing agency. It was fresh in my mind, so I figured — *eh*, why not?

Day 114: April 23, 2020 - 9:49 am (Thursday)

I've never been more excited for the NFL draft. Life has been bereft of sports for what feels like eons.

The world could use a good distraction right now — another four million people filed for unemployment last week…

Whenever I become fixated on earning more money with my writing, my mind wanders to copywriting. There's a higher income potential in copywriting than content writing.

Content writing and copywriting are similar, but they're not the same. The key distinction is the aspect of selling. Copywriting is selling with written words.

I have copywriting experience, but it's not a service I actively sell. Last summer/fall, I provided some email copywriting, product descriptions, and feature bullets to a consumer products company. I've also written a couple of landing pages — but that's about the extent of my copywriting portfolio.

Oh, guess who just emailed me back? Client D!

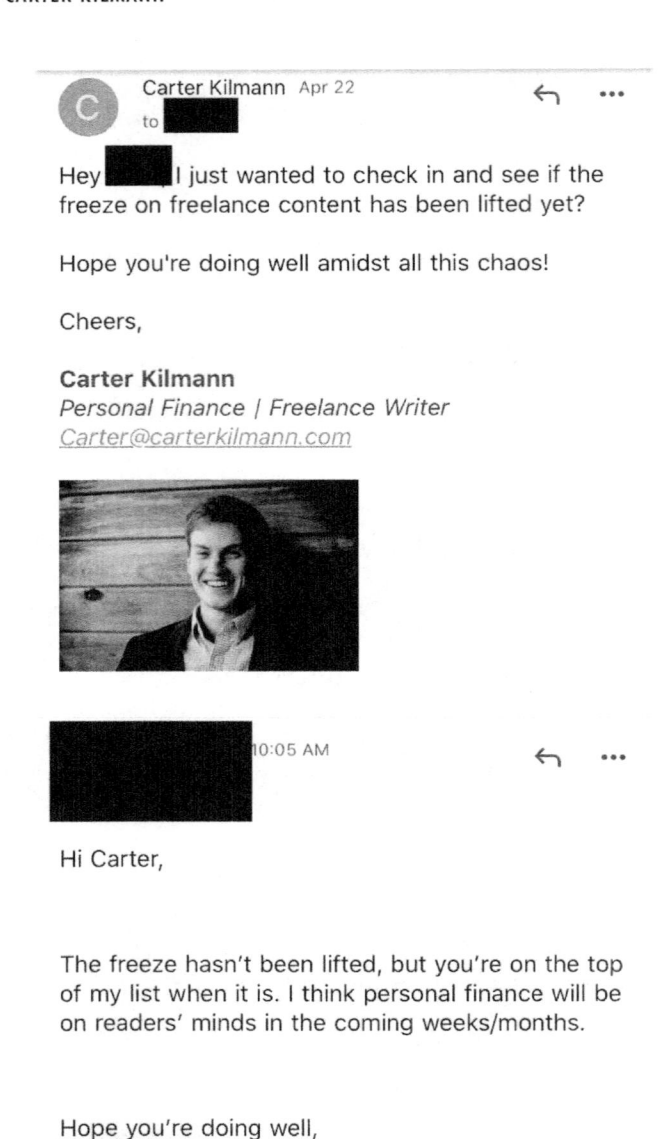

> **Carter Kilmann** Apr 22
> to ▮
>
> Hey ▮ I just wanted to check in and see if the freeze on freelance content has been lifted yet?
>
> Hope you're doing well amidst all this chaos!
>
> Cheers,
>
> **Carter Kilmann**
> *Personal Finance | Freelance Writer*
> *Carter@carterkilmann.com*

▮ 10:05 AM

> Hi Carter,
>
> The freeze hasn't been lifted, but you're on the top of my list when it is. I think personal finance will be on readers' minds in the coming weeks/months.
>
> Hope you're doing well,
>
> ▮

That's reassuring. After Client A delivered yesterday's bad news, I reached out to Client D to check on the content freeze. Now, I feel a little better.

Day 115: April 24, 2020 - 11:24 am (Friday)

Should I submit my work to a publication and give away some of my control or self-publish and risk publications not seeing it?

A perpetual question.

Publications position content in front of larger audiences, increasing the odds of adding followers and earning more money. On the other hand, self-publishing can attract more suitors (i.e. publication editors).

I submitted my "Tell Me About a Time You Failed" piece to one of Medium's publications, Marker.[30] Two weeks went by — nothing. So, I said screw that and self-published. Within 48 hours, two editors left private notes saying they'd like to add my story to their publications.

In my early Medium days, I didn't know publications existed. My first couple of posts were self-published. Fortunately, The Startup editors discovered both of them and asked if I'd like to publish on their platform.

Now, I submit 99% of my posts to publications, including my own. But I still find myself in a publishing pickle from time to time.

Earlier this week, I pitched a post to Better Marketing, a marketing-focused publication — if you couldn't tell by the name. It outlined my thoughts on how I wrote a $1,000+ post. I'd seen a number of these posts on their platform, and I couldn't get enough of them; I love reading about how to optimize Medium posts.

Well, an editor responded yesterday:

Medium post Inbox

Thu, Apr 23, 2:43 PM (1 day ago)

to me

Hey Carter, your post is really good, but we ran a quadrillion "How I made X on Medium" ones already, phasing them out for a bit. If you have anything else on writing, gladly!

So, now I'm in a pickle.

My backup option was to submit it to The Startup, which I did immediately after receiving that email, but I don't want to wait two weeks for them to review it. I'm usually a patient person, but not when it comes to having my content published. I put all this time and energy into writing, so it's frustrating to play wait-and-see.

I'll see how I feel on Monday.

Day 116: April 25, 2020 - 9:25 am (Saturday)

What are the Packers doing? These draft picks are so freaking questionable. Ask anyone with an ounce of NFL knowledge who the best three players for the Packer are, and you'll get the following list:

1. Aaron Rodgers
2. Davante Adams
3. Aaron Jones

Guess who we draft with our first two picks?

A quarterback and a running back.

WHY. Those aren't positions of need!

UGH. Anyway, I forgot to mention that the 365 Days of Freelance Writing Patreon page and Medium publication have officially been launched![31] *How exciting, right?*

Well, I'd launched the Patreon page a little while back, and I'd created the Medium publication even further back, but I hadn't finalized the Patreon tiers or started adding content. And the Medium page didn't have a post, so it didn't exist publicly.

As of today, both are up and running. I'm excited about it.

I need to clean up my Medium page's copy, which I'm hoping drives traffic to the Patreon page.

Editor's note: In case it isn't obvious, I uploaded each day of this book as an individual post on Patreon. The idea was to establish a concurrent revenue stream through Patreon donations as I wrote this book. As you'll see, this tactic did not work.

Day 117: April 26, 2020 - 2:15 pm (Sunday)

Losing internet connection when you have client work to do is no bueno, especially when it's editing.

That's what I get for procrastinating.

5:19 pm

The power is back. Life is restored.

Week 17 Lessons & Takeaways

#1: Client work has slowed a little…

#2: Believe it or not, I rarely cold pitch. The main reason is time. I've chosen to concentrate on my brands, Bacon Bits and 365 Days of Freelance Writing.

#3: I sent about 40 pitches over my first couple of months of full-time freelancing, but I've focused more on attracting inbound leads rather than chasing work. Out of those cold pitches, the most successful ones were more personalized. It's the little things — like looking up your contact's bio, complimenting a certain post, or offering a quick tip — that set pitches apart from the masses.

#4: I've delivered copywriting services before, but I think it's time to explore this offering a little further. Earning six-figures with content writing is a tall task; copywriting makes it more achievable.

#5: The editor from Client D was kind enough to let me know that I'm at the top of the list once "the freeze" is lifted. That was reassuring.

#6: I'm patient, but not when it comes to waiting for my Medium content to be picked up by a publication. Self-publishing has worked in the past — and by that I mean it's attracted editors to my content — but it feels risky. What if no editors see my post and it slips through the cracks? It would feel like a waste.

#7: The Packers made extremely questionable draft decisions.

#8: The Patreon page and Medium Publication for 365 Days or Freelance Writing are open for business.

#9: Procrastination almost got me in trouble. Don't procrastinate — especially when it comes to client work.

Day 118: April 27, 2020 - 8:27 am (Monday)

The weekend didn't clear up my indecision about self-publishing. April's been a big Medium month, but I'm still sitting on three unpublished posts. Time to figure out what I'm going to do…

10:34 am

Alright, alright, alright — I've got it.

Screw waiting, I'm going to self-publish to see if I can attract any suitors. If not, it'll be the inaugural post of my 365 Days of Freelance Writing publication. I think that's the best approach. Plus, I'm tired of updating the in-post stats. The title has changed from "How I Think I Earned **$1,000+** With One Post" to "How I Think I Earned **$1,250+** With One Post."

I'll give it a few days (or at least until it's curated) before I add it to my publication.

12:38 pm

Well, damn. It wasn't curated. That was fast (and disappointing). I think I missed the boat with this whole "how I made $1k+ on Medium" concept.

Day 119: April 28, 2020 - 10:46 am (Tuesday)

Soooooo, yesterday's post strategy didn't go as planned, but curation and views aren't the only indicators of a good article on Medium. A friend of mine — who's been dabbling in writing over the last five months or so — read my post and told me it inspired him to explore Medium a little further. He came across a comedy writing competition, which he's entering.

Inspiring someone to take action is pretty cool.

A couple of weeks after I quit my job (back in July 2019), I published my story on Medium — why I chose to pursue my dreams rather than stay shackled to a desk to earn more money. I shit you not, after reading my post, a college friend of mine gave me a call and told me he was inspired...

...and quit his job too.

I mean, DAMN. That was nuts to hear.

Day 120: April 29, 2020 - 11:17 (Wednesday)

I haven't had the best luck with Medium over the last couple of weeks. I submitted a post to Slackjaw, the largest humor publication on Medium. They didn't think it was the right fit.

The post's premise? Dissecting why curiosity killed the cat.

I don't know, I thought it was a funny concept. At least it was fun to research and write. Plus, now I know the origin of the phrase.

Unfortunately, I was counting on Slackjaw to accept the submission. I'm creating a series of idiom posts that are supposed to be funny, and I want them to be housed in the same place.

Hopefully, I can find another fitting publication that's interested in idioms and humor.

Sort of a unique niche, eh?

Day 121: April 30, 2020 - 12:11 pm (Thursday)

Hmmm...did I make a mistake? At the beginning of the month, I published two Bacon Bits posts — but then I let off the gas. I took a break from Bacon Bits.

Was that a strategic error?

On Day 109 (April 18), I mentioned riding the momentum I'd created with my budget-cutting post. But I wasn't talking about cranking out more financial content — I planned to diversify by trying new topics.

Over the last two weeks, I've finished three Medium posts:

1. Idioms Are Weird. Why Did Curiosity Kill the Cat?
2. My Peace of Mind Cracked Today
3. How I Think I Earned $1,250+ With One Post[32]

The first two are still unpublished. The last one has barely cracked 100 views over three days. I'm not giving up on my diversification tactic, but the results haven't been encouraging so far.

Especially during this financially stressful time, I need to get another Bacon Bits post written and published ASAP.

APRIL STATS

Relative to March, April zoomed by. I've had to navigate a few more client hurdles (content suspensions), but Medium has kept my total earnings in line with the last few months. But, if I don't land a couple more gigs this month, I think we might experience an earnings dip.

As a reminder, here's each client's description:

- Client A — Digital marketing agency
- Client B — Digital marketing agency
- Client C — FinTech startup (no longer a client)
- Client D — Online finance publication (content freeze)
- Client E — Auto finance company
- Client F — ClearVoice assignments
- Client G — SaaS company (no longer a client, for now)

365 Days of Freelancing - Monthly Stats

	Jan	Feb	Mar	Apr
Income				
Client A	960	960	960	640
Client B	329	119	153	189
Client C	500	-	-	-
Client D	350	350	-	-
Client E	-	450	450	900
Client F	-	225	-	-
Client G	-	200	-	-
Medium	32	21	719	734
Total Income	**$2,171**	**$2,325**	**$2,282**	**$2,463**
Growth (%)	-	7.1%	(1.9%)	7.9%
Blog Posts (Paid)				
Client A	6	6	6	4
Client B	3	2	2	2
Client C	1	1	-	-
Client D	1	1	-	-
Client E	-	1	1	2
Client F	-	2	-	-
Client G	-	1	-	-
Total Paid Posts	**11**	**14**	**9**	**8**
Blog Posts (Unpaid)				
Medium	1	-	-	1
Bacon Bits	1	2	4	2
365	-	-	-	2
Total Unpaid Posts	**2**	**2**	**4**	**5**
Total Blog Posts	**13**	**16**	**13**	**13**
Medium				
Views	1,151	1,352	19,466	11,052
Reads	439	468	7,413	4,220
Existing Followers	54	63	80	238
New Followers	9	17	158	133
Total Followers	**63**	**80**	**238**	**371**
LinkedIn				
Existing Followers	458	465	493	526
New Followers	7	28	33	44
Total Followers	**465**	**493**	**526**	**570**

Highlights

- Thanks to my biggest Medium month to date, my income rose by 7.9%. It's impossible to say for sure, but, sans a global pandemic, I think I would've been between $3,500 and $4,000 based on the projects I had lined up.
- My content output would've been higher without the production stall — and if two of my Medium posts would've been published.
- My Medium views and reads are returning from the stratosphere, as expected.
- I didn't add as many Medium followers as I did in March, but it was still a healthy increase of 133. If I can match April's performance, I'll hit 500 by the end of May!
- My LinkedIn following continues to grow at a healthy clip — by 8.4% in April.

MAY

Day 122: May 1, 2020 - 9:47 am (Friday)

Believe it or not, we're one-third of the way through this 366-day journey. Time is flying.

I'm compiling a list of potential publications and websites to submit pitches to. To date, I've prioritized my personal brands over landing more clients. But, ideally, I'd like to make $60k a year while I build my revenue-generating brands.

You can look at the numbers and see that, at least from a dollar standpoint, I'm a ways away. But it doesn't feel like it.

Pre-pandemic, I almost reached a normalized income level of $4,000 per month — before any Medium income and excluding ad-hoc projects.

- **Client A:** $960 for six blog posts each month (doesn't include ad-hoc case studies or white papers)
- **Client B:** $150 - $200 for two editing assignments each month
- **Client D:** $700 - $1,050 for two or three blog posts each month
- **Client E:** $900 for two posts each month
- **Client G:** $900 for two posts each month (eventually, but they suspended our arrangement before we finished the trial period)
- **Total:** $3,610 to $4,100

Client D's estimate might be a little idealistic, but the editor did commission two posts at once right before they put a freeze on freelancer work.

Overall, the timing just didn't click. BUT, it still could once this whole ordeal comes to an end. Fingers crossed that's sooner than later.

Day 123: May 2, 2020 - 11:02 am (Saturday)

My time in Florida has come to an end. ATL here we come.

I'm not sure how common this mistake is, but I made an embarrassing one last night. Have you ever received an email and misread or mistook it for good news when it was actually bad? I experienced some selective reading and whiffed the word "not" as in, "Your story was **not** published by The Writing Cooperative."

Which would normally be an okay slip up…except I announced to the table that my story was published.

Much to my chagrin, it was not published. But it's okay; there are plenty of publications to try. If not, I'll self-publish it and call it a day.

Day 124: May 3, 2020 - 7:09 pm (Sunday)

Today felt like a workday. I had a long editing assignment to knock out, which took a couple of hours. On top of that, I spent two more hours cleaning my apartment — so it's been quite the Sunday.

In other news, my unpublished Medium posts were picked up by Curiosity Never Killed the Writer — an apt name for my "curiosity killed the cat" post. Have I mentioned the other post? I don't think I have. I knocked it out in an afternoon actually (which is totally unlike me).

The title? "My Piece of Mind Cracked Today"[33]

I wrote it after Client A informed me that one of her clients was suspending content output. It was the first time I'd experienced any sort of financial worry about writing (that's the beauty of having runway established ahead of time).

I don't expect much from these posts in terms of views and followers. It just felt good to write about something besides personal finance on Medium.

Week 18 Lessons & Takeaways

#1: Over this past week, my Medium strategies were...hmm... *ineffective*.

#2: Views, reads, and claps aren't the only metrics of performance for Medium posts. Inspiring readers to act on their desires is another key indicator of successful writing.

#3: I'm concerned that I may have let off the gas too soon with respect to pumping out Bacon Bits content. That'll be a renewed focus in May.

#4: We're a third of the way through this 366 day writing journey. Time flies when you're having fun, right? *Damn right*.

#5: We can play the "what if" game for days, but I might've been pulling in a stable $4,000 per month by now if the pandemic hadn't occurred. And that's before Medium income and one-off projects.

#6: I'd say "read your emails carefully," but we're human — and prone to mistakes. I misread an email and thought my idiom post was published by The Writing Cooperative. Turns out my mind skipped the "not" in "not published." And I had announced to Kaileigh's family that my post was accepted before catching my mistake. Ugh.

#7: I'm glad I charge an hourly rate for my editing services because it's heavily dependent on the body of work. How can you determine a standard fixed rate?

#8: My unpublished Medium posts were finally picked up by a publication. I'm not expecting many views or reads though.

Day 125: May 4, 2020 - 9:49 am (Monday)

I like LinkedIn as a lead-generation platform, don't get me wrong, but I'm not the biggest fan of using it as a cold pitching platform. I receive salesy connection requests all the time. Like connecting is a ruse just so people can hit you with a sales pitch.

Here's an example that felt disingenuous. This person led with a pretty standard, but welcoming connection request. Nothing wrong with it. One week later (almost to the minute), he asked if my business had been impacted by the pandemic. We exchanged a couple of surface-level messages before the conversation died.

APR 17

6:51 am

Hey Carter,

I'm looking to grow my network with businesses like yourself. Would be great to connect.

I look forward to being part of your network.

Carter Kilmann · 6:52 am
Happy to connect,

APR 24

7:59 am

Hey Carter

I hope your keeping well and safe during this difficult time.

How's business going during this time?

Carter Kilmann · 8:03 am
Hey A few of my clients have been impacted, which has led to reduced volumes of work. But nothing extreme. How about you?

> **3:28 pm**
> Hey Carter we are good thanks and business is going well thanks for asking. I am sorry for the reduction in the work for your business and clients being impacted.
>
> Have you looked at ways of getting new clients for your business during this time?
>
> *APR 25*
>
> **Carter Kilmann** · 5:10 am
> That's good to hear.
>
> For sure, there's always a need for content.

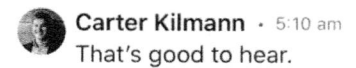

This morning, he led with this doozy of a sales pitch:

> *TODAY*
>
> **7:14 am**
> Question for you... What say if I could send you 10 qualified leads every week?
>
> **Carter Kilmann** · 8:19 am
> 10 leads would be appealing, but that also depends on the work and the rate
>
> **9:16 am**
> When you free this week to jump on a call so that we can go through this further with you?

I mean, what do you expect me to say to that? I can see that you're about to sell me something.

Next up, the request to hop on the phone. For me, I'd rather you take the time to spell out what you're selling me. Maybe that's just me (I'm a visual person, not auditory). I like transparency, not vague promises of personalized leads.

It could be legit, or it might be a total scam. I'll hear it out purely for the sake of writing a conclusion for this post.

Day 126: May 5, 2020 - 5:07 pm (Tuesday)

I had a super productive Tuesday, knocking out everything on my task list. Plus, Better Marketing accepted my submission, "How I Landed 3 Clients in My First Week of Self-Employment."[34]

I've tried to replicate the success of my budget-cutting post by sharing pertinent lessons through personal anecdotes.

How I Quit My Steady Job and Pursued My Entrepreneurial Dreams

320 views	159 reads	50% ratio	22 fans

How I Think I Earned $1,250+ With One Post

114 views	29 reads	25% ratio	12 fans

See the pattern? Hasn't worked as well so far.

Oh, continuing from yesterday's sales pitch, I still haven't heard from the guy. I sent, "Are you free right now?"

No response.

Editor's note: He never responded.

8:36 pm

It's been seven weeks since I've attended a public social gathering — ever since that weekend I spent in Nashville. Tonight, I went to the park and drank with some friends.

It was nice.

Day 127: May 6, 2020 - 10:38 am (Wednesday)

Ughhh...it's gonna be a slow day today.

Cinco de Mayo = staying up late + tequila = tired Carter

Here's an interesting observation though: now that I've been writing for a while, I've not only built up a portfolio but also a vault of unpublished posts and ideas. When I first started writing, that wasn't the case. It's convenient when my brain's moving slow on a particular day (oh, you know, like today).

Man, I need coffee.

12:47 pm

I had coffee, the day is looking up.

My Better Marketing post was distributed in three topics: Freelancing, Marketing, and Social Media. Good news, right? I'm not so sure.

From what I've read (and experienced with a couple of posts), distribution through multiple topics doesn't guarantee more engagement, which is super counterintuitive, right?

We'll see...

Day 128: May 7, 2020 - 11:42 am (Thursday)

It pays to do your research before pitching. Last week, I noticed that Writing Revolt is open to guest pitches, for which they're paying $100.[35]

1,000 words for $100 isn't amazing, but Writing Revolt holds a special place in my heart since it was integral to my development as a writer.

I read their pitch guidelines and perused existing guest posts. Nothing related to freelance finances whatsoever. So, I decided to pitch a post about managing money as a freelancer.

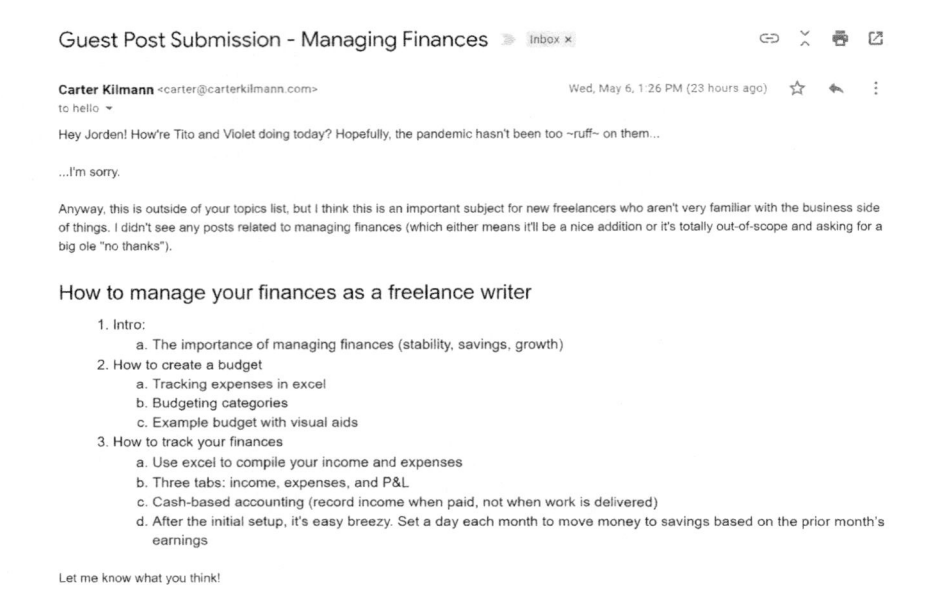

Guest Post Submission - Managing Finances Inbox

Carter Kilmann <carter@carterkilmann.com>   Wed, May 6, 1:26 PM (23 hours ago)
to hello

Hey Jorden! How're Tito and Violet doing today? Hopefully, the pandemic hasn't been too ~ruff~ on them...

...I'm sorry.

Anyway, this is outside of your topics list, but I think this is an important subject for new freelancers who aren't very familiar with the business side of things. I didn't see any posts related to managing finances (which either means it'll be a nice addition or it's totally out-of-scope and asking for a big ole "no thanks").

How to manage your finances as a freelance writer

1. Intro:
    a. The importance of managing finances (stability, savings, growth)
2. How to create a budget
    a. Tracking expenses in excel
    b. Budgeting categories
    c. Example budget with visual aids
3. How to track your finances
    a. Use excel to compile your income and expenses
    b. Three tabs: income, expenses, and P&L
    c. Cash-based accounting (record income when paid, not when work is delivered)
    d. After the initial setup, it's easy breezy. Set a day each month to move money to savings based on the prior month's earnings

Let me know what you think!

Well, they liked the idea — and they're willing to pay $200 for an even more comprehensive guide.

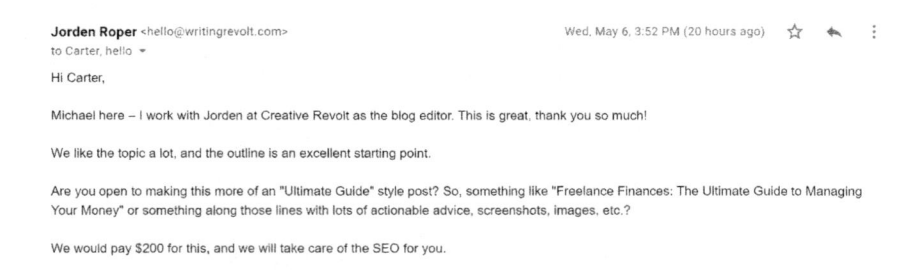

Jorden Roper <hello@writingrevolt.com>   Wed, May 6, 3:52 PM (20 hours ago)
to Carter, hello

Hi Carter,

Michael here – I work with Jorden at Creative Revolt as the blog editor. This is great, thank you so much!

We like the topic a lot, and the outline is an excellent starting point.

Are you open to making this more of an "Ultimate Guide" style post? So, something like "Freelance Finances: The Ultimate Guide to Managing Your Money" or something along those lines with lots of actionable advice, screenshots, images, etc.?

We would pay $200 for this, and we will take care of the SEO for you.

It pays to pitch content ideas that haven't been published on a site yet.

Day 129: May 8, 2020 - 3:14 pm (Friday)

I'm trying to get better at warm pitching. If you're unfamiliar, it's the process of developing a relationship with an editor, marketing director, etc. before pitching your services. The easiest way to get a response from an editor is if they know you — or, at least, recognize your name. Even if it's a fleeting thought like, "Hmmm...Carter Kilmann...that name seems familiar."

I'm determined to post on Business Insider and Supermaker. The former is a prominent business publication (if you couldn't tell) and the latter brands itself as "new school business media."

I've started following editors for these publications on Twitter. I'm hoping to nurture digital relationships by promoting or engaging with their tweets.

My first attempt at engaging with an editor from Business Insider has...well...gone unnoticed thus far.

It was an eerie moment of synchronicity.

Earlier today, I published the following post on Bacon Bits: "Monopoly: Board Game or Our Current Reality?"[36] It compares elements of Monopoly and the current economy/economic fallout. It was fun to write, I incorporated my sense of humor.

Anyway, while searching for header images, I came across Ms. Monopoly, a 2019 female rendition of Monopoly.

Well, within an hour of publishing my post, Stephanie Hallett (who I started following **this morning**) quote tweeted an unbelievably bizarre Ms. Monopoly advertisement, saying "What! The! Eff!!!!!!!!!!!!!!!" (I didn't shortchange the number of exclamation points.)

For 1 minute and 48 seconds, we hear the stories of three girls aspiring to be inventors. It feels like it's going to be some sort of startup incubator ad.

Except it's Ms. Monopoly...

So, of course, I have to tell her about this weird experience. It's like a weird sign from the Monopoly gods, who am I to ignore that?

My response:

"1. That was totally unexpected. I'm so thrown.

2. It's eerie. I posted something on Medium a few minutes ago about Monopoly, and I noticed the Ms. Monopoly game in my search for a header image...I thought, 'I didn't know there was a Ms. Monopoly,'

And here it is on my feed..."

No response. Awesome.

Day 130: May 9, 2020 - 10:14 am (Saturday)

I think it's time to sit down and reassess my business goals — specifically how my daily and weekly tasks align with them.

Client B, my editing client, is a digital marketing agency. While reviewing one of her posts on goal-setting, I realized I need to reconsider how my task list advances my progress towards my goals. I have the big picture figured out, but my day-to-day life feels somewhat arbitrary.

It's also time to push for copywriting work.

In other news, Kaileigh stepped in dog shit...

Day 131: May 10, 2020 - 3:50 pm (Sunday)

It's the first work-free Sunday I've had in a few weeks. My editing client altered her strategy/schedule a bit, so she'll provide drafts on Tuesday/Wednesday rather than Thursday/Friday.

In a bit of personal news, I'm moving in with Kaileigh (a big step, I know). My lease expires on May 25, so stage one of my move-out process commenced today. Stage one: selling furniture, which means I put on my photographer hat and snapped some pictures to upload on Facebook.

There's a bit of a silver lining — sharpening my copywriting skills. Hopefully, I can craft compelling product descriptions that buyers can't resist.

5:07 pm

Update: I had fun writing these descriptions.

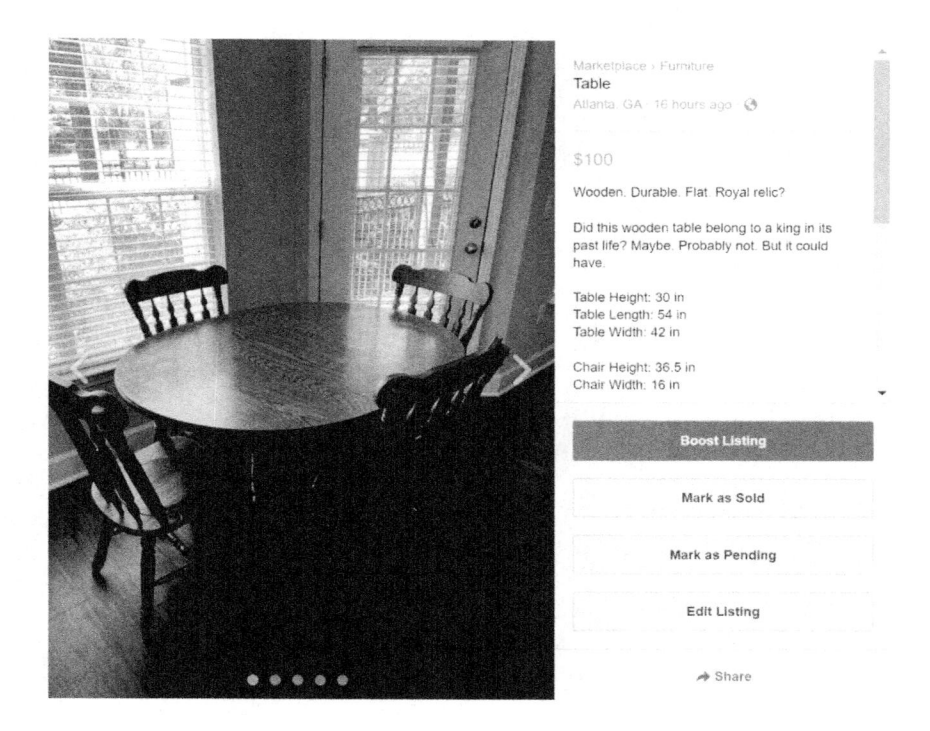

Week 19 Lessons & Takeaways

#1: LinkedIn is an excellent platform for networking and lead generation, but I don't like sending (or receiving) cold pitches via LinkedIn. Warm pitches, sure. Establish a relationship first. But cold pitches rarely pique my interest.

#2: I tried to replicate my budget-cutting post's success by blending anecdotal lessons into my writing. It hasn't worked as well as I expected.

#3: After two months of quarantine, I finally did something social. It was nice.

#4: Since last July, I've accumulated a respectable inventory of ideas and rough drafts. It's nice to have when I'm not sure what to work on.

#5: Medium posts distributed in two or more topics are not guaranteed to outperform posts only distributed in one.

#6: It pays to send unique post ideas to publications. I sent Writing Revolt a pitch about managing freelance finances, and they asked for a comprehensive guide and offered to pay double.

#7: Warm pitching generates more conversions than cold pitches — but it takes much longer since you have to build a relationship with the prospect first. My first attempt to engage with one particular editor on Twitter crashed and burned (i.e. no response).

#8: What time is it? Goal-setting time. Or...I guess the better answer would be "goal-reassessing time." I haven't touched my goals since my first month of self-employment. My weekly tasks should be tied to these goals. I need to do a better job of this.

#9: Want to practice copywriting? Sell something on Facebook Marketplace and write a killer product description.

Day 132: May 11, 2020 - 10:36 am (Monday)

Copywriting requires a deeper knowledge of consumer psychology and marketing. There's an adage about successful writers (I might butcher it): good writers make you laugh, great writers make you cry, and the best writers make you buy.

In short, it's a much taller task to persuade someone to purchase something. So, this is going to take some time to digest.

For the last two hours, I've looked for an answer to the following questions:

1. How should I learn copywriting?
2. How do I find copywriting clients?

While I know copywriting basics, I could use a refresher and holistic overview of the process, including where to find clients or gigs, how to engage with them, and how to prove my worth as a copywriter. Somewhat surprisingly, Reddit came through with the best content for my needs.

This Reddit post outlines a pretty comprehensive process for getting started (including recommended readings and a general schedule).[37]

4:46 pm

Just got Medium's monthly newsletter and…oh…my…god.[38] Look at these numbers…

> **April earnings payouts**
>
> By the 8th of each month (so in this case May 8), we initiate the payments for the prior month's earnings. Please allow 3-7 business days to receive the April earnings payouts in your Stripe account. Based on member engagement from this period:
>
> - 61.3% of writers or publications who wrote at least one story for members earned money.
> - 5.4% of active writers earned over $100.
> - $28,622.44 was the most earned by a writer, and $12,797.13 was the most earned for a single story.

$28,622?! That's bananas.

Day 133: May 12, 2020 - 2:38 pm (Tuesday)

I reviewed and refined my 2020 goals yesterday. I started by listing six measurable goals.

2020 Goals

1. Have 1,000 Medium followers
2. Have 100 Bits subscribers
3. Have 100 "365 Days of Freelance Writing Newsletter" subscribers
4. Write "365 Days of Freelance Writing"
5. Earn $5,000 in one month
6. Earn $40,000

As you can see, the first three relate to converting readers into followers/subscribers, the fourth is just the completion of this book, and the last two relate to income.

Here's the tricky part though: the first three work against the last two. In other words, if I spend time building my Medium following by writing posts, I have less time to focus on paid gigs — and vice versa.

Medium earnings aren't guaranteed. I'm far more likely to make $3 from a post than $1,200. Part of me wonders if I should have primary goals and secondary goals, allocating more time toward primary goals. For example, the first four could be primary while the income goals could be secondary. That's been my strategy so far, at least. I haven't concentrated on earning as much money as possible — instead, I've been more concerned with building my following on Medium.

That same part of me wants to set a steep, steep goal, like "be the top-earning writer on Medium." Obviously, that would take years. But the thought excites me.

I mean, I saved up a year of runway for a reason — to have the liberty of not worrying about money. I know you can do the math, you probably have already. If you annualized my year-to-date earnings, you're not getting a bank-breaking annual income.

Of course, I'd like to make more. At any time, I could start a profile on Upwork and make pennies per word. But I'm not trying to grind for 12-hours a day, writing about topics I don't care about, only to make 10 cents a word.

I know I could grind if I needed to; I've proved it to myself before when I worked in banking. I viewed every day as a challenge and worked myself into the ground. I had a lot of success — but I burnt myself out.

I'm not trying to do that again.

Day 134: May 13, 2020 - 7:58 am (Wednesday)

The weather has been so sporadic lately. The temperature has been in the 40s in the morning before rising to the 70s in the afternoon. *No, I'm not trying to make bland small talk, I'm going somewhere with this.*

The inconsistent weather messed with my sinuses and caused post-nasal drip, so I was up at 2:30 this morning. I abhor sore throats, and post-nasal drips can cause them. I'll sacrifice sleep to ensure that doesn't happen.

Which got me thinking, I rarely sacrifice sleep anymore. Back in my banking days, I'd sacrifice sleep all the time. Now, I can't operate at full creative capacity without my eight hours.

Sans a restful night's sleep, my productivity is a fraction of what it usually is. It's bizarre because that wasn't the case before. Maybe it's the type of work (or that I drank inordinate amounts of coffee back then).

4:48 pm

In other news, I eclipsed 400 Medium followers today!

Day 135: May 14, 2020 - 2:14 pm (Thursday)

I'm still having trouble deciding between whether to submit posts to paid publications or to publish them on Medium.

I strayed from the usual casual blog post to more of an in-depth article. It's a piece on the current and future economy from a psychological perspective. I enjoyed writing it, and I think it's pretty good. So, why not shoot for the stars?

I sent it to the New York Times.

According to their submission guidelines, they'll decide whether to accept it (or more likely decline) in three days. If that's the case, I'll try to find it a home on a Medium-owned publication, such as Marker.

If *that* doesn't play out, I'll pitch it to a few other non-Medium publications. It doesn't feel like something I'd include in Bacon Bits, and I'm hesitant to self-publish because I think this can make money.

We'll see, one day at a time.

Day 136: May 15, 2020 - 2:27 pm (Friday)

I'm trying to balance work and life responsibilities today. We (Kaileigh and I) toured an apartment. We had high expectations (a dangerous frame of mind), and it didn't quite live up to the hype.

Plus, I'm still trying to sell my furniture, so there are a lot of moving pieces. *See what I did there?*

In turn, I didn't come close to accomplishing what I wanted to this week.

Wait, should I start sharing my weekly task list?

Hmm, not a bad idea...I'll start sharing that on Mondays.

In other news, my Patreon page is up to date as of today's entry!

Day 137: May 16, 2020 - 1:03 pm (Saturday)

Why do I always forget how much stuff I have until I start packing? It's like, "Oh, I didn't think about all of my dishware and glasses."

This is going to be a rough week. I'm not looking forward to balancing a work schedule and my move.

It's looking like a deadline-filled week too. I told Writing Revolt that I'd deliver that comprehensive guide to them by next Friday. I also need to finish posts for Client A and Client E.

Ugh.

Day 138: May 17, 2020 - 7:44 am (Sunday)

I'm starting to second guess Mailchimp — and maybe even Patreon.

Editor's note: I inadvertently left out the fact that I started my Bits newsletter on Mailchimp, an email marketing automation platform. It's free up until a certain number of email contacts (2,000 as of this writing). I express my frustrations with this platform in the ensuing days.

I like Patreon's platform as both a creator and a subscriber. But it might not be the best visual platform for writers. All of my Patreon posts are text entries (with a few images), but it's not the easiest font or formatting to read.

May 13 at 4:12pm

Day 116: April 25, 2020 - 9:25 am (Saturday)

What are the Packers doing? These draft picks are so freaking questionable. Ask anyone with an ounce of NFL football knowledge, who're the best three players for the Packers?

1. Aaron Rodgers
2. Davante Adams
3. Aaron Jones

Guess who we draft with our first two picks?

A quarterback and a running back.

WHY. Those aren't positions of need!

UGH. Anyway. So, I forgot to mention that the 365 Days of Freelance Writing Patreon page and Medium website have officially been launched! *How exciting, right?*

Well, I'd launched the Patreon page a little while back, and I'd created the Medium publication even further back. But I hadn't finalized the Patreon tiers or started adding content. And the Medium page didn't have a post, so it didn't exist publicly.

Now, both are up and running. I'm really excited about it.

Hmm, it's not too bad on my phone. But I know it's tougher to read on the computer. Let's compare this to Medium's phone layout.

> Unparalleled frustration. Uncharacteristic avarice. Unbridled, boisterous showboating. Questionable investments and ensuing bankruptcies. Blunt accusations of unethical behavior.
>
> All standard occurrences during the family-favorite board game: Monopoly.
>
> Without fail, Monopoly turns into a four-hour endeavor that only one person truly wants to finish. What starts as good-natured play inevitably devolves into a ruthless competition.
>
> One-by-one, Monopoly dishes out financial blows to its wanna-be real estate tycoons. Its colorful currency disappears faster than you can say Pennsylvania Avenue. Until that fatal dice roll arrives — and an exorbitant $1,400 hotel bill shafts you. Your funds run dry.
>
> Monopoly drills the final nail into your cardboard coffin.

It's the spacing and font size. I think Medium's spacing is better for differentiating line breaks and their font is a little larger. I need to compare the computer interfaces later.

Anyway, I need to dig into Substack now, which is another platform that supports email newsletters.[40] I've seen it gaining traction on Medium — in terms of people writing about it. I hear good things, including that it has a post archive that's easy to filter through to find older posts, which would be ideal for 365 Days of Freelance Writing since posts are frequent.

Although it's an added time commitment, I suppose I could utilize both Patreon and Substack.

We'll see.

Week 20 Lessons & Takeaways

#1: Copywriting can be lucrative, but it's not something you can pick up and be good at. It takes a deeper understanding of marketing and human psychology. And it must be practiced over and over and over. It's time to start practicing.

#2: I refined my 2020 goals and realized my goals sort of work against each other. Some are income goals, others are building the readership of Bacon Bits and 365 Days of Freelance Writing. The latter are investments — hopefully, they earn money one day. But they don't make me much today.

#3: Don't sacrifice sleep unless you have to. Writing is so much harder when you're tired. I used to sacrifice sleep in my old job. Now, I ensure I get my eight hours.

#4: Dream big, right? I wrote a somewhat formal article (versus a casual blog post) that I'm excited about. So excited that I submitted it to the New York Times.

#5: I'll start sharing my weekly task lists on Monday so that you can hold me accountable for getting my shit done.

#6: Moving isn't fun, but I do have the benefit of a flexible schedule.

#7: It's time to check out Substack. Ultimately, it could be a better platform for what I'm trying to do.

Day 139: May 18, 2020 - 3:30 pm (Monday)

Ohhhhh boy. This will not be an enjoyable week. My move-out has been accelerated, as Mother Nature decided to bless Atlanta with 10 consecutive days of thunderstorms, starting Wednesday. Tomorrow might be my only window to move with clear skies.

On top of that, I have several imminent client/personal deadlines. As promised, here's my task list for the week:

This Week (5/17 - 5/23)

1. 365 Days of Freelance Writing (x7)
2. Writing Revolt post
3. Client B edits
4. Client A post
5. Gaming Nexus review
6. Freelance emotions post
7. Better Marketing post - Scarcity
8. Better Marketing post - Don't cold pitch on LinkedIn
9. Bacon Bits post - Beware of a bear market rally
10. Find homes for old posts

My guest post for Writing Revolt is due on Friday, which should be enough time. As usual, I'll have edits for Client B due on Friday as well. And I have a game review due today for Gaming Nexus.

Have I mentioned that? I'm a staff writer (unpaid) for Gaming Nexus, a gaming news and review site. It's a fun side thing I do since I enjoy video games.

Anyway, I also want to maintain a steady flow of Bacon Bits and Better Marketing content. PLUS, I need to find publications for a few old posts.

So, as you can see, I've got a busy week ahead of me.

Day 140: May 19, 2020 - 10:42 am (Tuesday)

I think it's fair to say that the New York Times isn't biting. Time to look elsewhere. I don't expect to hear anything from Marker either. I think it has a better chance of being seen by Medium editors if I self-publish it and attract a lot of viewers.

My task list might be a little too aggressive. I've underestimated the amount of time it takes to sift through belongings and pack.

11:16 am

Alright, I've pitched my post to two big-name sites (Forbes, CNBC) and Supermaker. I've now submitted three posts to Supermaker — I am determined to write for them.

It's time to brave the storm of moving. Wish me luck.

10:14 pm

I. Am. POOPED. Moving is exhausting.

Day 141: May 20, 2020 - 11:26 am (Wednesday)

I have an idea. You know how I want my writing to be published right away and that I'm fidgety until it is? Instead of pulling the trigger and self-publishing after a couple of days, I'm thinking I'll allow roughly two weeks before self-publishing or publishing via my publications.

This will only apply to evergreen content that has the potential to be posted elsewhere, like on Supermaker or The Penny Hoarder. Topical content has a deadline since it's related to current events.

At first, my published content output will likely decline due to the lag effect of this wait-and-see approach. But it will eventually become a rolling schedule of content.

Day 142: May 21, 2020 - 7:51 pm (Thursday)

It's been a freaking DAY. I spent another five hours moving.

The rest of my day has been concentrated on that Writing Revolt post. "Post" doesn't feel accurate anymore. It'll be a full-scale guide to freelance finances, probably 4,000+ words with step-by-step screenshot examples.

Hopefully, this amount of effort pays dividends in other ways because I've outworked my pay…

Oh, I almost forgot, I spent the first 45 minutes of my day calculating how much I earn per word on Medium. The results were…troubling.

Across all of my posts, I make $0.04 per word on average. If you nix my budget-cutting post, that number drops to a measly penny. Remember how I said my goal of building a Medium following contradicts my income goals?

Yeah. That's why.

Day 143: May 22, 2020 - 5:42 pm (Friday)

It's been ANOTHER exhausting day, and I haven't even contributed to my move-out process today.

My comprehensive guide wound up being 4,278 words. It's totally on me for going way more in-depth than I was expected to, but I asked if they'd be willing to up the price from $200 to 10 cents per word.

I'm so mentally pooped. But, if there's a silver lining, it's that I can pump out words when it comes to personal finance. That sort of validates that I know what I'm talking about.

The downside is that I've completely shunned my other work...

Day 144: May 23, 2020 - 12:49 pm (Saturday)

Woah, my Medium views have SPIKED over the last 24 hours or so.

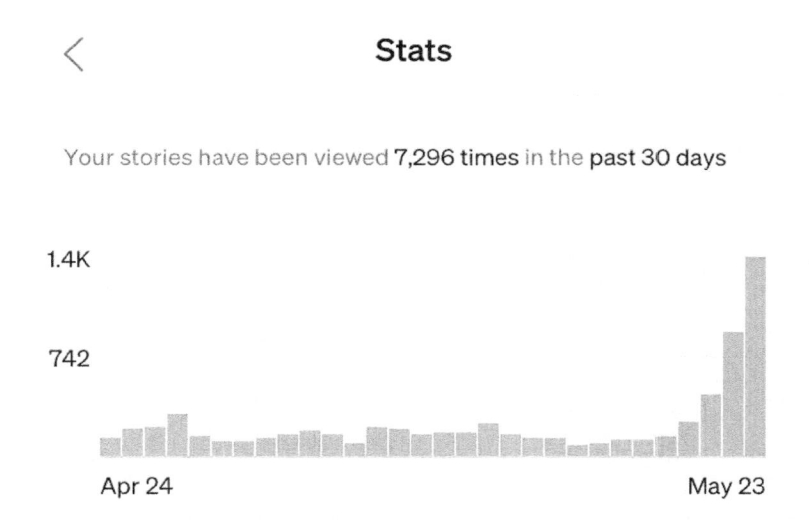

Stats

Your stories have been viewed **7,296 times** in the **past 30 days**

[Bar chart showing views from Apr 24 to May 23, with values ranging up to 1.4K, peaking at May 23]

It's 100% due to my budget-cutting post, which has surged back with 30 hours of reading time today. It's not like I promoted it or anything. I guess Medium started distributing it again.

It's back under the "Top Posts" for the money tag, currently sitting at #7.

I didn't have to do anything. So that's cool.

Day 145: May 24, 2020 - 11:52 am (Sunday)

I'm still dumbfounded over this, but my budget-cutting post reached new heights yesterday. I have no idea why.

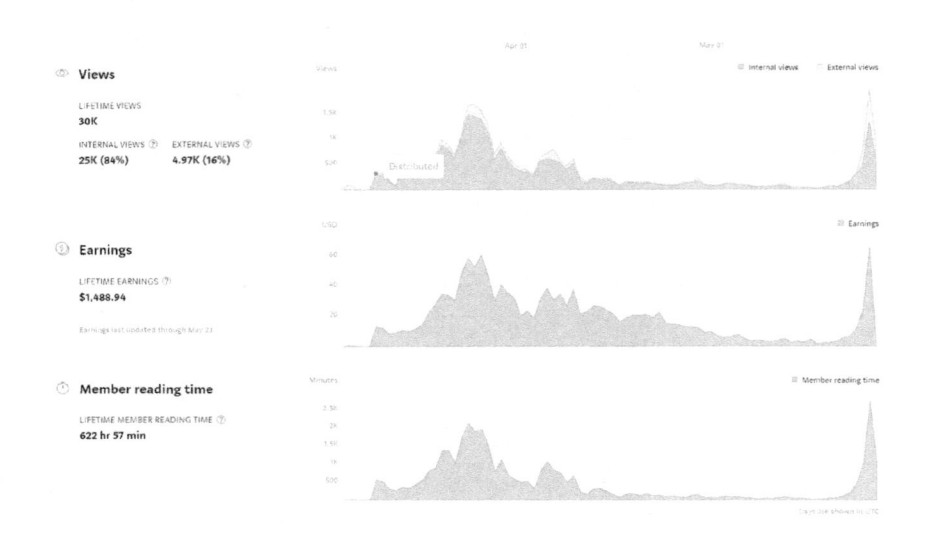

This spike boosted my follower count too. Ten days ago, I surpassed 400 followers. As of today, I'm at 464. Not too shabby.

I've noticed something interesting: I don't care about the negative comments as much as I used to. I've only received two or three...*confrontational*...responses during my time writing for Medium. The first one bothered me. Now, I'm not as concerned. Even with a noncontroversial topic, people will find a way to disagree. It's unavoidable.

Two months ago, when the post initially peaked, one gentleman responded to my post with a somewhat abrasive comment.

> **Phillip Long**
> Mar 25
>
> I had to stop reading once you revealed that you were paying $8 for a single smoothie! No wonder you need serious work on your budget! Is it not completely apparent from the outset that ONLY rich people have any business paying even once $8 for a f#*ing smoothie!?!? How is it possible to think that that is normal?

I think you can imagine how it felt to receive this. How would you react? My mind jumped to firing back. Fight fire with fire — that sort of thing. But I know better.

You don't put out a fire with gasoline (emotion). You cut off the fire's oxygen by dumping water on it (logic).

I did a little reconnaissance and read through this guy's response history. (I probably spent way too much time on this, but whatever.) He's an opinionated guy. My story wasn't the first to receive his contention.

This guy thrives on heated debates, so I wasn't going to give him that. Instead, I admitted my previous ignorance and added more context. No jabs or retorts.

Carter Kilmann
Mar 25 · 1 min read

Well, Phillip, I wasn't smart about how I spent my money while I worked in banking. Yes, I made a very comfortable paycheck—but I was far from being "rich."

We're all human. We all have something we indulge in. Fortunately for me (and my bank account), I got my shit together and put a stop to my excessive smoothie purchases.

I cook 95% of my meals, so I don't spend much money on dining out. So, I treat myself to smoothies every now and then (32 oz. smoothies from Smoothie King get pricy, I agree).

To answer your question, it was normal for me because I didn't know what "normal" was. You just don't know what you don't know, until you figure it out and do something about it.

And it worked.

Phillip Long
Mar 25

Well Carter, that is a very reasonable response!

Now if we could just get the rest of the country to get some type of clue about how we live in an outrageous Disney Land of a world that cannot possibly be sustained, and that we better all realize our wasteful ways and act on conserving our money and resources.

As much as I wanted to stoke the fire, it wasn't worth the time or energy to get in a back-and-forth virtual yelling match. But, even though I nailed the response, I couldn't help but feel irked by the initial comment at the time.

That sentiment has changed over the last two months. This morning, I received another confrontational comment. This person argued that I contradicted myself.

Mitchell Posluns
May 24

At the end you said pay in cash, which contradicts one of your first points:

"So long as you use credit and debit cards for your purchases, it'll be easy to consolidate your expenses."

Do you really mean, don't accrue debt aka don't buy things you can't afford? Big difference here

No one likes to be accused of contradiction. But, honestly, I wasn't phased this time. To clear his confusion, I tried to provide a straightforward explanation:

Carter Kilmann
May 24 · 1 min read

Hey, Mitchell. Thanks for reading!

The earlier statement you've referenced merely points out that it's easier to consolidate your expenses if you use a credit or debit card—not that you should avoid paying in cash. Downloading your activity is a quicker process than manually entering your cash purchases from saved receipts.

I'm assuming this is the later statement you're referring to:

"I know we're living through the gradual transition to a cashless world. But stick to cash when you can."

Context matters here. If you read the previous paragraph, you'll see that this piece of advice only applies to people who can't control their credit card spending.

"But if you can't control your spending, using a credit card will be counterproductive. Because credit cards make it so easy to make purchases."

I hope this helps!

I don't think the sting of criticism will ever subside altogether. But it's getting easier with time.

Week 21 Lessons & Takeaways

#1: I shared my weekly task list, which wound up being pointless because my move took up way more of my time than I expected.

#2: Just because I love my work, doesn't mean a big-name publication will. No one's scrambling to publish my psychology/economics post.

#3: I'm toying with a different content publishing approach. To potentially land guest posts on other sites, I'm going to send Medium post drafts to other publications first. If they don't get picked up, I'll post them to Medium.

#4: Guess who went overboard and wrote a 4,250-word post when the ask was 2,000? *This guy!* I should have communicated earlier that I was trending toward a massive guide. But I didn't, and I had to ask in retrospect if they'd be willing to pay more. I'm not expecting them to, but I feel like I went above and beyond the expectation.

#5: If you can, avoid moving. It's awful. I know that's not realistic, so, if you have to move, don't expect to get a lot of work done. Although I've completed my move-out, I'm pretty behind on content output.

#6: Don't call it a comeback. My budget-cutting expense has been revitalized. For whatever reason, it attracted a hair under 2,000 views on Saturday. I guess the lesson here is to never count your Medium posts out. The algorithm might decide to share it with the masses again.

#7: As creators, we're subject to criticism. It still sucks to hear, but it's getting a little easier to accept and process. I dealt with a couple of critiques on Medium, and I'd say my retorts were on point.

Day 146: May 25, 2020 - 10:15 am (Monday)

Alright, last week wasn't an ideal week for sharing my task list. My move pretty much shot any chance I had of accomplishing the majority of my tasks.

The second time's the charm:

This Week (5/24 - 5/30)

1. 365 Days of Freelance Writing (x7)
2. Client A post (x2)
3. Client B edits (x5)
4. Client E post
5. Self-publish 90% Economy post
6. Edit & submit Freelancing Emotions post
7. Send Bits newsletter #2
8. Bacon Bits post

I have several client posts to crank out over the next couple of days. Once I complete those, I'll try to find a home for a post about the many emotions of freelance writing. Plus, it's about time for the second Bits newsletter to be distributed. (I've gained a few more Bits subscribers from my post's resurgence.)

Day 147: May 26, 2020 - 2:14 pm (Tuesday)

Great news: I'm getting paid more.

When I delivered that ridiculously long guide on Friday, I tacked on a request at the end of my email.

> **Carter Kilmann** <carter@carterkilmann.com>
> to michael
>
> May 22, 2020, 5:33 PM (4 days ago)
>
> Hey Michael, hope you had a great week.
>
> So, this became even more comprehensive than I imagined it would be (I guess I got kind of carried away).
>
> It's roughly 4,250 words...
>
> Is this too long? Let me know what you think. I'd be happy to discuss ways to shorten it if need be. As crazy as it sounds, I could also add more to the investing section (like specific accounts or tools that could be useful).
>
> Would you guys be open to increasing the rate from $200 to mirror the 10 cents per word pay structure? I know it's totally on me for going more in-depth, but I was hoping we could at least discuss it.
>
> Let me know your thoughts!

I tried to pose the pay increase as logically as possible. Thankfully, it worked.

> On Tue, May 26, 2020 at 11:31 AM Michael K <michael@writingrevolt.com> wrote:
> Hi Carter,
>
> Thanks for this! Great post, I just read it and am going to go in and edit now.
>
> As far as length, it's totally fine that it ended up being longer. We may want to shorten some sections, which I'll take care of as I edit – or I'll add notes if it's more of a significant change so you can take care of it.
>
> We can absolutely increase the rate! Does $400 for this work for you?
>
> – Michael

Phew. I feel so much better.

In other writing news, I decided to self-publish my 90% economy post.[39] I pitched it to **ten** publications, and no one responded. But that's okay! I'll see how it fares on Medium.

It was curated in "Business" and "Economy," so that's a good start.

Day 148: May 27, 2020 - 2:48 pm (Wednesday)

I haven't resolved my goal confusion. I'm still torn — should I focus on increasing income to better sustain myself or building my brands, which I enjoy more.

I'm trying to convince myself (and I'm winning, I think) that I can do both, but my scope needs to be more narrow. In other words, beyond my current clients, my future gigs should pertain to financial copywriting.

That'll provide more income than blog posts, so I won't feel as conflicted when I focus on personal stuff.

That makes sense, right?

Ugh. I hope so.

In client news, I've cranked out assignments — I'm nearly caught up. I just have to review a post for Client E, edit my Writing Revolt post, and finish a post for Client A. Oh, and I still have two posts to edit for Client B.

Alright, maybe I'm not as close to catching up as I thought.

In Medium news, The Startup asked if I'd like to publish my 90% economy post on their platform. I did, somewhat absent-mindedly. After I hit submit, I had second thoughts.

Maybe I didn't give a couple of publications enough time to respond…

Day 149: May 28, 2020 - 6:51 am (Thursday)

Well, what a pleasant surprise. I woke up to 500 followers on Medium.

I've never cared much — at least, not any more than the average person — about social media followings. Twitter, Instagram, Facebook friends, etc. The high school version of me cared, but not really since then.

Medium is different though, it's one thing to say, "Hey, you're amusing or interesting, I'll read your tweets" or "Hey, you post cool pictures, I'll 'like' your posts."

Following someone on Medium establishes a deeper connection in my opinion. It's more complimentary. You have to like someone's writing — their inner thoughts, feelings, and perspectives — enough to want to continue reading them indefinitely.

I strive to gain more followers because I want people to enjoy my writing. It's validating. It's a metric that conveys whether my writing is readable or not.

1:52 pm

I think I'm going to ditch Mailchimp. The formatting is so frustrating. It's not a simple transfer from a Google Doc to the platform's text editor.

I signed up for Substack and imported my email list (which is up to 52). I'll keep you posted on my review of Substack.

Day 150: May 29, 2020 - 7:11 am (Friday)

Smartphones are so perplexing. They have obvious benefits for freelance writers, but they're also such a detriment to productivity.

I grab for my phone whenever I hit a lull. I incessantly check it for no reason whatsoever.

Sure, my phone has apps I need to access — like my work email and Google Docs.

But I don't need to scroll through Facebook or Twitter as much as I do.

2:59 pm

Damn, I just had the most gratifying "I know what I'm talking about" moment.

I was editing a landing page for free webinars (so, a copyediting assignment since it's ultimately trying to drive an action that leads to sales).

In my first round of edits, I suggested adding transparent benefits to justify why my client is providing free education and materials. She nailed what I was asking for — benign (versus greedy and brash) benefits that assuage any doubt or suspicion as to why she's providing a free service.

But, I nixed a couple of sentences that essentially made it sound like, "Yes, this is free — but I might earn your business and money later." Which, in all honesty, isn't the worst statement. It's transparent, that's for sure.

But I'd rather the reader reach that conclusion on their own.

So, I responded with...

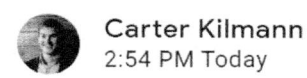

> **Carter Kilmann**
> 2:54 PM Today
>
> I'm hesitant to keep this, since it's sort of like saying "Yeah, this is free - but hopefully you wind up paying me later"
>
> Hopefully, it's unconsciously inferred that they benefit from paying you - rather than you benefit from getting their business.

I wrote that last sentence...and I was like, "Damn...I know what I'm talking about."

It was glorious.

Day 151: May 30, 2020 - 11:34 am (Saturday)

Client B has been killing it this month (to my benefit since I edit her work). Thanks to her and Medium, I made about $1k this past week.

On top of that, she's referred me to two people for writing/editing work. That's the benefit of delivering high-quality service.

> **A new contact/project** — Inbox
>
> May 30
> to me
>
> Hi Carter!
>
> A contact of mine, Cherlyn, is interested in possibly hiring you for some help editing a PowerPoint presentation. I gave her your email but thought I'd give you a heads up. Feel free to let her know if you aren't interest in that kind of thing, but hopefully, she'll have some other projects for you as well!

Editing a PowerPoint seems a little out-of-scope. But, hey, it's money, right? Plus, it could lead to more work.

Day 152: May 31, 2020 - 11:24 pm (Sunday)

I significantly underestimated how long it would take me to edit a blog post for Client B. I'm up way later than I should be for a work night. (I'm a morning person, not a night owl.)

Anyway, let's take a look at how I did last week.

This Week (5/24 - 5/30)

1. ~~365 Days of Freelance Writing (x7)~~
2. ~~Client A post (x2)~~
3. ~~Client B edits (x5)~~
4. ~~Client E post~~
5. ~~Client H edits~~
6. ~~Self-publish 90% Economy post~~
7. ~~Edit & submit Freelancing Emotions post~~

8. ~~Send Bits newsletter #2~~
9. Bacon Bits post

It was still a hectic week, as I finished moving out of my apartment. Nonetheless, I completed all of my client assignments. I had originally anticipated three editing assignments for Client B at the beginning of the week, but that number rose to *five*.

I also added "Client H edits" (i.e. Writing Revolt) to this list, which I didn't realize I had received until Wednesday. For whatever reason, I didn't get the Google Docs email alert when the edits were shared with me.

As I mentioned earlier this week, I decided to self-publish my 90% economy post, which I eventually added to The Startup. It's produced pretty pedestrian numbers. Nothing exceptional.

ECONOMY · Show in chart · Show in chart			
The 90% Economy: Indefinitely Temporary?	169	73	43%
8 min read · In The Startup · View story · Details			

I sent my freelancing emotions post to Supermaker, but — per usual — I haven't heard back. *Is a reply so hard?!*

Issue #2 of the Bits newsletter made its way around my email list. I'm going to transfer everything to Substack before #3 publishes. I'm just not a fan of Mailchimp's interface.

Here's how it's performed so far:

	Bits Newsletter #2	Sent	40.0%	6.0%
	Regular · The Bits Newsletter		Opens	Clicks
Sent Thu, May 28th 1:51 PM to 52 recipients by you				

Unfortunately, I wasn't able to complete a Bacon Bits post. I came up with a couple of topic ideas, but I didn't have time to write anything for them beyond rough outlines.

All in all, it was a pretty successful week considering the circumstances.

Week 22 Lessons & Takeaways

#1: Speak up for yourself. If you did more work than expected, it doesn't hurt to ask for a pay bump. I cranked out 4,000+ words for my Writing Revolt guest post, and I requested a higher rate. They recognized the extra value I provided and raised my rate from $200 to $400.

#2: I'm still figuring out my goals. More specifically, which ones to focus on. I'm leaning toward my Medium goals while experimenting with financial copywriting.

#3: I eclipsed the 500 followers threshold this week!

#4: Mailchimp might not be for me. I spend so much time optimizing my text on their platform (e.g. tinkering with the font sizes and headers). It's a cumbersome process.

#5: Smartphones can be great for on-the-go work, but they also stifle productivity if you keep them nearby when you work.

#6: Have you ever written a sentence and thought, "Man, that's an awesome sentence"? I had one of these moments recently while editing a client's landing page.

#7: When your clients succeed, you reap the benefits too. Client B has been killing it, so I've had plenty of editing assignments come across my figurative desk.

#8: Some publications (maybe most) will refuse to be responsive. It happens. It only takes one good pitch idea to get your foot in the door though. *I'm looking at you, Supermaker. I will be published on your site. Editor's note: I gave up on Supermaker.*

#9: Overall, my week was a success. I knocked out all of my client work, including a few unexpected assignments. The only task I couldn't complete was a Bacon Bits post.

MAY STATS

In all honesty, I thought May would be a down month. I expected a semi-lag effect after a couple of clients cut back content needs in March and April. But, over the final week, I benefited from additional editing assignments from Client B and a resurgence of my budget-cutting post. I'll take it.

As a reminder, here's each client's description:

- Client A — Digital marketing agency
- Client B — Digital marketing agency (editing work)
- Client C — FinTech startup (no longer a client)
- Client D — Online finance publication (content freeze)
- Client E — Auto finance company
- Client F — ClearVoice assignments
- Client G — SaaS company (no longer a client, for now)
- Client H — Writing Revolt

365 Days of Freelancing - Monthly Stats					
	Jan	Feb	Mar	Apr	May
Income					
Client A	960	960	960	640	480
Client B	329	119	153	189	741
Client C	500	-	-	-	-
Client D	350	350	-	-	-
Client E	-	450	450	900	450
Client F	-	225	-	-	-
Client G	-	200	-	-	-
Client H	-	-	-	-	400
Medium	32	21	719	734	505
Total Income	**$2,171**	**$2,325**	**$2,282**	**$2,463**	**$2,576**
Growth (%)	-	7.1%	(1.9%)	7.9%	4.6%
Blog Posts (Paid)					
Client A	6	6	6	4	3
Client B	3	2	2	2	9
Client C	1	1	-	-	-
Client D	1	1	-	-	-
Client E	-	1	1	2	1
Client F	-	2	-	-	-
Client G	-	1	-	-	-
Client H	-	-	-	-	1
Total Paid Posts	**11**	**14**	**9**	**8**	**14**
Blog Posts (Unpaid)					
Medium	1	-	-	1	4
Bacon Bits	1	2	4	2	1
365	-	-	-	2	-
Total Unpaid Posts	**2**	**2**	**4**	**5**	**5**
Total Blog Posts	**13**	**16**	**13**	**13**	**19**
Medium					
Views	1,151	1,352	19,466	11,052	15,778
Reads	439	468	7,413	4,220	6,320
Existing Followers	54	63	80	238	371
New Followers	9	17	158	133	159
Total Followers	**63**	**80**	**238**	**371**	**530**
LinkedIn					
Existing Followers	458	465	493	526	570
New Followers	7	28	33	44	20
Total Followers	**465**	**493**	**526**	**570**	**590**

Highlights

- Consistent with that lag effect I mentioned, I had one less blog post for Client A this month. That was due to one of her clients putting a temporary stop on content. It seems like it'll just be three posts per month for the foreseeable future.
- Client B came out of nowhere with nine editing assignments, which ultimately drove my income growth.
- I asked Client E if they'd be open to sending me two writing assignments at a time. (This would enable me to consistently make $900 a month from this client.) No response yet.
- For consistency, I've labeled Writing Revolt as "Client H." The renegotiated rate helped a ton.
- From the ashes, my budget-cutting post returned, earning $414 in May. This led to a huge boost in views, reads, and followers. Last month, I predicted that I'd hit 500 followers this month — but I didn't expect to set a new record for "New Followers."
- Not a bad month for Medium content output, but only one of those posts generated noteworthy results. (It was the Better Marketing post.)
- I wasn't as active on LinkedIn this month, so my following only grew by 20 in May.

JUNE

Day 153: June 1, 2020 - 2:30 pm (Monday)

Alright, it's time to refocus on Medium content. Here's my task list for the week.

Week (5/31 - 6/6)

1. 365 Days of Freelance Writing (x7)
2. Transfer Bits newsletter to Substack
3. Send invoices
4. Bacon Bits post (x2)
5. 365 DFW post (x2)
6. Better Marketing post
7. Client B edits
8. Read three chapters of The Copywriter's Handbook

One of those 365 Days of Freelance Writing posts is the freelancer emotions post I mentioned last week. I want to hold off on publishing that one until I've added an in-depth post about the "why" behind my 365-day journey.

Otherwise, I want to get back to consistently publishing on Bacon Bits. And it wouldn't hurt to land a post on Better Marketing. It's only one sample, but my first post for them attracted over 1,000 views.

Day 154: June 2, 2020 - 9:31 pm (Tuesday)

Good news: Client E is happy to send me two assignments at once. That's a reliable $900 of monthly income right there.

I get the vibe that I could even take on three if I wanted. *Editor's note: My vibe was incorrect.*

Anyway, I started scoping out some possible financial copywriting clients to pitch. I mainly used Google and LinkedIn to look up wealth management firms. I don't think I'll have a problem finding *potential* clients. It'll just take a lot of pitching to find companies that need a writer right now.

Which reminds me, I came across a few helpful tips for finding gigs in the Writing Revolters Facebook Group.

> You can get some awesome #writing gigs by following this method.
>
> 1) Go to Twitter. Type "need freelance writer." You will come across many tweets of the potential clients. Pitch them your service. Just reply to the tweet with something awesome.
>
> 2) Take help of Linkedin. Go there and type "need a writer," amid tags choose "content." You will see so many people who are in need of a writer. Add them, talk to them. But don't sound too salesy.
>
> 3) Go on Instagram. Type #digitalmarketingagencies and just open them one by one. Leave a voice note. Don't type. Say Hi, and tell them about your services."
>
> I wish you good luck!

I tried the Twitter and LinkedIn routes, but those didn't yield much. I came across a couple of "help wanted" ads for writers, but they both had at least 50 responses already. It might have been a timing issue. I think I came across this advice when it was circulating, so lots of people acted on it simultaneously.

But I haven't tried the Instagram approach to finding digital marketing agencies. I need to give that a try.

Day 155: June 3, 2020 - 3:38 pm (Wednesday)

Today has been all over the place. I've had phone calls with clients, a bank, and Microsoft support. I've sent and responded to a bunch of emails. I completed edits for a few older blog posts too.

I'm exhausted, yet I feel like I've barely accomplished anything.

You know what — I'm calling it a day.

Day 156: June 4, 2020 - 11:56 am (Thursday)

From day one of this adventure, I've been confident in my finances.

Why? Because I had (a) an emergency fund and (b) a year of runway. They've provided total peace of mind, which you can't put a price on. I couldn't imagine the stress of working and living without these two reserves.

Sure, it'd be motivating in a sense. Like an "I HAVE to get this done" sort of thing. That's a heavy burden to carry every month though.

But those were my "pre-business venture" finances. All of that money came from my previous occupation. So, despite entering this entrepreneurial journey with financial stability, it's not the same thing as establishing a stable income.

My income has been steady for a while, at least in terms of breaking even. But, until this morning, I hadn't taken a step back to appreciate this. I'm not making a significant amount — but I'm earning *and* saving. That's important.

I'm not even remotely close to my ultimate revenue goals, but it's reassuring to know that I'm making more than I'm spending.

Day 157: June 5, 2020 - 6:51 pm (Friday)

Hey, here's a killer recommendation: prioritize content that's even remotely time-sensitive. And by that I mean if your content's message could change based on news or scheduled events, make sure you finish it ahead of time.

I'm writing a post about the weirdness of the stock market's rally and the direction of the economy. Except I pretty much rewrote half of it because a new jobs report came out today and unemployment dropped, which is great...but it was a total surprise. So I had to reword my paper (errr...post) to accommodate this positive sign.

You know what I just realized when I accidentally called it a paper. *Why am I writing about this?* It's topical but...is it going to grow my audience? Do enough people care about economics?

I called it a *paper*...

Economics ties into personal finance in a big picture sense, but I don't know...my two economics pieces to date haven't performed particularly well.

The 90% Economy: Indefinitely Temporary?

189	81	43%	14
views	reads	ratio	fans

Monopoly: Board Game or Our Current Reality?

159	79	50%	14
views	reads	ratio	fans

Decent read ratios, but they're not exactly expanding my reach.

I'll finish this one and see if it's worth continuing this content trend.

Day 158: June 6, 2020 - 10:45 am (Saturday)

I'm still not very enthusiastic about my stock market/economics post — "What's Going On With the Stock Market?"[41] I enjoyed assessing different bear markets and comparing the COVID-19 pandemic to previous epidemics. But I'm just not vibing with it; I don't think it'll perform well.

And I worry that my uncertainty shows in my writing...

I guess we'll see. Usually, I'm antsy about getting my content posted, but I'm not in a big rush to post this (other than the fact that it's tied to current events).

I've also spent time updating Patreon today (I'd fallen a little behind) and transferring my Bits newsletters to Substack. The more I compare Mailchimp — and even Patreon — to Substack, the more I feel inclined to switch.

I'll look into it more tomorrow.

Day 159: June 7, 2020 - 12:38 pm (Sunday)

We're commencing Operation Substack. In the day or so that I've spent interacting with the platform, I've realized Substack is better for what I'm trying to accomplish. *Sorry, Patreon.*

It just makes more sense for writers to use Substack. The platform is more accommodating, and it's easier for viewers to find and filter through previous content.

Plus, I never truly "launched" my Patreon platform. Just like I haven't really "launched" my 365 Days of Freelance Writing Medium publication. So, switching won't be an ordeal.

Other than having to upload each post again...

Week 23 Lessons & Takeaways

#1: Along the same lines as "you miss 100% of the shots you don't take," you have to ask questions and propose alternatives if you want to improve workflow processes. I asked Client E's editor if she'd be alright with sending me two assignments at once, and she was happy to. This locks in at least $900 per month (versus back-and-forth swings between $450 and $900 due to timing issues).

#2: Social media platforms can be bountiful sources of gigs, so long as you're willing to dig for opportunities.

#3: As a business owner, I'm in charge of every facet of my operation — which can be overwhelming. That's why I decided to take a half-day on Wednesday.

#4: Organized finances = peace of mind. Since day one of my freelancing journey, I've kept my finances neat and tidy. It's been a HUGE advantage. Financial stress can be debilitating. I can't say it enough: it's so reassuring to know I'm making and saving money. It proves my business is viable.

#5: Prioritize your time-sensitive content. I dilly-dallied (I don't think I've ever written this term) publishing my "What's Going On With the Stock Market?" post. As a result, I've had to update sections of the post a couple of times now. I'm not super confident about it anyway. I don't have a good reason. Maybe it's because I've updated it like four times since it's tied to current economic events. *Sigh.* My gut tells me it'll perform like my previous economics posts.

#6: Sorry, Patreon. I've elected to switch to Substack. *No hard feelings.*

Day 160: June 8, 2020 - 1:14 pm (Monday)

Alright, I think I have a large enough sample size to make a semi-confident declaration: Tagging your Medium post with "Covid 19" or "Coronavirus" increases your odds of being curated in one of your other tags.

At least, that's been my experience so far. I published my "What's Going On With the Stock Market?" post this morning, which included the "Covid 19" tag.

And it was curated under "Money" and "Economy."

If you recall, I introduced this possibility back on Day 101. It could be a completely unfounded proclamation — it might not factor into Medium's curation algorithm whatsoever.

However, to date, I've tagged six posts with either "Covid 19" or "Coronavirus" and all six have been distributed (usually in "Money" or "Economy").

Again, it could be a coincidence. But who knows?

1:29 pm

I have impeccable timing. This morning's post happens to discuss the impending recession.

Within a couple of hours, the National Bureau of Economic Research — the organization that officially decrees economic recessions in the US — announced that we entered a recession in February.

I'm so glad I didn't procrastinate this morning, or else I'd have even more rewriting to do.

On another note, here's how we did last week in terms of knocking out tasks...

Week (5/31 - 6/6)

1. ~~365 Days of Freelance Writing (x7)~~
2. ~~Transfer Bits newsletter to Substack~~
3. ~~Send invoices~~
4. Bacon Bits post (x2)
5. 365 post (x2)
6. Better Marketing post
7. ~~Client B edits~~
8. ~~Client E edits~~
9. Read three chapters of The Copywriter's Handbook

It doesn't look like the most productive week, but I did knock out some admin work (I applied for a PPP loan). I also made some headway on my Bacon Bits posts, one of which I posted this morning, but there's still work to be done on the next one.

This week should be better:

This Week (6/7 - 6/13)

1. 365 Days of Freelance Writing (x7)
2. Update Substack with 365 DFW (2 months)
3. Client A post
4. Client B edits
5. Client E post
6. Bacon Bits outline
7. Bits newsletter #3
8. 365 DFW post
9. Better Marketing outline
10. Gaming Nexus post

As you can see, I'm going to be busy.

On top of my typical client assignments, I have a few personal work tasks to complete this week. I want to update my 365 Days of Freelance Writing Substack so that it can run concurrently with my daily entries. This will be my second time updating a platform with all of these posts...*can't wait*.

It's also time for the third installment of the Bits newsletter, and I've got plenty of topical content to work with.

Lastly, I want to outline a couple of Medium pieces to keep progressing toward my follower goals.

Day 161: June 9, 2020 - 1:55 pm (Tuesday)

I just received an exciting email from Client E.

In addition to sending me two writing prompts at once, she also raised their rates to $500 per piece since these are supposed to be more complicated (they're about lemon laws and liens). So, I'll deliver at least $1,000 of work for Client E this month (with the potential for more since it's still early June).

If I can knock these out quickly, I could set myself up for a solid payday.

On top of THAT, she concluded the email with a flattering note:

> Finally, our CEO ▮▮▮▮▮▮▮ really liked your article about secure loans! Just thought I'd pass along the compliment to you, that was passed along to me by my manager. :) I've been hearing great things overall from our executive team about the high-quality content we're producing, so thank you for your hard work! I appreciate it. People are noticing.

That was AWESOME to read. I might not be the fastest writer, but I'm meticulous. So it's cool to see that my work is appreciated.

In other news, my "What's Going On With the Stock Market?" post is performing better than expected.

What's Going On With the Stock Market?

326	188	58%	17
views	reads	ratio	fans

Not too shabby after one day. Just goes to show you can't predict how posts are going to perform.

In *other* other news, I like Substack's platform so much better for both Bacon Bits and 365 Days of Freelance Writing. It's cleaner and more user-friendly. Creating and formatting posts is much easier.

Day 162: June 10, 2020 - 5:43 pm (Wednesday)

Hitting publish.

Beyond calls or meetings with prospective clients, hitting publish is one of the more nerve-wracking elements of freelance writing. So much goes into the creative process — brainstorming, planning, researching, writing, editing — and it all comes down to pushing "submit," "publish," or "send."

Is my title good enough?

Did I catch sneaky mistakes?

Will people read it?

Will people *get* it?

Will people like it?

These questions are exhausting, but they're always present in some form. That's the challenge of writing for the benefit of others (versus writing purely for creative purposes). You have to consider how your writing will be received and deciphered.

It was a much steeper challenge at first. Oh man, hitting publish on my first post? That was scary. But guess what was even harder? Sharing it on my social media platforms.

That was a real hurdle.

It's one thing to post on Medium or some other publication and just let it be. It's public, but mainly for the eyes of strangers. You're turning up the emotional-involvement dial when you share it with your friends, family, old coworkers, random people from your hometown, college acquaintances, and whoever else lurks in the shadows of your followers/friends list.

So long as you've done your due diligence and put meaningful time into crafting and refining your product, your post will be well-received.

But, the time will come when you have a **hater**.

Haters get under people's skin and make their blood boil.

But, as many writers will attest, you can't "make it" without having haters. The key is to use their ill-will as motivation. Their critiques can bother you, but you can't let them see that. That's fueling their fire.

Instead, harness that ire and use it to write. Prove them wrong.

Day 163: June 11, 2020 - 1:59 pm (Thursday)

I suck at juggling. I'm pretty coordinated, but maintaining fluid motions and keeping each ball in the air is beyond my capabilities.

In terms of juggling tasks, I'm a little bit better. It's necessary if you want to be a full-time freelance writer (or any type of business owner I suppose). But I'm feeling the heat right now. *Literally and figuratively, I'm on a walk and it feels like 97 degrees.*

There are so many moving pieces, sometimes it's hard to keep up with everything. I'm semi-responsible for my troubles since I tend to bite off more than I can chew. This became more apparent today when I landed two one-off gigs — which is great news and not something to complain about, but the next week will be more stressful than usual.

Client B — you rock, Hannah — referred the first gig to me. It's that PowerPoint editing project I mentioned last week.

> Hi Carter!
> I understand that you are an editor. I have a very very important PowerPoint presentation to give on June 8th and I want to make sure it's perfect. Not a lot of narrative but I want to make sure no typo's etc. Do you do this type of review? If so how much would you charge? There are 35 slides.
> Thanks!

She meant June 18th

I haven't reviewed PowerPoint slides before — at least not in a paid editorial capacity. But, whatever, I'm sure it'll be straightforward. I offered my services at $100 per hour, which wasn't questioned. I have a feeling I'm either drastically underestimating or overestimating how long this will take me.

The second gig is a ClearVoice assignment. I get notifications at least four or five times a week for potential assignments from Rev, a transcription company. Except 95% of their assignments have nothing to do with my background, interests, niches, etc. They're usually about adding subtitles to various video platforms or something like that.

Anyway, ClearVoice notified me of a $337.50 gig for an 800-word post on market research.

ClearVoice

Carter,

Congrats! Rev has hired you for *How Coronavirus is Impacting Market Research*. The deadline is Friday, Jun 19, 12:59am EDT

Questions about this assignment? Use the "Messages" tab in the sidebar.

Go to assignment

I'd be foolish to turn that down. But I have a litany of assignments due next week, so, again, I'm embracing higher levels of stress. Here's what I've got in the client pipeline:

1. PowerPoint edits are due by Monday
2. Client A post due sometime next week (not a hard deadline, but I have to deliver three posts this month, and I haven't turned in any yet)
3. Client E post due next Thursday
4. Client B edits due by Friday
5. ClearVoice assignment is due by Friday

Alone, my client work isn't overwhelming, but I also have personal content I need to produce, such as...

1. Bacon Bits posts
2. 365 Days of Freelance Writing posts and daily entries (AND uploading over *five months* of posts to Substack, which takes forever)
3. Better Marketing posts (I know this publication can be a game-changer for building my following)

It's a lot, but I perform better under pressure. My productivity levels skyrocket when I'm overwhelmed. That's always been the case.

Day 164: June 12, 2020 - 3:32 pm

HOLY. SANTA. CLAUS. The latest Medium writers newsletter just came out.[42]

Want to guess how much the highest-earning writer made in May?

May earnings payouts

By the 8th of each month (so in this case June 8), we initiate the payments for the prior month's earnings. Please allow 3-7 business days to receive the May earnings payouts in your Stripe account. Based on member engagement from this period:

- 60.7% of writers or publications who wrote at least one story for members earned money.
- 5.4% of active writers earned over $100.
- $35,379.72 was the most earned by a writer, and $6,844.29 was the most earned for a single story.

That's absolutely bananas. Over $35,000 in one month? I wish they provided a wee bit more information — like how often this writer posted. Although, I see how that could unmask who the writer is.

It's motivation. Fuel to the fire. I want that. Not just for the money (although that'd be sweeeeeet) but also because that's some serious influence. To make that much money, you'd need millions of views and reads.

It's almost unfathomable.

4:37 pm

People can be so exhausting. Here's a response to my budget-cutting post that was just posted.

> **Ronald**
> Jun 12 · 1 min read
>
> A Budget did help me as well a few years ago. But one thing I am wondering: You wrote that you did work 70+ hours a week (which is 10 hours every single day) and that yiur income was great.
>
> But then again it was 4'000$? I mean, I work 40 hours a week and make around 8–9k. Which based on the hours is nearly 4 times more. I think some of your numbers aren't right or you need to find a far better job.
>
> 1 response

> **Carter Kilmann**
> Jun 12 · 1 min read
>
> Hi Ronald, thanks for reading. I never mentioned my actual income. I think you might be mistaking my example chart's income for my own. As I stated in the paragraph before the chart, those numbers are random (purely there to support the step-by-step guide).
>
> Glad to hear you make a solid income and only work 40-hour weeks, congratulations! That's no small feat.
>
> Thankfully, I did find a far better job—I'm now a self-employed freelance writer (which I also mentioned).

You might have to open my post for context, but c'mon. I blatantly said right before the chart that the numbers were arbitrary.

Ugh. Some people.

Day 165: June 13, 2020 - 11:54 am (Saturday)

Yep, I underestimated the time it'll take to edit these slides. They aren't content-rich, it's just that there are so many little things to clean up. An extra space, mismatched font sizes, misalignments, misformatted lists, and so on.

But, again, I quoted at $100 per hour, so I'm earning a solid rate.

In other news, I received an email about guest posting on Bacon Bits.

> Hey Carter,
>
> Are you accepting authors other than yourself to submit writing for the Bacon Bits publication on Medium?
>
> I'm in the process of familiarizing myself with the platform and have some writing ready to tidy up and publish.

This marks the third time someone has inquired about posting on my publication. It's flattering that someone would want to use my platform to share their work, but Bacon Bits isn't far enough along to accept guest posts quite yet.

On one side, there are benefits to opening it up to the public — like broader reach and accelerated growth. On the other side, that's also a bigger time commitment (editing, scheduling posts, corresponding with applicants, etc.)

I think I'll open it up to submissions one day — once the site has a few thousand followers and maybe 50-75 posts from yours truly.

Day 166: June 14, 2020 - 2:30 pm (Sunday)

Damn, I should add PowerPoint editing to my portfolio of services. That assignment took 2 hours and 39 minutes, resulting in a crisp $265 payment.

Not too shabby.

It's also a different form of editing. I was thinking, "Hmm, 35 slides shouldn't take too long since there isn't a ton of narrative." But I didn't consider the formatting tweaks, font resizing, image alignment, etc.

3:15 pm

I've recommended it before, but I want to reiterate that the Write Jobs newsletter is a worthwhile (and affordable) investment. While catching up on this past week's newsletters, I found a "writers wanted" ad from IGN, one of the best-known video game publications.

In case you don't remember, I've written for a gaming publication (Gaming Nexus) for the last 14-ish months. It's somewhat of a voluntary gig — I don't get paid, but I get free copies of the games I review.

IGN, on the other hand, pays ~$400 per review. Plus, it's a huge brand.

It would be AWESOME to write for their platform. I've followed Dan Stapleton, their Executive Editor (and the author of the ad), on Twitter for quite some time. That's not relevant — more of a fun fact.

Anyway, here's the email I sent:

> **Game Review Writer**
>
> **Carter Kilmann** 8:32 AM
> to dan
>
> Hey Dan, how's your weekend going?
>
> I came across your ad for additional news and review writers. Admittedly, I don't have a great PC (Xbox is my system of choice) - but I'm familiar with multiplayer shooters. I'm also open to playing most genres (even horror, but I can't promise I won't play with the volume down and lights on).
>
> Anyway, I've been writing for Gaming Nexus for the last 14ish months. Here are a few of my reviews:
>
> Super Mega Baseball 3
> Need for Speed Heat
> Age of Wonders: Planetfall
>
> I'd love to write for IGN in any capacity, I've relied on your site since I can remember for reviews and updates on my favorite games. Let me know if you're interested!

Fingers crossed.

Editor's note: Dan never answered.

Week 24 Takeaways

#1: I'm going out on a limb here and hypothesizing that Medium posts with the "Coronavirus" or "Covid 19" tags have a higher chance of curation. I've tagged six of my posts with either of these tags, and all six have been curated.

#2: Man, talk about great timing. I posted my "What's Going On With the Stock Market?" which talks about the impending recession, and the NBER announced a recession less than two hours later.

#3: Words of affirmation can be excellent motivational boosts. Client E's editor relayed some kind words from her CEO. It's nice to know my work is valued.

#4: Much to my surprise, my "What's Going On With the Stock Market?" post is doing quite well. My feelings of hesitation were unfounded. Go figure.

#5: I've become more accustomed to it, but sharing personal work with the public takes time to adjust to. It's an emotional hurdle. As writers, we open ourselves up to criticism and negativity when we share our content. Thick skin is a must.

#6: Freelancing is like juggling. There are a bunch of moving pieces. Task lists are your friend.

#7: Medium. Can. Make. You. SERIOUS. Cash. Medium's latest newsletter shared some ridiculous earnings figures. The highest-earning writer made over **$35,000**. It takes a helluva long time to get to that point. But this demonstrates the viability of writing for Medium. Plenty of people do it full-time.

#8: People are exhausting sometimes. I had a very...*ignorant*... response to my budget-cutting post.

#9: Starting a Medium publication has perks, such as receiving inquiries about guest posts. I'm not open to featuring other writers on Bacon Bits right now, but I think it's flattering that people want to post on it.

#10: If you're familiar with PowerPoint, you could add "Presentation Edits" or "Presentation Reviews" to your list of services. I haven't done a thorough search, but I doubt it's a saturated market.

#11: For only a few bucks a month, you can subscribe to the Write Jobs newsletter. I highly recommend it. It's been a source of relevant and recurring opportunities. It paid for itself and then some. Plus, it's helped me find ways to get my foot in the door with big-name publications.

Day 167: June 15, 2020 - 10:02 am (Monday)

Maybe it's the caffeine coursing through me, but I've planned an aggressive task list for the week. *Typical me.*

But first, let's review my progress from last week.

This Week (6/7 - 6/13)

1. ~~365 Days of Freelance Writing (x7)~~
2. Update Substack with 365 DFW (2 months)
3. Client A post
4. ~~Client B edits~~
5. Client E post
6. ~~Bacon Bits outline~~
7. ~~Bits newsletter #3~~
8. ~~365 DFW post~~
9. ~~Better Marketing outline~~
10. ~~Gaming Nexus post~~

Not bad, but nothing astounding. A few comments:

- I wish I would've gotten a post finished for Client A or Client E because this upcoming week is flushed with client work.
- As I've mentioned, updating Substack takes SO long. It's worth it in the end, but man it's a tedious process. Silver lining: this is the second time I've gone through my old posts and uploaded them to a site (the first was Patreon), so it's a thorough editing review at least. I've caught small, difficult-to-spot errors.

- I'm giving myself credit for completing a 365 Days of Freelance Writing post. To fill out my Substack landing page, I had to write an about page and "Start Here" post that added context to my page. I'll use most of that language to create an intro post for the 365 Medium publication — I just have to format and convert it.
- My Bits newsletter and Gaming Nexus post took a while to complete (I'd estimate the better half of a workday each). So they took away from client work time.

Let's take a look at the upcoming week:

Week (6/14 - 6/20)

1. 365 Days of Freelance Writing (x7)
2. Client A post (x2)
3. Client B edits
4. Client E post
5. Client E outline
6. Client F post
7. ~~Client I edits~~
8. Bacon Bits post
9. Better Marketing post
10. Update 365 Substack (February)

As you can see, it's loaded with client work. Hopefully, those outlines from last week help me knock out a couple of Medium posts though. If you're wondering why I'm aiming for a Better Marketing post versus a 365 Days of Freelance Writing post, I'm waiting until my Substack entries are up to date.

I don't want to drive traffic to Substack if it isn't current.

Day 168: June 16, 2020 - 10:02 am (Tuesday)

Do you want to hear something sort of ridiculous?

If you're not familiar with Medium, the platform tracks the stats for your posts *and* responses. I rarely check how my responses perform because there's no reason to. They don't earn money or, generally speaking, attract much attention.

However, I happen to have one response that's attracted more views than some of my full-fledged posts...

Here's the response:

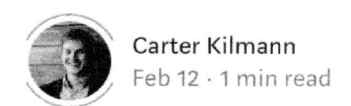

Carter Kilmann
Feb 12 · 1 min read

> Great read, Tim. Have you ever heard of binaural beats? It's kinda trippy "music," but it makes for effective background noise.
>
> Also, you're totally right about comparing yourself to other writers. I ventured down the rabbit hole of doubt about ten days ago doing this. Not a fun experience.

69

And here are the stats:

250	218	87%	9
views	reads	ratio	fans

Isn't that ridiculous? I mean, it makes some sense. Tim Denning, the author of the post, has over 97,000 followers, so his comment sections are bound to receive a sizable flow of traffic.

I think this insight can be exploited. By responding to the posts of prominent writers, you could drive additional traffic to your profile. Responses have to be thoughtful and valuable — not self-promotional.

Could be an effective tactic.

2:32 pm

What are your words worth? What are fair prices for your services?

It's no secret that setting your rates as a freelancer is a tough task. First, writers have to pick the type of rate to charge — such as per word, fixed, or hourly. Then they have to pinpoint an amount that's fair to all parties. It's a balancing act.

Charge "too little" and you feel like you're cheating yourself. Charge "too much" and you feel like you're cheating your client.

So, what's the right answer?

It's surprisingly simple: it's whatever price you can confidently charge and justify. What dollar figure can you promote and persuade prospects to pay for your services? The higher your rates, the more you have to demonstrate your value.

Your rate doesn't have to be a static number — it can (and should) change over time. With repetition, you'll get a feel for your "number."

If you're thinking something spurred this topic today, you're absolutely right. The company that requested the ad hoc PowerPoint review was surprised by the final bill.

> Hi Carter!
> I will have to break your payment up into two parts. Your invoice came in a little higher than I expected. One payment will come from my company and the balance from me personally. I will probably use PayPal.
> Thanks!

To establish some context, here's my response to her initial request:

> me Jun 10
> to ▮
>
> Hi ▮
>
> Did you mean June 18? I'd be happy to review your slides. Are your main concerns grammar, formatting, usage, etc.? Or are you looking for holistic feedback on flow and continuity?
>
> Generally, my editing rate is $100 per hour - but I wouldn't expect slides to take very long to review (especially if the narrative is limited).
>
> If that works for you, feel free to send them my way. I can have them back by EOD Friday.
>
> Let me know what you think!
>
> Cheers,
>
> Carter

In her response, she confirmed the June 18th presentation date and asked if I could have the revisions to her by Monday. But she didn't answer the editing questions or refute my rate.

So, I operated off of my assumption that she wanted a holistic review. I made formatting suggestions on top of standard grammar corrections and fixed typos. I'm proud of my edits because I believe they enhanced the presentation.

Now, it's worth mentioning that I'm just using this situation as an example. It's not like she complained or demanded a lower rate. She simply explained her payment would be in two installments. When I saw that she was a little surprised, I thought, "Hmm, did I charge too much?"

But I quickly dismissed that notion. I told her my rate — she didn't dispute it. I told her it wouldn't take long — but I didn't specify an exact amount of time.

The moral of the story is that it's easy to get in our heads as writers, but we can't let second thoughts discredit our hard work.

Day 169: June 17, 2020 - 1:50 pm (Wednesday)

This was a fun email to receive:

Bacon Bits has 500 followers Inbox
Newsletters/Medium

Medium 1:26 PM
to me

Medium

Your publication has 500 followers on Medium

#proudofmyself

I certainly have high aspirations for Bacon Bits and my Bits newsletter, but I never would have imagined having 500 followers by this point.

Sure, I wish I posted more frequently, but I tend to set unrealistic expectations.

Considering the milestone, I figured today would be a good day to highlight my thoughts about starting a Medium publication.

- It's worth starting a publication for several reasons:
    o You have a platform that can help you reach a specific, segmented audience.
    o Your platform establishes your authority on a subject.
    o You maintain total control of your publication schedule (i.e. you don't have to wait for an editor to approve and publish your work).
    o You can grow your personal following while growing your publication's following.
- Looking back on it, I'm glad I waited to launch Bacon Bits until I had five ready-to-publish posts. From the onset, my page has looked like it has a decent amount of content. If I would've spaced out my first five posts, I might've missed out on early followers.
- One high-performing post can put your publication on people's radar, but a consistent output of posts will ultimately drive people to follow.
- I don't recommend opening up your publication to guest posts immediately. I'm still not sure when the best time is, but I'm not ready yet.
- Organization is key. Your publication needs to be easy to navigate — or else people will get confused and leave. I've spent a ridiculous amount of time toying with my page's layout and tabs. But I'm glad I did.

Day 170: June 18, 2020 - 6:57 am (Thursday)

So, on Tuesday, I proposed an idea for piggybacking off another Medium author's large following by responding to their posts with valuable insights or perspectives. If you're the first response, even better — more people will see it.

If there was a disclaimer, it's that I based my theory on one example.

Well, I decided to try it again shortly after Tuesday's entry.

This highlight will look questionable out of context. It's from a Tim Denning post, and it relates to holding yourself accountable for meeting deadlines by allowing your friends to share embarrassing (or lewd) photos of you if you don't succeed.[43] I'd argue that's more of an exercise of trust versus accountability...

> Find a friend who has embarrassing photos of you — ideally nude photos. Tell them you need help. Tell them that you need them to hold you accountable. Tell them your writi...
>
> The Blueprint I Gave My Friend W... 2.5K 27
> Tim Denning

Carter Kilmann
Jun 16 · 1 min read

Oh boy, that's certainly an unconventional motivator! I'd beat my deadlines by days if I tried this method.

Great advice, Tim.

36

And stats thus far:

> **Oh boy, that's certainly an unconventional mo...**
>
> | 13 | 11 | 85% | 4 |
> |---|---|---|---|
> | views | reads | ratio | fans |

Against my own advice, I didn't strain to add much value. But I noticed no one had commented yet, so I got antsy.

While the stats haven't been anything crazy (which doesn't matter since responses can't earn money), I gained a follower from this brief comment. One of those claps came from someone who followed me immediately after clapping, so they left a quasi-paper trail.

Now, imagine the potential results of taking an extra five minutes to add substance. Replicate this process once a day for a month. If the assumption/goal is to gain one follower from every response, that's 30 new followers for roughly an hour and a half of time.

Not bad considering some actual posts don't have that kind of success.

1:41 pm

Hey, it's National Freelancer's Day! I'm going to reward myself by continuing to work because I have a deadline.

Yaaaaaaay!

Day 171: June 19, 2020 - 2:31 pm (Friday)

Man, oh, man. What a hectic week. I have *one* more assignment to submit. Once I do, I will have delivered over $1,500 worth of content this week.

To be honest, I'm pretty pumped about it.

The money isn't even the most exciting part. While the week felt busy, it wasn't overwhelming. It felt like a personal challenge — it was *fun*.

The one downside: I won't make much headway on my Medium content this week, which is a bummer.

Ohhh, I have to tell you about my ClearVoice assignment. So, since receiving the assignment last week, the platform has displayed a clear due date of June 19. Here's proof:

How Coronavirus is Impacting Market Research

In Progress

Rev.com Blog

Due Jun 19th, 2020

Context: I like to operate as if my due date is a day closer than it is. When other stuff preoccupies my time, I'm still prepared to meet deadlines. It's like a 24-hour cushion.

I had already planned to submit this market research post by yesterday (June 18). I'm cranking out the post, my fingers rattling off words about market research and the pandemic. Smooth sailing.

Well, as I'm wrapping up, the editor reaches out and asks for an update. "Hi Carter, checking on this assignment and when today you think it will be finished?"

I'm thinking, "when *today?*" This is due tomorrow.

Turns out, ClearVoice's platform had the wrong date. If I would've scheduled my week assuming the post was due today, I would've missed my deadline. Now, is that a big deal? Probably not since I had a good reason.

But, from a professional standpoint, I look much better.

Lesson of the day: don't strive to meet deadlines, beat them by at least 24 hours.

Day 172: June 20, 2020 - 11:39 am (Saturday)

Client work kept me from hitting my Medium objectives this past week, but I should be able to prioritize Medium content next week.

What's been cool though is that my posts are still receiving a moderate amount of traffic — even though I've only published one post this month. I don't know if this will hold true forever. I'm guessing my budgeting-cutting post still boosts my stats.

Which, by the way, topped $2,000 of lifetime earnings yesterday.

Lifetime summary

VIEWS **41K**

EARNINGS ⓘ **$2,004.98**

AVG READING TIME ⓘ **2 min 35 sec**

I can't even imagine what it's like for the big-name Medium writers who routinely make thousands of dollars from their posts.

On top of that, historical content continues to make money. A library of posts can continue generating income. Not a ton, but it all adds up. I'm not sure how the algorithm works, but Medium circulates old content depending on people's preferences.

If you post four times a month for a year, you'll wind up with 48 posts, which become passive, money-making assets. If you repeat that process for five years, you're looking at 240 posts!

How much passive income depends on a few things, like the type of content (evergreen versus topical) and audience size.

But it's still something.

Day 173: June 21, 2020 - 9:02 pm (Sunday)

I wonder what it's like to have employees.

As a freelance writer, it makes sense to start as a business of one. But you'll see a lot of successful writers recommend outsourcing certain tasks like editing, bookkeeping, website development, and graphic design. In turn, there's more time and resources available to concentrate on the creative side of this business.

Outsourcing is integral to scaling, or so they say.

I'm not inclined to outsource anything beyond my taxes at this point. But...maybe one day...

I like to control every aspect of my creative process, so I couldn't imagine subcontracting my assignments to other writers. I also don't see myself hiring an editor. From a value perspective, I understand why people do it. I just haven't warmed up to the idea yet.

Plus, I'd need a seriously good editor to justify paying for the service.

Anywho, let's look at how we did last week:

Week (6/14 - 6/20)

1. ~~365 Days of Freelance Writing (x7)~~
2. ~~Client A post (x2)~~
3. ~~Client B edits~~
4. ~~Client E post~~
5. Client E outline
6. ~~Client F post~~
7. ~~Client I edits~~
8. Bacon Bits post
9. Better Marketing post
10. Update 365 Substack (February)

It was a huge week for client work. I didn't get to my Bacon Bits and Better Marketing posts, but I should have more time next week for them. Speaking of next week, here's what we're looking at:

This Week (6/21 - 6/27)

1. 365 Days of Freelance Writing (x7)
2. Client A post
3. Client B edits
4. Client E post
5. Bits newsletter #4
6. Bacon Bits post
7. Better Marketing post
8. 365 DFW post
9. Update Substack (March)

I still have some client work to wrap up for the month, but then I will devote my time to Medium content.

Week 25 Lessons & Takeaways

#1: What's the right rate to charge clients for your services? The answer: whatever you can convince them to pay. If you can demonstrate the value behind a $1,000 price tag for a blog post, then by all means charge $1,000. Just keep in mind that your prospect pool shrinks as you increase your rate.

#2: Bacon Bits hit 500 followers!

#3: I put my "comment on a popular author's post to gain followers" theory to a test. I commented on Tim Denning's post, and I gained a follower. *Neat!*

#4: I delivered $1,500 of content this week. It was an awesome feeling.

#5: Submit content a day ahead of schedule. It'll alleviate stress and ensure you meet every deadline. There was a mix-up with my post for ClearVoice — the due date on the platform was listed a day later than the client was expecting. But I was prepared since I added a 24-hour cushion to my writing schedule.

#6: My budget-cutting post cracked $2,000 of earnings!

#7: Writing creates assets (your posts). Why are they assets? They continue to make money over time. The bigger your portfolio, the better chance you have of establishing passive income from your archive.

#8: Freelancing starts as a business of one, but that doesn't mean you have to stay a lone wolf forever. One day, I'll probably test the waters of outsourcing — at least beyond my taxes.

Day 174: June 22, 2020 - 9:27 pm (Monday)

Today just didn't feel productive. We're not off to a great start this week. Considering it's a Monday, I'm a little annoyed that it wasn't.

Monday is the tone-setter. A kickass Monday lines you up for a kickass week.

Oh well, I just need to rebound with a big Tuesday.

Day 175: June 23, 2020 - 9:01 am (Tuesday)

Remember that ClearVoice assignment from last week? I decided to see if it was posted yet, and I stumbled across a Rev landing page for freelance transcriptionists and captioners.[44]

The payouts seem pretty decent.

Transcriptionists earn $0.30 to $1.10 per audio/video minute, while captioning earns $0.54 to $1.10 per audio/video minute. So, if you transcribe an hour-long video, you're looking at somewhere between $18 and $66.

Let's assume you're earning the median rate for transcription ($0.70). If you transcribed an hour of video from Monday through Friday, that's $210 per week. That's not too bad.

There's no minimum or maximum number of assignments — it seems to be totally up to you. Plus, they distribute payouts every week.

I'm curious how rates are determined. Do you start at the bottom end and get rate increases over time? I might explore this more.

If you need a little income bump, that's not a bad option.

12:25 pm

I don't know what's up with me today, but I'm drained. I'm having occasional bouts of lightheadedness. So much for a productivity rebound.

Day 176: June 24, 2020 - 1:58 pm (Wednesday)

I woke up feeling achy and sore. Plus, I've had off and on headaches.

So, guess who's about to be tested for COVID?

This guy.

I'm at a drive-in testing facility. It's an eerie experience seeing a single-file line of cars waiting to be tested. It's like a scene out of Contagion.

The good news: when I take ibuprofen and Emergen-C, I feel practically 100%. So, I'm still able to concentrate on work.

The thought of being incapable of working is kind of scary.

2:28 pm

Oh man, those cotton swabs are uncomfortable. It's like they're tickling your brain.

Day 177: June 25, 2020 - 10:38 am (Thursday)

Dude, what a weird week. It doesn't feel like it should already be Thursday. I've managed to keep up with most of my work despite my soreness, fatigue, and occasional headaches.

Today's a big day though. I need to get A LOT done. I don't even want to type it out. It may stress me out a little.

Ahh whatever, here's the list:

1. Client A post by 6/30
2. Client B edits by tomorrow
3. Client E post by 6/30
4. Bits newsletter by this afternoon
5. Bacon Bits post before the Bits newsletter (best case) or by Monday (worst case)
6. Better Marketing post by 6/30

I know, those last two are self-imposed deadlines, but I'll be a little disappointed if I end June with only one Medium post.

Day 178: June 26, 2020 - 2:35 pm (Friday)

UGH. It's one of those days where I'm stuck in a writing loop. I'm working on a post for Client E, and I've rewritten the same concept in seven different ways. It's beyond frustrating. I can't satisfy my perfectionism.

I know it's counterproductive, but I can't help it.

AND THERE'S A MOSQUITO IN HERE.

No, sir. Not for long. You picked a bad time, Mr. Mosquito.

Ceases the mosquito's existence

Alright. Time to shift gears and work on something else.

4:26 pm

In much better news, I don't have COVID.

Why the aches and fatigue then? Who knows!

Day 179: June 27, 2020 - 6:01 pm (Saturday)

I have SO MANY tabs open right now, it's unsettling.

I have 53 tabs open across five browsers...

That hurt to type. I honestly feel like I'm committing a crime.

Anyway, I figured today would be a good day to share my Substack stats. Since switching from Mailchimp, I've published two Bits newsletters on Substack. Here are the results:

Well, the stock market finally woke up.
Jun 11 at 4:38 pm

116
TOTAL VIEWS

64
EMAIL RECIPIENTS

→

41%
OPEN RATE
108 OPENS

CLICK RATE

12% of openers clicked a link

  4% https://medium.com/bacon-bits/whats-going-on-with-...

  4% https://www.businessinsider.com/delta-flight-one-pass...

  4% https://www.usatoday.com/story/money/2020/06/08/r...

Consumers? More like consavers, amirite?
Jun 25 at 3:36 pm

34
TOTAL VIEWS

66
EMAIL RECIPIENTS

→

26%
OPEN RATE
33 OPENS

CLICK RATE

12% of openers clicked a link

  6% https://networthify.com/calculator/earlyretirement?inc...

  6% https://www.barrons.com/articles/the-10-cheapest-sto...

I don't think "total views" is very relevant since one person can open an email a bunch of times and skew that figure. That was the case with the first newsletter — one person is responsible for 36 of those opens. Don't ask me why.

Instead, I'm focusing on open rate. The average email open rate is 15-25%, so I'm pretty satisfied with my results so far.[45]

I think the first email's subject line was way more effective. In retrospect, I rushed June 25's subject selection process.

"Consavers"? *What were you thinking, Carter?*

Day 180: June 28, 2020 - 3:10 pm (Sunday)

I'm positioned to finish up my client assignments by EOD Tuesday. *Yay!* But I'm seeing the repercussions of only publishing one Medium post this month. *Boo!*

My Medium notifications have been quieter than usual. Fewer claps, responses, and followers. Catching this bug, whatever it is, didn't help. I've had much less energy. Much less resolve and determination to knock out work.

July will be different. I don't want to see my Medium momentum dwindle.

This might sound surprising, but I think I'd prefer to push out more Medium content than to make an extra $500-1,000. Am I crazy?

Maybe.

Probably.

Week 26 Takeaways

#1: Did you know that Rev.com hires freelancers to transcribe videos? It doesn't sound like a bad gig.

#2: Fatigue + soreness + headaches = less-than-stellar productivity

#3: Guess who got tested for COVID? *This guy.* Guess whose test came back negative? *This guy.* Guess who has no idea why they feel crappy? *THIS GUY!*

#4: Writing can be so mental. I couldn't help my perfectionist ways — I kept rewriting the same section of a client post over and over and over. It's painfully counterproductive.

#5: I'm drowning in tabs this week. I can't wait for the sweet endorphin release when I close them all.

#6: Through four newsletters, Bits is ahead of the curve. The average email open rate is between 15% and 25%. I've topped that range each time (47.2%, 42%, 41%, and 26%).

#7: My income will be higher this month, but my Medium stats will be down. Weirdly enough, I think I'd trade income for better Medium performance.

Day 181: June 29, 2020 - 7:53 am (Monday)

Let's take a look at how we did last week.

This Week (6/21 - 6/27)

1. ~~365 Days of Freelance Writing (x7)~~
2. Client A post
3. ~~Client B edits~~
4. Client E post
5. ~~Bits newsletter #4~~
6. Bacon Bits post
7. Better Marketing post

8. 365 DFW post
9. Update Substack (March)

I know, I know — it doesn't look great, but I'm in position to complete most of the above this week. I was sick (I think?), so my productivity was a little off.

With that in mind, here's what I'm looking to accomplish this week:

This Week (6/28 - 7/4)

1. 365 Days of Freelance Writing (x7)
2. Client A post (edits)
3. Client B edits
4. Client E post
5. Send invoices
6. Bacon Bits post (edits)
7. Better Marketing post (edits)
8. Update Substack (March & April)

I anticipate a short week since it's a holiday, so there's less on this list than usual. I'll have Client A's and Client E's posts completed by tomorrow, so then I'll finally prioritize my Medium content.

Day 182: June 30, 2020 - 7:59 am (Tuesday)

I finished my client work for the month! Now I have the rest of the day to knock out these Medium posts.

In other news, I've corresponded with a company called Baseplay. They're a digital media company based in London. I'd never heard of them before they reached out, but that's not surprising considering their main operations are in Europe and Africa.

They originally emailed me on May 8:

Hi Carter,

I came across your articles on Medium and really liked them. If like many independent creators, you've been busy making awesome content and you want to reach the most number of people and generate the maximum revenue possible.

You can easily make more revenue from your content by submitting to more platforms like Baseplay, this is known as revenue maximization.

Baseplay is a perfect revenue maximisation channel because it:

- Hosts over 8 million users
- Is growing by 200k users monthly
- Supports most forms of content (music, video, games, apps, illustrations)
- Owned by Basebone ltd, a trusted company that's been around since 2007

We want to exceed your expectations which is why we're our offer is :

- Completely free membership
- 80% revenue share on ads
- Monthly payouts
- No channel exclusivity
- Automatic upload of your existing content
- Free advertising on select content items

How do you qualify:

- Your content complies with our Ad policies
- Your content meets our quality standards

... that's it

While this in itself might sound too good to be true, we're offering so much more. As this is a new program the first 50 creators registered will be classified as Pioneers and will be included into our PR and advertising.

This translates to great content marketing for you and your brand, free advertising, and increased revenues.

While we think this is a no-brainer for creators, If you're having any doubts please let us know, we'd be delighted to connect and answer your questions.

Any platform that's free to join and doesn't require new content is worth looking into. So, I signed up. I'm still not sure how it's going to work, but the platform is supposed to launch in July.

I guess we'll see where this goes. They've made it clear that it won't cost me anything and that I can use the platform to share published content.

Editor's note: It didn't go anywhere.

JUNE STATS

In terms of income, June was a great month. The crazy thing is that it was also my lowest output month. Isn't that wild? I'm not happy about my Medium production, but I'm not going to beat myself up over it.

As a reminder, here's each client's description:

- Client A — Digital marketing agency
- Client B — Digital marketing agency (editing work)
- Client C — FinTech startup (no longer a client)
- Client D — Online finance publication (content freeze)
- Client E — Auto finance company
- Client F — ClearVoice assignments
- Client G — SaaS company (no longer a client, for now)
- Client H — Writing Revolt
- Client I — Consulting firm (editing work)

365 Days of Freelancing - Monthly Stats

	Jan	Feb	Mar	Apr	May	Jun
Income						
Client A	960	960	960	640	480	480
Client B	329	119	153	189	741	430
Client C	500	-	-	-	-	-
Client D	350	350	-	-	-	-
Client E	-	450	450	900	450	1,000
Client F	-	225	-	-	-	338
Client G	-	200	-	-	-	-
Client H	-	-	-	-	400	-
Client I	-	-	-	-	-	265
Medium	32	21	719	734	505	496
Total Income	**$2,171**	**$2,325**	**$2,282**	**$2,463**	**$2,576**	**$3,009**
Growth (%)	-	7.1%	(1.9%)	7.9%	4.6%	16.8%
Blog Posts (Paid)						
Client A	6	6	6	4	3	3
Client B	3	2	2	2	9	4
Client C	1	1	-	-	-	-
Client D	1	1	-	-	-	-
Client E	-	1	1	2	1	2
Client F	-	2	-	-	-	1
Client G	-	1	-	-	-	-
Client H	-	-	-	-	1	-
Client I	-	-	-	-	-	1
Total Paid Posts	**11**	**14**	**9**	**8**	**14**	**11**
Blog Posts (Unpaid)						
Medium	1	-	-	1	4	-
Bacon Bits	1	2	4	2	1	1
365	-	-	-	2	-	-
Total Unpaid Posts	**2**	**2**	**4**	**5**	**5**	**1**
Total Blog Posts	**13**	**16**	**13**	**13**	**19**	**12**
Medium						
Views	1,151	1,352	19,466	11,052	15,778	8,562
Reads	439	468	7,413	4,220	6,320	3,651
Read Ratio	38%	35%	38%	38%	40%	43%
Existing Followers	54	63	80	238	371	530
New Followers	9	17	158	133	159	65
Total Followers	**63**	**80**	**238**	**371**	**530**	**595**
LinkedIn						
Existing Followers	458	465	493	526	570	590
New Followers	7	28	33	44	20	9
Total Followers	**465**	**493**	**526**	**570**	**590**	**599**

Highlights:

- I'm not going to complain about a 16.8% income increase. I attribute the jump to (1) rate increases for Client E, (2) a high-paying assignment on ClearVoice, and (3) a high-paying editing gig for Client I.
- Receiving double assignments from Client E has been and will continue to be huge. That locks in $900 to $1,000 each month.
- If you want to take a glass-half-empty perspective, the gigs with Client F (ClearVoice) were ad hoc projects. So, I can't expect to replicate that income going forward.
- Oh, Medium. I apologize for my neglect this month. At least my lone post did well.
- My views practically halved in June relative to May. Not surprising considering the lack of content.
- Modest follower gains across the board — July will be different. BET ON IT.

JULY

Day 183: July 1, 2020 - 4:47 pm (Wednesday)

WOW. What a huge day. We're officially halfway through this 366-day year.

Even though 2020 packed a decade's worth of events into six months, the writing journey has flown by.

I'm floored. I can't believe we're here. Writing every day is cathartic. It's an outlet to voice my frustrations and concerns. It's also a blank canvas for me to play with ideas and strategies.

If you traveled back in time to this moment and told me this quasi-journal would be a total bust, I'd still keep it going. Every aspect of my writing process has improved (in my biased opinion). Idea generation, consistency, organization, timeliness, editing — everything.

Sure, it's a challenge. Sometimes it's the last thing I want to do. But nothing worth having comes easy.

Rant over.

In other news, we're back in the Medium saddle. I published "How to Save an Extra $4,187 in the Next 6 Months" on Bacon Bits and submitted "Not All Time Is Equal" to Better Marketing.[46]

After submitting the Better Marketing piece, something dawned on me: I rarely write short-form Medium content. I didn't have the numbers in front of me (*now I do*), but I didn't need them. It felt weird to submit something that only takes four minutes to read, according to Medium's analysis.

If you're familiar with Medium, you know that they display reading time for each post. Here's an example:

What's Going On With the Stock Market?

Is this a new bull or a deceptive bear market rally?

Carter Kilmann
Jun 8 · 8 min read ★

I'm usually around seven minutes. To date, my average Medium post is 1,530 words. Of my 30 posts, only four have been under 1,000 words. On top of that, today's Better Marketing post is my first post under 800 words.

Post	Month	Words
Quitting Corporate: Why I Chose Happiness Over Money	Aug-19	1,466
3 critical lessons from my first month of freelancing	Aug-19	1,045
Finding Your (Writing) Voice	Sep-19	1,273
5 simple financial principles you need to know	Sep-19	2,094
A Mistake New Freelancers Need to Avoid	Nov-19	1,160
Why You Need to Take Command of Your Money	Dec-19	1,016
How to Take Command of Your Money	Dec-19	1,127
Get Your Finances Organized	Dec-19	1,570
The Sexiest 15-Minute Budget	Dec-19	1,046
Get Comfortable with Credit	Dec-19	1,323
5 Lame Excuses You're Making to Avoid Manaing Your Money	Jan-20	1,224
"Tell Me About a Time You Failed"	Jan-20	1,456
Why Every Freelancer Needs to Organize Their Finances	Feb-20	1,361
4 Financial Tasks You Need to Prioritize as a Freelancer	Feb-20	1,884
How I Cut My Monthly Expenses by 32%	Mar-20	2,109
How to Save Money as a Freelancer Without a Steady Paycheck	Mar-20	1,884
How My Emergency Fund Is Keeping Me Sane During the Pandemic	Mar-20	816
5 Financial Lessons to Learn From the Pandemic	Mar-20	1,177
How to Invest When You Know Nothing about Investing	Apr-20	3,608
How to Take Advantage of the Down Market Before It Rebounds	Apr-20	1,549
How I Quit My Steady Job and Pursued My Entrepreneurial Dreams	Apr-20	1,918
How I Think I Earned $1,250+ With One Post	Apr-20	2,960
Idioms Are Weird. Why Did Curiosity Kill the Cat?	May-20	1,070
My Peace of Mind Cracked Today	May-20	815
How I Landed 3 Clients in My First Week of Self-Employment	May-20	1,468
Monopoly: Board Game or Our Current Reality?	May-20	948
The 90% Economy: Indefinitely Temporary?	May-20	1,840
What's Going On With the Stock Market?	Jun-20	1,687
How to Save an Extra $4,187 in the Next 6 Months	Jul-20	2,287
Not All Time Is Equal	Jul-20	706
		39,367

There's nothing wrong with any of these figures. They're just observations. I've seen four-minute posts earn thousands of dollars. A reader might feel inclined to thoroughly read or finish a four-minute post versus an eight or ten-minute post.

What baffles me is that I'm usually much longer winded with my Medium content.

Day 184: July 2, 2020 - 12:02 pm (Thursday)

My "Not All Time Is Equal" title turned into "How to Charge More Based on Urgency." But that can happen when you submit to publications — you forfeit a little bit of control.[47]

I noticed something strange though. *And I promise this isn't a humblebrag.* My post was immediately curated and distributed in "Money," "Freelancing," and "Writing." I mean, as soon as they published it. Meanwhile, my Bacon Bits post is still under review.

It's not like Better Marketing is a Medium-owned publication. But one or more of their editors might be curators...

Just a thought.

Day 185: July 3, 2020 - 9:00 am (Friday)

The writing process is slow, and that goes beyond brainstorming, writing, and editing. I'm also referring to pitching. It can take weeks just for a publication to accept a pitch — and then there's editing and scheduling too.

Why bring this up?

Well, you probably pieced it together on your own, but I've pitched several publications this year and never received responses. My Money.com pitch (see Day 64) is one example. Or my "referees are the unsung heroes of sports" idea (Day 69), which I sent to a few platforms.

I don't mean to hide my losses under the rug — I just forget to share that certain sites still haven't responded.

There's a silver lining though. I have an inventory of solid pitches. If I wanted to, I could try to find homes for these ideas.

The pitching process is so frustrating and time-consuming though. I'd rather create my own platforms and share my ideas there.

3:03 pm

Ahaaaa, we've crossed 600 followers on Medium.

Sweet.

Day 186: July 4, 2020 - 11:54 am (Saturday)

Happy birthday, America.

I'm not big into politics, so I can't say this next statement with the utmost certainty, but the geopolitical scene of 2020 has to be the most bizarre of all time, no?

From an international perspective, the United States' feuds with Russia, China, and North Korea are enough to capture headlines. But, throw all the national noise into the mix, and you've got a messy ass situation.

It's just been a weird year, and it doesn't look like that'll change with the upcoming elections.

7:29 pm

I don't know what's up with me today, I just feel off.

I'm not motivated to do anything, but I also want to avoid doing nothing. It's quite a frustrating predicament.

Doubt infiltrated my thoughts earlier. I started questioning whether this book is worthwhile.

"Will it even help anyone?"

"Who cares about my Medium performance?"

"Why would anyone want to read about my prune juice experience?"

These are just a few of the doozies that crossed my mind out of the blue. Not a fun sequence of thoughts.

Day 187: July 5, 2020 - 9:47 am (Sunday)

You know, I've been thinking more about my self-doubts from last night. Who cares if this newsletter/book doesn't succeed?

I mean, obviously, I care. But if it fails — so what?

We learn more from failure than we do from success anyway. So, either it gains a lot of traction and succeeds or it goes nowhere and fails.

Editor's note: Of course, modest success is an option too.

I'm committed to building this brand and spotlighting the experience of freelance writing. I try to provide a perspective that'll resonate with you. Whether that's through practical tips, lessons via narratives, or emotional expectations.

Am I doing a good job? It's hard to say…since I haven't shared this with anyone yet.

I have confidence in my writing, but I don't expect people to gobble up every word I spout. I have high goals, but I don't have misguided expectations for achieving those goals. I'm well aware that it can take years to gain a notable following. And even longer to make any profit…

For now, there's no reason to get caught up in doubt. Whatever happens, happens.

Week 27 Lessons & Takeaways

#1: A company called Baseplay reached out to me about showcasing my content on their platform. I'm still in the dark in terms of how this process will play out. But, hey, why not give it a try?

#2: We're halfway through our 366-day journey!

#3: I realized something: I rarely post short-form Medium content. My average Medium post's word count is 1,530 words.

#4: I think one or more of the Better Marketing editors are Medium curators. I've had two posts published on their platform. Both were curated immediately upon publication. Meanwhile, I still have a Bacon Bits post that hasn't been assessed.

#5: The pitching process can take forever, so please excuse me if I don't report if my pitches succeed or fail. It's safe to assume that a pitch never garnered a response if I don't mention it.

#6: We crossed the 600-follower threshold on Medium!

#7: 2020 has been the most bizarre year of my lifetime. We're halfway through it, but I don't anticipate any less craziness.

#8: Screw self-doubt. It's irrational and counterproductive. I had a bout of self-doubt on Saturday — I questioned if this 365-day journey would even be valuable to readers. What good does worrying about that do? *Nada*.

Day 188: July 6, 2020 - 2:16 pm (Monday)

We're rapidly approaching the marketing phase of this writing journey. I expect my entries to be up to date on Substack by tomorrow. Then I'll be able to start publishing content on my

365 Days of Freelance Writing Medium publication, which I'm expecting to be the main driver of traffic to my newsletter.

I might also try helping people on platforms like Twitter, Reddit, and Quora to broaden my reach.

I'm not sure about paid advertising yet…the jury's still out on that one.

Anywho, let's see how we did last week:

This Week (6/28 - 7/4)

1. ~~365 Days of Freelance Writing (x7)~~
2. ~~Client A post (edits)~~
3. ~~Client B edits~~
4. ~~Client E post~~
5. ~~Send invoices~~
6. ~~Bacon Bits post (edits)~~
7. ~~Better Marketing post (edits)~~
8. ~~Update Substack (March & April)~~

Not. Too. Shabby.

Although, as I mentioned last Monday, I didn't plan for a task-intensive week. Plus, a lot of those were edits — not start-to-finish posts.

This week, I'm prioritizing the "launch" of my 365 Days of Freelance Writing Medium publication. I know, it has existed for a little while, but I didn't market it or anything.

Week (7/5 - 7/11)

1. 365 Days of Freelance Writing
2. Finish updating Substack
3. 365 DFW Medium Post (the "Why")
4. 365 DFW Medium Post (Freelancing Emotions)
5. 365 DFW Medium Post (How to start)

6. Bacon Bits post (Gamblers are investing)
7. Client A post
8. Client B edits (x2)

Day 189: July 7, 2020 - 11:12 am (Tuesday)

So, as you know, I decided to transition to Substack. The platform is well-suited for sharing my writing journey with an email list, but uploading each daily entry is time-consuming. I just reached Day 159 (June 7), which was the first day of "Operation Substack." After one month of uploading, I've gotten through 186 entries (daily posts, weekly reviews, and monthly stats).

It'll be such a relief when I'm finished.

5:29 pm

FINISHED. The sweet relief is flowing through me. That was such an onerous task.

Now, I can redirect my attention to Medium content.

Since my daily entries will be sent to subscribers, I have to decide when I'll upload posts. Do I upload today's entries (July 7) before I go to sleep so that it's shared on the same day? Or should upload and share tomorrow morning since the morning is a more natural time for email newsletters?

Hmmm...I need to think about this...

I'll get Kaileigh's opinion. She'll know what to do.

Day 190: July 8, 2020 - 10:55 am (Wednesday)

Somehow, I managed to forget that my next Bits newsletter is set to release this week. So, add that to the task list.

I'm pumped that I finished uploading my entries to Substack, but it took longer than expected. Yesterday's task list included writing 1,000 words of a 365 Days of Freelance Writing Medium post on how to start freelancing (seems like a solid initial post topic for the publication).

Since I didn't get to it yesterday, I have to write **2,000** words today. *Yay.*

As I've said before, I'm a meticulous writer — content doesn't pour out of my fingertips. But, today, I'm going to try.

After I format a couple of Medium posts, I'm going to set a 90-minute timer and power through it.

11:40 am

Alright, let's do this. Timer…SET.

1:10 pm

Phew. That was a grind.

BUT, guess who wrote 1,833 words? *This guy.*

It's much easier to produce high volumes of words in short periods when you know the material. I could write 2,000 words on freelance writing much much quicker than I could write 400 words on molecular biology or some other complex, unfamiliar subject.

I need a break though.

Day 191: July 9, 2020 - 10:05 am (Thursday)

You know what? Yesterday's writing exercise felt liberating.

On any given day, I allow myself to jump around from task to task. I let distractions get the better of me. But sitting down and pumping out roughly 2,000 words (including yesterday's entry) in 90 minutes was empowering.

My creative process is slower. So, it's reassuring to prove I can write a lot when I want or need to.

A well-organized outline is the difference-maker. It's just enough structure to provide direction without limiting creativity. (I shared my creative process back on Day 64, which included a summary of my outlining process.)

From there, it's just letting thoughts flow without editing or formatting interruption. You can't stress about word choice or typos. *That's my biggest obstacle. I want it to be perfect.*

But that's why editing is a separate task — write now, clean up and reformat thoughts later.

Yesterday's example motivated me. Going forward, I'll use that technique every workday. It's a bit more of a challenge when the content is research-oriented, but I think it'll still be more effective than my usual task-to-task dance.

Day 192: July 10, 2020 - 9:27 am (Friday)

Dude. Medium editors must be seriously overloaded right now. My Bacon Bits post from July 1 still hasn't been processed.

How to Save an Extra $4,187 in the Next 6 Months

We are processing this story. Hang tight!

It's not the first time Medium's taken a while to review a post of mine; Medium curators didn't review my first post-corporate Medium story until 18 days after its publication.

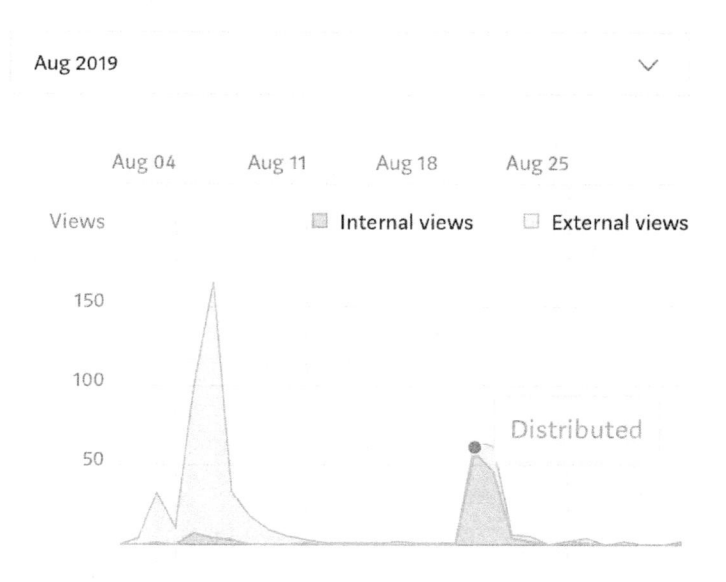

And that's just one example. It's pretty common. As frustrating as it is, there's nothing I can do.

Anyway, I thought more about yesterday's entry — and the importance of solid prep work before writing a post. Although I've written about the initial phase of my creative process before, I haven't shared a visual example.

My process and organization are the same for just about every post I write. Here's a screenshot of the Google Doc for my latest Bacon Bits post.

How to save during a recession

Title Ideas

1. How to save during a recession
2. How to save $4,187 during a recession
3. 12 ways to save money over the next six months
4. How to save up to $4,187 over the next 6 months

Resources

1. https://www.cnbc.com/2018/05/30/top-tips-from-a-28-year-old-who-made-2400-selling-things-online.html (Sell old stuff)
2. https://www.rev.com/freelancers (Transcribe)
3. https://www.reddit.com/r/WagWalker/comments/anxj5u/new_wag_walker_how_much_do_you_guys_earn/ (Dog walking info)

Unused

We have a tendency to buy things just because they're on sale - even though we don't need them.

We're in a recession. And it's a pretty unusual one.

While they're far from unusual, recessions brought about by a pandemic certainly are.

COVID-19 continues to rattle national economies and transform the global economy.

Recessions are tough. They're emotionally and financially draining. Salary cuts and layoffs lead to financial stress.

Outline

1. Introduction
    a. Two ways to increase savings
        i. Save more
        ii. Spend less
2. 5 ways to earn more money
    a. Sell old stuff
    b. Transcribe
    c. Write
    d. Walk dogs
    e. Book reviews
3. 7 ways to spend less money
    a. Source of stats
    b. Link for creating a budget
    c. Categories:
        i. TV
        ii. Clothing
        iii. Dining Out
        iv. Streaming subscriptions
        v. Groceries
        vi. Car Insurance
        vii. Alcohol
4. The big picture
    a. Table that consolidates the above recommendations

I brainstorm a few title ideas before and after my first draft. This gives me general direction before I start writing. Then, once I complete the initial draft, I'm better positioned to come up with a relevant title.

My "Resources" and "Unused" sections are pretty intuitive. *This post had more resources, but I didn't want to bore you with links.* Tracking your resources is a smart time-saver — it creates an easy list to return to later when you're trying to recall a stat or relevant article you've used before.

Along the same lines, relocating unused language from your draft to an "Unused" section prevents hindsight 20/20 moments. For instance, if you decide to delete a particular paragraph that doesn't fit with your post's theme, you can always add it back later if you realize it could be repurposed elsewhere.

Lastly, my outline enables me to drop a header into the "Draft" section of my document and start typing. It's a simple but effective guide.

For client work, I'll also include an executive summary section that discusses the purpose of the post, any guidance from the client, keywords, and word count. This just keeps me on track. It's less imperative for personal posts since I'm dictating most of that anyway.

Day 193: July 11, 2020 - 5:00 pm (Saturday)

I know I sound like a broken record, but sharing the stats from Medium's monthly newsletter has become a habit. Why stop?

> **June earnings payouts**
>
> By the 8th of each month (so in this case July 8), we initiate the payments for the prior month's earnings. Please allow 3-7 business days to receive the June earnings payouts in your Stripe account. Based on member engagement from this period:
>
> - 63.1% of writers or publications who wrote at least one story for members earned money.
> - 5.7% of active writers earned over $100.
> - $33,617.89 was the most earned by a writer, and $6,386.48 was the most earned for a single story.

The numbers are still staggering. I wonder if the highest earner is consistently the same person every month. I mean, realistically, how many writers make over $30,000 on Medium?

Which makes me curious...does Medium make money?

quick Google search

As of 2019, apparently not.[48]

That would be most unfortunate if Medium closed its doors out of the blue one day. I guess it wouldn't be the end of the world, but a lot of my writing aspirations are tied to the platform.

Then again, could a platform with over 60 million readers fold in the blink of an eye? Probably not.

Day 194: July 12, 2020 - 6:02 pm (Sunday)

I'm hoping Medium's curation delay is an aberration. I'm planning to launch my 365 Days of Freelance Writing Medium publication this week, so it'd be less than ideal if curation isn't a thing right now.

In other news, I came across an interesting Medium post just now — "How I Grew a Twitter Account to 40,000 Followers in 2 Days."[49] It's a simple story about a man who took advantage of a cultural fascination to grow his social media following.

Despite the title, it's not exactly a "how-to" article. But it does cast light on identifying trends and piggybacking off of them to expand your reach. Jared, the post's author, leveraged a scene from Michael Jordan's latest documentary, *The Last Dance*, to create viral videos. If you're familiar with the documentary, it's the scene where Jordan is vibing to an unknown song on his Walkman.

Jared exploited this by reposting this scene with superimposed songs from various artists. Each song targeted a different audience. And, as the title shares, he achieved virality and grew his social media following to 40,000 in two days.

Week 28 Lessons & Takeaways

#1: I managed to pump out roughly 2,000 words in 90-minutes, which is unlike me. I've experimented with timed writing sessions before, but I'm going to take this approach every workday going forward. It's way more efficient than sporadic task-jumping.

#2: Medium curators seem to be on vacation…

#3: As backward as it sounds, creativity needs a little structure. Before you even start writing, it's important to compile resources and create a brief outline. Once you initiate the actual writing phase of your creative process, you'll have a guide that keeps you moving in the right direction.

#4: Did you know that Medium isn't profitable? At least, it wasn't in 2019. Maybe it is now.

#5: Viral content doesn't need to be complex.

Day 195: July 13, 2020 - 10:58 am (Monday)

It's still early, but I don't expect to surpass last month's income results. That's not a total surprise since I've allocated so much time to my personal brands thus far, but I need to start mentally preparing for that reality.

Anyway, let's review last week's progress.

Week (7/5 - 7/11)

1. ~~365 Days of Freelance Writing~~
2. ~~Finish updating Substack~~
3. ~~365 DFW Medium Post (the "Why")~~
4. ~~365 DFW Medium Post (Freelancing Emotions)~~
5. 365 DFW Medium Post (How to start)
6. Bacon Bits post (Gamblers are investing)
7. ~~Bits newsletter #5~~
8. Client A post
9. ~~Client B edits (x2)~~

As minor as it seems, updating Substack with all of these entries took a painful amount of time. So, I'm very glad that's out of the way. Otherwise, my week was so-so in terms of productivity.

When I first created my task list, I accidentally left off my Bits newsletter, which takes half of a day to write, edit, and publish. Beyond that, I completed editing assignments and primed my 365 DFW publication for its launch — I just need to finish my "How to start freelance writing" post.

This week isn't going to be very productive. I'm moving into an apartment with Kaileigh on Wednesday, so I won't be working as much Wednesday through Friday.

This Week (7/12 - 7/18)

1. 365 Days of Freelance Writing (x7)
2. Client A posts (x2)
3. Client B edits
4. Client E post
5. 365 DFW post (How to start)
6. Bacon Bits post (Gamblers investing)

Half of this week's task list consists of wrapping up tasks from last week. Considering the move, I'll be happy with a successful launch of the 365 DFW publication.

Also, I'm not sure if I'll have an assignment brief from Client E this week, but I threw it in there just in case.

Day 196: July 14, 2020 - 9:30 am (Tuesday)

I read another interesting post this morning — "How I Write 20,000 Words in a Single Day."[50] It's from our good pal, Tim Denning.

First of all, that's an absurd volume of words. At that rate, you could write a full-length book in a matter of **days**. In my opinion, the biggest lesson from this post is the importance of exercising your writing muscles.

You can't expect to write 20,000 words in a day without loads of practice. The same concept applies whether it's 10,000 words or even 2,000 words. You have to constantly push your limits if you want to write more.

Another key element Tim discusses is the idea of writing from multiple writer perspectives — such as a personal finance writer, a productivity writer, a psychology writer, and so on.

The more perspectives you take, the easier it is to write about various topics.

2:05 pm

A potential opportunity popped up in my inbox just now.

> Hi Carter,
>
> Hope you are well! We have an opportunity at the Federal Reserve Bank in Atlanta for an Editor. This is a contract through the end of the year that could be extended.
>
> They would like an Editor with Financial Services experience. This person will be editing materials from short paragraphs to 20-30 page reports and will be working on multiple assignments at the same time.
>
> If you'd like to see more details, please let me know.

That could be interesting. My initial questions:

1. Is this a remote position?
2. Is this a part-time position?
3. What's the pay?

Anything full-time is a nonstarter. As you're well aware, I have other clients and personal projects. Unless this position pays a ridiculous amount of money, I wouldn't cut ties with my current clients.

Let's see what they say.

Day 197: July 15, 2020 - 9:17 pm (Wednesday)

Did I mention that I hate moving? I'm exhausted...and we have so much left to do.

Sometimes I wish I was a minimalist.

Anyway, it turns out the Federal Reserve job is a full-time position. *Eh, no thanks.*

That would mean dropping each of my current clients and putting my personal ambitions on hold. It'd be a legit resume padder, but I don't think it's worth it.

From the sound of it, I don't think it'd be a borderline 40 hour per week job either. Here's the word for word response to my part-time question:

"It is 40 hours/week. There are 2 other Editors on the team and they are very busy!"

Hard pass.

Day 198: July 16, 2020 - 8:07 pm (Thursday)

Moving + Internet problems = Zero productivity

I spent about five minutes reading through an editing assignment, and I paid my state tax estimate. Otherwise, I spent all day moving and organizing.

Looks like I won't be rolling out the Medium publication this week. Especially since I still don't have an internet connection...

Day 199: July 17, 2020 - 5:03 pm (Friday)

FINISHED. *Sort of.*

Everything has been moved into the new apartment, and I'd estimate that we're 90% unpacked and organized. I feel like I've moved nine times this year.

Good news though, we have internet! So I was able to complete my editing assignment for the week. *Yay!*

We're already 17 days into July, and I feel like I haven't accomplished anything. I need a huge week next week. Maybe I'll hit a creativity-high and pump out like nine Medium posts.

That'd make me feel better.

Day 200: July 18, 2020 - 3:41 pm (Saturday)

Hey, we made it through 200 days. That's pretty cool.

A bit of disappointing news: my latest Bacon Bits post was **not** distributed. Downer.

I'm not sure why, but at least I can stop checking.

My Medium stats took a hit over the last six weeks or so. I think it's a result of reduced post quantity. Assuming the read ratio is a reliable indicator of quality, my posts have done alright. I haven't had anything below 42% in quite some time.

How to Charge More Based on Urgency

199	99	50%	15
views	reads	ratio	fans

How to Save an Extra $4,187 in the Next 6 Mo...

147	69	47%	16
views	reads	ratio	fans

What's Going On With the Stock Market?

938	483	51%	34
views	reads	ratio	fans

The 90% Economy: Indefinitely Temporary?

306	128	42%	18
views	reads	ratio	fans

Monopoly: Board Game or Our Current Reality?

218	123	56%	16
views	reads	ratio	fans

How I Landed 3 Clients in My First Week of Se...

1.8K	866	48%	97
views	reads	ratio	fans

If I can push out another four or five posts in July, I think I'll get my numbers up again.

Day 201: July 19, 2020 - 11:02 am (Sunday)

Writers have to exercise their writing muscles just like any other body part.

It's similar to working out or playing sports. If you play golf and take a break from it for a while, you'll be rusty the next time you play. Likewise, if you hit the driving range every day and work on your mechanics, you'll see your skills improve. The same principles apply to writing.

Since I've been moving since Wednesday, it feels like I'm a little out of practice. Thankfully, my 365 Days of Freelance Writing responsibilities keep me writing — even if it's just a small blurb.

I still have a couple of moving chores left for tomorrow, but once that's done, I'm dedicating my week to pumping out content.

12:45 pm

I highly recommend hiking. On top of good physical exercise and serene views, hiking clears the mind and opens the door for creative thinking.

Week 29 Lessons & Takeaways

#1: A potential editing gig with the Federal Reserve of Atlanta surfaced, but it was full-time. As legit of a role as that would be, I don't want to sacrifice my freelance business for that type of role. Plus, it sounded like it would be a heavy workload.

#2: If you embrace multiple perspectives, you'll never run out of topics to write about.

#3: Writing is like a muscle. It has to be exercised regularly and pushed to the limit if you want to strengthen it.

#4: Hiking is walking on steroids in terms of clearing mental distractions. Serene views and peaceful nature sounds reinvigorate the soul.

Day 202: July 20, 2020 - 4:14 pm (Monday)

"Write when you feel overpowered by your emotions."

I've seen many writers preach this concept over the past few months. The idea is that emotion-driven writing has a better chance of connecting with readers. Plus, when you channel your emotions into your writing, you enter a state of mind (commonly referred to as "flow") that enables high volumes of lucid content.

The only challenge is that emotions are unpredictable. You can't schedule an emotional writing session for Monday at 2 pm — it just doesn't work that way.

The best we can do is keep a phone or computer nearby for when inspiration strikes.

But enough about feelings, let's take a look at last week's progress and the week ahead. *Disclaimer: last week's task list is **not** a sight to behold...but that was expected.*

This Week (7/12 - 7/18)

1. ~~365 Days of Freelance Writing (x7)~~
2. Client A posts (x2)
3. ~~Client B edits~~
4. Client E post
5. ~~365 DFW post (How to start)~~
6. Bacon Bits post (Gamblers investing)
7. Bacon Bits post (Is money the solution?)

A few thoughts:

- I finished one post for Client A. If I wanted to make myself feel better, I could separate that into two tasks and cross out one.
- I didn't complete a post for Client E because I still haven't received my assignment briefs yet.
- While I didn't add to my speculative-gamblers-turned-investors post, I did come close to finishing a philosophical post about money.

Since my move is 95% done, this week should be more productive.

This Week (7/19 - 7/25)

1. 365 Days of Freelance Writing
2. Client A post
3. Client B edits
4. Client E post
5. Launch 365 publication
6. 365 DFW post
7. Bacon bits post
8. Bits newsletter
9. Medium post

Day 203: July 21, 2020 - 4:33 pm (Tuesday)

You know what I haven't explored much? Converting newsletter content into blog posts and repurposing Medium stories for LinkedIn.

From what I can tell, there's nothing wrong with either approach.

For newsletters, subscribers still have early access to your content and thoughts, so it's not like you're nullifying the extra value of your newsletter.

To date, I've published five Bits newsletters, covering a range of topics like the stock market, saving, consumer spending, debt, and so on. It's all original — nothing was pulled from existing Bacon Bits posts. So, I could easily modify, restructure, and add to these newsletters to bolster my content output.

I could apply a similar process to my other Medium content. I know I reference him often, but I noticed Tim Denning routinely adds Medium content to his LinkedIn page. After he posts a story on Medium, he adds it to LinkedIn roughly one to two weeks later.

When you think about it, how is this any different from a video content creator posting a video on Facebook and then uploading it to YouTube? Or a clothing store selling clothes to customers in Georgia even though they're based out of South Carolina?

To reach the widest range of people, you have to leverage multiple platforms.

Day 204: July 22, 2020 - 2:26 pm (Wednesday)

Over the last 204 days, I've acknowledged select milestones, such as hitting 500 Bacon Bits followers or reaching the halfway point of my 366-day journey. But, as strange as it may sound (at first), day 204 might be the biggest.

Why? Because it's been exactly one year since I started working for myself.

On Friday, July 19, 2019, I walked out of my corporate banking job for the last time. That following Monday, I started freelance writing full-time.

In honor of this milestone, I publicly announced my 365 Days of Freelance Writing platforms and published three posts on my Medium publication. I've got another "year in review" type post on the way that I'll publish later this afternoon.

Day 205: July 23, 2020 - 2:59 pm (Thursday)

A fellow writer reached out to me on LinkedIn this morning. She asked if I'd be willing to take a survey, which would help her assess freelance writers' perspectives and ambitions. One of the questions stuck out to me.

"What is the #1 goal you want to achieve with your writing career?"

That'll get you thinking.

So, I thought about it for a minute or two. I have a long list of goals. But, as the question stated, I had to choose my *top* goal.

I wrote, "Earn a six-figure income from my personal writing projects."

Whenever I think about dream levels of income, I think back to a 2010 Princeton study on happiness and money.[51] The study concluded that there's a correlation between income and happiness up to $75,000 per year. Beyond that level, additional income did not suggest an increase in happiness.

Obviously, that's just one study. So, I hit up the Google machine in search of an updated result.

A 2018 Purdue study came to the rescue.[52] From a global standpoint, the study found that annual income levels between $60,000 and $75,000 satiate our emotional well-being, while $95,000 satisfies our life evaluation.

Simply put, if we make $75,000, we're emotionally satisfied. If we make $95,000, we feel accomplished and successful. *According to the study.*

I don't even think I'd even need to earn six figures to be content with my occupation and financial situation. For instance, if my personal writing and projects (like Medium stories, Bacon Bits, and this book) generated $75,000 of income every year, I'd take that in a heartbeat.

It may not be an insane amount of money, but that type of work and that income would enable me to live an ideal lifestyle.

Day 206: July 24, 2020 - 9:35 am (Friday)

There's no question that Medium is a popular writing platform, but the underlying algorithms and inner workings are a mystery — even to the most successful writers.

I came across an insightful, well-organized analysis of a writer's Medium performance. Amardeep Parmar, who's an editor for Entrepreneur's Handbook, dives deep into his earnings stats in his post, "A Statistical Breakdown of $4,345 in 6 Months on Medium."[53]

While it's just one person's data, here are his takeaways:

- Most stories fail to earn much money. And you can't predict which ones will go viral on Medium.
- If you happen to have success, don't assume your next posts will replicate that performance (you know what they say about assuming).
- There isn't an ideal length for a Medium post. Amardeep's longest posts are 15-minute and 20-minute reads. Their average read times were both below three minutes, meaning people tend to skim these articles pretty quickly. He's had five-minute posts exhibit longer average read times.
- Some stories don't gain traction until well after they're published. This happened with me when my budget-cutting post resurged a couple of months after peaking.
- **Curation is essential.** If there's one aspect of a post to focus on, it's not padding word length or choosing a fancy header image — it's getting curated.

It's easy to get carried away with your stats. On more than one occasion, I've extrapolated assumptions from my previous posts and tried to replicate success. But the results aren't consistent.

As lame as it sounds, the most effective way to generate success is to write well-thought-out, organized, and valuable content (i.e. from the perspective of the reader). *Also, don't be overly self-promotional and don't break Medium's curation policies.*

Day 207: July 25, 2020 - 9:13 am (Saturday)

I'm thinking about constructing some sort of personal writing challenge. You know, one of those where you have X days to earn Y amount?

Something like a 60-day, $10,000 copywriting challenge.

I'd commit the initial 15 days to sample creation. Then, I'd spend the next 15-20 days pitching as many prospects as possible (personalized pitches, of course). Finally, I'd have about a month to earn as much as possible.

I know, I know. I act like a dog chasing squirrels. *Commit to one project, will ya??*

It's just something I'm considering. It would motivate me to pursue more copywriting gigs. Maybe I'll save it for September or October.

Day 208: July 26, 2020 - 9:25 pm (Sunday)

I came across an inspiring story this past week — *which I meant to share earlier (oops).*

$500,000 at 30: I Hit My FIRE Number![54]

It's a post from A Purple Life, the blog of a financially focused writer who just hit her retirement number. She's incredibly detailed and an excellent writer. Her tone is friendly and energetic, which is easier to read.

By minimizing spending and maximizing savings, she's managed to build a net worth of over $500,000 in only nine years of work. She plans to leave her full-time job in September (I can't figure out what her job is though).

From her post:

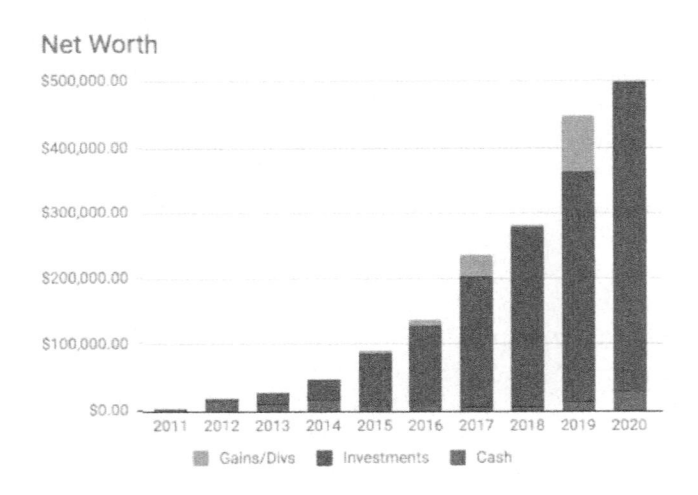

Net Worth

[Bar chart showing net worth growth from 2011 to 2020, rising from near $0 to approximately $500,000, with categories for Gains/Divs, Investments, and Cash]

Can you imagine retiring at 30? Based on the average US life expectancy of 78, that's almost 50 years of retirement.

50. Years.

Good for her. That's the power of compound interest working in tandem with minimal lifestyle expenses.

Week 30 Lessons & Takeaways

#1: Many writers preach the importance of writing when you're overwhelmed with emotion, which I stand by as well. Emotional writing is relatable, meaning you have a better chance of connecting with readers.

#2: Who says content has to stay on its initial platform? Newsletters can be redesigned into blog posts. Medium posts can be reposted on LinkedIn. All to reach a broader audience. Nothing wrong with that.

#3: Money is a funny subject. We spend so many of our waking hours dedicated to earning more of it — but many people don't enjoy their income-generating activity (i.e. their job). A couple of studies determined that emotional fulfillment does not increase past a certain income threshold (~$75,000). So, is a draining, six-figure job worth the emotional toll?

#4: Medium is one of the most popular writing platforms out there, but it has its fair share of secrets. No one knows how to construct the perfect post for virality. It's simply unpredictable. But, if there's one thing to strive for, it's curation.

#5: Writing challenges can be fun and profitable. I'm thinking of taking on a self-imposed copywriting challenge in a month or two.

#7: Saving money is like investing in your future self. You grant future-you the power to live a more robust life. One writer, the author of A Purple Life, will retire in September with a net worth of $500,000 at age 30. Not too shabby.

Day 209: July 27, 2020 - 9:52 am

It's a busy day today, so let's review last week's task list.

This Week (7/19 - 7/25)

1. ~~365 Days of Freelance Writing~~
2. Client A post
3. ~~Client B edits~~
4. Client E post

5. ~~Launch 365 publication~~
6. ~~365 DFW post~~
7. Bacon bits post
8. ~~Bits newsletter~~
9. Medium post

Notes:

- I just have to wrap up a few final touches for Client A's post.
- I finally received my assignment from Client E on Friday afternoon, so I didn't have a chance to start it.
- I had a successful public launch of my 365-day writing project (by my standards I suppose).
- I nearly finished a post for Bacon Bits, which I'll publish this morning.
- I started another Medium post, which discusses emotional intelligence. Hopefully, I can complete that this week too.

Aaaaaaaand the week ahead:

This Week (7/26 - 8/1)

1. 365 Days of Freelance Writing (x7)
2. Client A post (x2)
3. Client B edits
4. Client E post
5. Bacon Bits post (x2)
6. Better Marketing post
7. Medium post

Day 210: July 28, 2020 - 12:11 pm (Tuesday)

If you start a Medium publication, you get additional stats and insights. In addition to your personal stats page, you'll also have a publication stats page.

Here's my stats page for Bacon Bits.

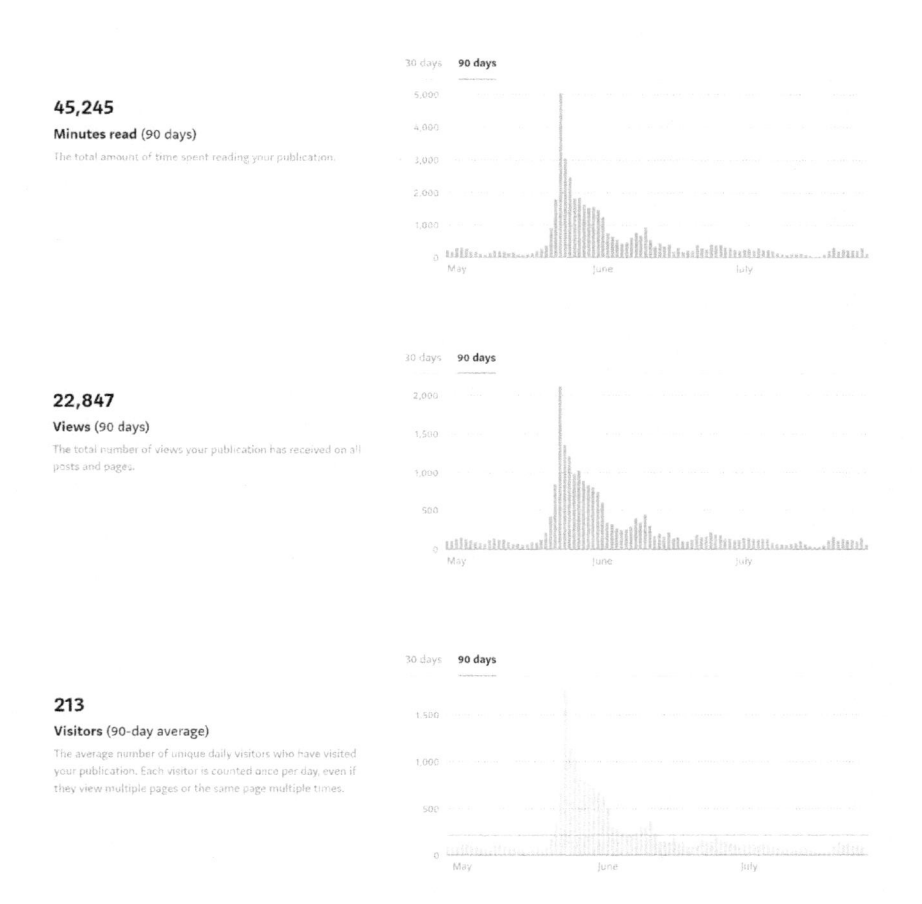

45,245
Minutes read (90 days)
The total amount of time spent reading your publication.

22,847
Views (90 days)
The total number of views your publication has received on all posts and pages.

213
Visitors (90-day average)
The average number of unique daily visitors who have visited your publication. Each visitor is counted once per day, even if they view multiple pages or the same page multiple times.

Similar to your personal stats, you can track reading time and views, but you also access a unique stat: visitors.

I like seeing my publication's average daily visitors. I can better quantify the traffic I'm generating.

2:57 pm

You can learn a lot from other content creators — not just writers.

Sometimes, I watch video game streamers during my breaks. Obviously, writing and streaming are different forms of content creation, but there's some overlap.

If you're unfamiliar, streamers broadcast their gaming sessions while viewers watch and comment. It's not a requirement, but streamers are usually better than the average bear at the games they play — but not always. Personality and community engagement can compensate for ability.

I was watching a popular gaming streamer, Average Dad (his real name is Dean), during my lunch break today. During his stream, he dished out a solid piece of simple wisdom. One particular viewer said he was jealous of Dean's job. In response, he said jealousy is fruitless. Playing the comparison game isn't productive. Instead, focus on you and your content.

I've fallen into the "doubt trap" before, where I'll compare myself to other successful writers. It's not fun.

We just have to combat it with logic and remember everyone's journey is unique.

7:38 pm

Well, this was a surprise.

Medium

Hi there,

Our curators just read your story, *How to Save an Extra $4,187 in the Next 6 Months*, that you submitted for review. Based on its quality, they selected it to be recommended to readers interested in Money across our homepage, app, topic page, and emails.

I'm not sure why Medium said my post wasn't distributed back on July 18. We officially have a new record for the longest post curation review at 27 days.

I mean, I'll take it. But that's bizarre.

Day 211: July 29, 2020 - 2:31 pm (Wednesday)

It's funny how time changes things. A year ago, I was so focused on building a portfolio — I had maybe ten pieces of content to my name. Now, I have no idea what that number is. I lost count a while ago.

So, let's count.

adds up totals in a spreadsheet

Old clients	17 posts + assignments
My website	4 posts
Guest posts	10 posts
Client A	65 posts
Client B	33 posts + website pages
Client C	11 assignments
Client D	2 posts
Client E	8 posts
Client F	3 posts
Client G	1 post
Client H	1 guest post (hasn't published yet)
Client I	1 PowerPoint review
Medium	37 posts
Bits	7 newsletters
Gaming Nexus	7 reviews
Total	**207 portfolio pieces**

By "old clients," I mean clients that I haven't worked with this year, so they aren't listed in my monthly stats analyses.

Not bad, eh? Honestly, I'm not sure what my numbers should be after a year of full-time writing. BUT I did set portfolio goals way back when I started writing full-time.

Dusts off old goal list

Weirdly enough, I set my initial business goals exactly one year ago (7/29/19). *I promise I didn't plan this.* One of my goal categories was "Portfolio"; I aimed to have 100 portfolio pieces by the end of this year.

Have 100 posts in portfolio	Portfolio	Long-term	12/31/2020	

Goal CRUSHED.

That date was somewhat arbitrary though. I had no idea how long it would take to write 100 posts.

So, that's neat.

Day 212: July 30, 2020 - 10:12 am (Thursday)

Yesterday's counting exercise got me thinking about the number of words I've written. *No, I'm not about to calculate that mountainous figure.* That would be so tedious and such a time burn. But I have tracked the word counts of my Medium posts.

My aggregate word count across Medium posts is just below 55,000 words.

Post	Month	Publication	Words
Quitting Corporate: Why I Chose Happiness Over Money	Aug-19	The Startup	1,466
3 critical lessons from my first month of freelancing	Aug-19	The Startup	1,045
Finding Your (Writing) Voice	Sep-19	Writing Cooperative	1,273
5 simple financial principles you need to know	Sep-19	Bacon Bits	2,094
A Mistake New Freelancers Need to Avoid	Nov-19	The Startup	1,160
Why You Need to Take Command of Your Money	Dec-19	Bacon Bits	1,016
How to Take Command of Your Money	Dec-19	Bacon Bits	1,127
Get Your Finances Organized	Dec-19	Bacon Bits	1,570
The Sexiest 15-Minute Budget	Dec-19	Bacon Bits	1,046
Get Comfortable with Credit	Dec-19	Bacon Bits	1,323
5 Lame Excuses You're Making to Avoid Manaing Your Money	Jan-20	Bacon Bits	1,224
"Tell Me About a Time You Failed"	Jan-20	The Startup	1,456
Why Every Freelancer Needs to Organize Their Finances	Feb-20	Bacon Bits	1,361
4 Financial Tasks You Need to Prioritize as a Freelancer	Feb-20	Bacon Bits	1,884
How I Cut My Monthly Expenses by 32%	Mar-20	Bacon Bits	2,109
How to Save Money as a Freelancer Without a Steady Paycheck	Mar-20	Bacon Bits	1,884
How My Emergency Fund Is Keeping Me Sane During the Pandemic	Mar-20	Bacon Bits	816
5 Financial Lessons to Learn From the Pandemic	Mar-20	Bacon Bits	1,177
How to Invest When You Know Nothing About Investing	Apr-20	Bacon Bits	3,608
How to Take Advantage of the Down Market Before It Rebounds	Apr-20	Bacon Bits	1,549
How I Quit My Steady Job and Pursued My Entrepreneurial Dreams	Apr-20	The Ascent	1,918
How I Think I Earned $1,250+ With One Post	Apr-20	365 DFW	2,960
Idioms Are Weird. Why Did Curiosity Kill the Cat?	May-20	Curiosity	1,070
My Peace of Mind Cracked Today	May-20	Curiosity	815
How I Landed 3 Clients in My First Week of Self-Employment	May-20	Better Marketing	1,468
Monopoly: Board Game or Our Current Reality?	May-20	Bacon Bits	948
The 90% Economy: Indefinitely Temporary?	May-20	The Startup	1,840
What's Going On With the Stock Market?	Jun-20	Bacon Bits	1,687
How to Save an Extra $4,187 in the Next 6 Months	Jul-20	Bacon Bits	2,287
How to Charge More Based on Urgency	Jul-20	Better Marketing	706
5 Unavoidable Emotions If You Want to Be a Freelance Writer	Jul-20	365 DFW	1,537
365 Days of Freelance Writing	Jul-20	365 DFW	1,620
How to Be a Successful Freelance Writer With No Experience	Jul-20	365 DFW	2,864
What You'll Learn in Your First Year of Freelance Writing	Jul-20	365 DFW	1,684
Is Money the Solution to Life's Problems?	Jul-20	Bacon Bits	977
			54,569

Hmm...considering 90% of my writing covers either personal finance or freelance writing, I might have enough existing content to create a couple of eBooks. I think it's a fairly common practice for people to compile and convert their blog posts into eBooks.

But I'll need to confirm that.

What's the benefit? From a reader's perspective, it's centralized information. For instance, let's say I wrote a general eBook about taking control of your finances. If someone wants to organize their finances, cut expenses, and start investing, they don't have to find and read 15 different articles. It's all in one place.

From my perspective, I'm able to assemble a marketable product that can become an income stream.

I'll have to dig through my old posts and see if there's enough there to create a single cohesive product.

Man, who would've thought counting would trigger business ideas?

Day 213: July 31, 2020 - 6:57 am (Friday)

Soooo, I received a client email last night that threw a wrench in my Friday work schedule.

Some context: I delivered a post on Tuesday about the state of the U.S. mortgage industry. The topic seemed fitting because the client works with companies in healthcare and financial services. Or, so I thought.

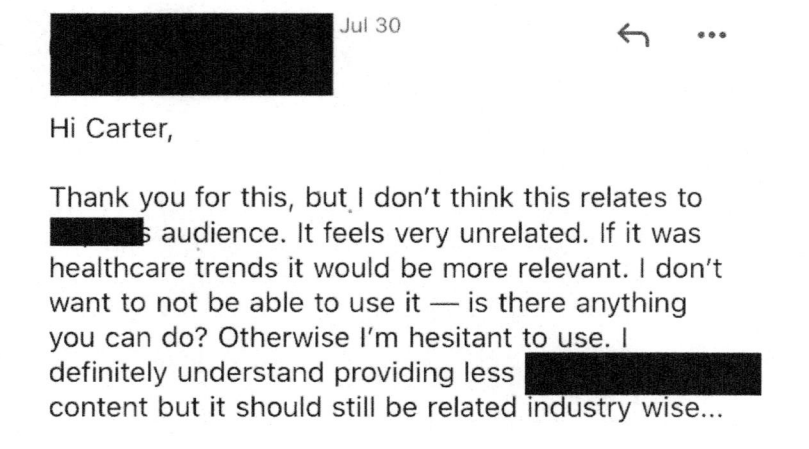

> Jul 30
>
> Hi Carter,
>
> Thank you for this, but I don't think this relates to ███'s audience. It feels very unrelated. If it was healthcare trends it would be more relevant. I don't want to not be able to use it — is there anything you can do? Otherwise I'm hesitant to use. I definitely understand providing less ███ content but it should still be related industry wise...

A bit of miscommunication, they *used* to work with financial services companies, but I never got that update. So, now I need to write another post before the end of the day.

Sigh...

JULY STATS

July. A lovely month in many respects. We celebrated the USA's independence. Sports returned after a *painfully* long absence. I moved in with Kaileigh. We took a trip to the mountains.

These are all great things.

But July was also a down month from an income perspective. No need to panic. It was somewhat expected.

As a reminder, here's each client's description:

- Client A — Digital marketing agency
- Client B — Digital marketing agency (editing work)
- Client C — FinTech startup (no longer a client)
- Client D — Online finance publication (content freeze)
- Client E — Auto finance company
- Client F — ClearVoice assignments
- Client G — SaaS company (no longer a client, for now)
- Client H — Writing Revolt
- Client I — Consulting firm

365 Days of Freelancing - Monthly Stats	Jan	Feb	Mar	Apr	May	Jun	Jul
Income							
Client A	960	960	960	640	480	480	480
Client B	329	119	153	189	741	430	415
Client C	500	-	-	-	-	-	-
Client D	350	350	-	-	-	-	-
Client E	-	450	450	900	450	1,000	450
Client F	-	225	-	-	-	338	-
Client G	-	200	-	-	-	-	-
Client H	-	-	-	-	400	-	-
Client I	-	-	-	-	-	265	-
Medium	32	21	719	734	505	496	147
Total Income	**$2,171**	**$2,325**	**$2,282**	**$2,463**	**$2,576**	**$3,009**	**$1,492**
Growth (%)	-	7.1%	(1.9%)	7.9%	4.6%	16.8%	(50.4%)
Blog Posts (Paid)							
Client A	6	6	6	4	3	3	3
Client B	3	2	2	2	9	4	6
Client C	1	1	-	-	-	-	-
Client D	1	1	-	-	-	-	-
Client E	-	1	1	2	1	2	1
Client F	-	2	-	-	-	1	-
Client G	-	1	-	-	-	-	-
Client H	-	-	-	-	1	-	-
Client I	-	-	-	-	-	1	-
Total Paid Posts	**11**	**14**	**9**	**8**	**14**	**11**	**10**
Blog Posts (Unpaid)							
Medium	1	-	-	1	4	-	1
Bacon Bits	1	2	4	2	1	1	2
365	-	-	-	2	-	-	4
Total Unpaid Posts	**2**	**2**	**4**	**5**	**5**	**1**	**7**
Total Blog Posts	**13**	**16**	**13**	**13**	**19**	**12**	**17**
Medium							
Views	1,151	1,352	19,466	11,052	15,778	8,562	4,552
Reads	439	468	7,413	4,220	6,320	3,651	1,947
Read Ratio	38%	35%	38%	38%	40%	43%	43%
Existing Followers	54	63	80	238	371	530	595
New Followers	9	17	158	133	159	65	50
Total Followers	**63**	**80**	**238**	**371**	**530**	**595**	**645**
LinkedIn							
Existing Followers	458	465	493	526	570	590	599
New Followers	7	28	33	44	20	9	14
Total Followers	**465**	**493**	**526**	**570**	**590**	**599**	**613**

Highlights:

- My income took an uppercut to the jaw, halving relative to June. But no need to fret, we're resilient. We can take a few blows. Why the down month? Moving, vacationing, publicly launching my 365-day writing project. An assortment of reasons.
- From a high level, my Medium numbers look bizarre. I published more posts in July than ever before...but my earnings, views, reads, and follows suffered. I think that's largely due to March's budget-cutting post running out of steam. I quickly compiled this table, which demonstrates that sentiment. *Note the numbers below are in thousands and a little understated because Medium abbreviates numbers.*

	March	April	May	June	July	Aggregate
Total Views	19.5	11.1	15.8	8.6	4.6	**59.4**
Budget-Cutting Post	17.2	7.8	12.3	5.8	2.5	**45.6**
Rest of Portfolio	**2.3**	**3.3**	**3.5**	**2.8**	**2.1**	**13.8**
BC Post % of Total	*88%*	*71%*	*78%*	*68%*	*55%*	*77%*

- I haven't spent as much time on LinkedIn lately, but I'm planning to republish a few Medium posts on LinkedIn to expand my audience. We'll see if that helps.

AUGUST

Day 214: August 1, 2020 - 9:13 am (Saturday)

The problem with creative freedom is...the freedom?

There are so many things to explore. To date, I feel like I've mentioned nine different projects I'm either working on or want to work on. Whether it's Bacon Bits, the Bits newsletter, this 365-day writing experience, or an eBook, I feel this urge to pursue everything.

And I know that's not feasible.

There isn't a universal approach to freelance writing. I think there are loose parameters, but that's about it. No two careers look the same.

Choosing what to focus on becomes a real challenge. Since the start of this year, I've concentrated the majority of my time on personal projects. I haven't been constantly cold pitching. I don't want to fill my plate with client work.

But, from what I've seen, that's an atypical approach to starting a freelance writing business. If there were a freelance writing handbook — and, who knows, maybe there is — it wouldn't say "avoid pitching and landing clients." Because that's ridiculous advice.

Client acquisition is typically the initial priority. More clients equate to more income. That was my original strategy, but it shifted as I came up with my personal projects.

I guess the main purpose of this rant is to point out there isn't a clear cut path to follow. Strategies and goals can transform with time.

Also, it goes without saying that creative freedom is a privilege, not a problem.

Day 215: August 2, 2020 - 12:25 pm (Sunday)

As a freelancer, I'm the last one to learn about developments at my clients' companies. If a client is having financial trouble or is switching to another space or cutting its marketing budget, they're not going to think, "Oh, let's get Carter looped in immediately."

And I understand that. I'm not a traditional employee.

That can lead to some sudden workflow changes, which I've had a few of this year due to the pandemic.

Fortunately, the freelance universe tends to balance itself out.

July was a down month for a variety of reasons — moving, taking a vacation, and timing issues with a Client E assignment — but August should be up again. Client B is creating a digital marketing course, and she needs help reviewing and editing the content.

> Well, I need to create a bunch of incredible marketing content for this and will be essentially creating another website for it. I would love your help editing and creating the copy. I'd like to talk to you about this and see if you have time in your schedule to edit the content I want to put out. I'm thinking this would include website copy, email marketing copy, and social media ad captions.

I'm not sure about the details yet, so who knows what the rate will be — but it'll be a fun project.

Week 31 Lessons & Takeaways

#1: You can learn a lot from other content creators — not just writers.

#2: In a dramatic turn of events, my Medium post was curated after almost a month of review...even though Medium said it wasn't curated a while ago. I'm not sure what happened there.

#3: Count your portfolio now and then. I lost count of my portfolio's size months ago, so I decided to figure it out. Turns out, I recently crossed the 200-piece portfolio milestone, which is well beyond the goal I set for 2020 back in July 2019.

#4: If you write enough about a certain topic, you might be able to compile and convert your blog content into an eBook or course. I realized I've written 55,000 words on Medium so far, which is plenty of material to work with.

#5: More often than not, freelancers are the last ones to know about company issues or strategic shifts. I wrote a post for a client regarding the state of the US mortgage market. Little did I know, they haven't worked within the financial services industry in quite some time. So, my post was irrelevant, and I had to write another.

#6: Creative freedom is a blessing and a curse. It's hard to decide what to do sometimes. Should I focus on Medium content or client work? Should I write an eBook? What about converting newsletters into blog posts? The list grows every day.

#7: Freelancing is an up-and-down job. This year has been chaotic with plenty of down moments (like content freezes and work cessations), but the freelancing universe has a knack for rebalancing. July was a low-income month, but August is looking promising after Client B announced a big project.

Day 216: August 3, 2020 - 9:30 am (Monday)

Man, what a start to the week. I just brewed up a fresh batch of coffee...except I left out the ground coffee beans. What's worse is I drank about a third of a cup before realizing it was just hot water and old coffee remnants...

Happy Monday!

2:34 pm

Hey, my comprehensive freelance finances guide finally posted on Writing Revolt![55] Jorden's editor let me know I could post it in the Writing Revolt Facebook group, so I did.

> **Jorden Makelle**
> You absolutely killed it with this blog post, **Carter**!! Thank you so much and please pitch our editor if you have any more ideas, we loved working w/ you! 😊
>
> Like · Reply · 22m

Considering I learned a lot about freelance writing from Jorden, this was pretty cool to see.

6:55 pm

Alrighty, let's look at task lists for last week...

This Week (7/26 - 8/1)

1. ~~365 Days of Freelance Writing (x7)~~
2. ~~Client A post (x2)~~
3. ~~Client B edits~~
4. ~~Client E post~~
5. Bacon Bits post (x2)
6. Better Marketing post
7. Medium post

- It might as well say "Client A post (x3)" since I had to redo a post.
- I only finished one Bacon Bits post, but I should be able to complete the other one this upcoming week.
- I started a post about emotional intelligence, which I just think is an interesting psychological concept. That's the "Medium post" since I'm not sure where I'll publish it.

Aaaaand this upcoming week...

This Week (8/2 - 8/8)

1. 365 Days of Freelance Writing (x7)
2. Client B edits
3. Client E post
4. Bits newsletter
5. Better Marketing post
6. Bacon Bits post
7. Medium post

Day 217: August 4, 2020 - 4:44 pm (Tuesday)

What's the latest you've ever returned a library book? I finally cemented my all-time latest return this afternoon when I dropped off a pair of books that Kaileigh and I rented...in January.

I can't even blame COVID-19. I had plenty of opportunities before social restrictions went into effect.

I'm the worst.

On a business note, LinkedIn connections seem less and less genuine these days. Not that I haven't connected with some cool writers and such, but for every solid connection I also have three sales-oriented people.

In fact, 13 of my last 16 messages are from randoms that pushed some sort of agenda — selling leads, promoting platforms, blah, blah, blah.

I don't know if irrelevant sales pitches are like a *"hey we made it!"* milestone or what. I got one yesterday that was totally out of leftfield.

> Hi Carter,
>
> Would you be open to exploring potential offers from motivated buyers for your company?
>
> We work with middle market buyers who are actively looking to acquire new business ventures.
>
> Carter, let me know if this is something you are open to discussing? Thanks!

Excuse me, what? I run a one-man freelancing business.

What're you going to buy? My year's worth of Medium content? Rights to this unfinished book?

My soul?

This is the exact reason I don't use LinkedIn to randomly solicit business.

Day 218: August 5, 2020 - 11:39 am (Wednesday)

I HATE waiting on people — particularly when someone sets up a call and then proceeds to not show up.

Freelance writing is a pretty reclusive line of work. It doesn't have to be if you don't want it to be, but it's sequestered by default. Back in my banking days, I was on calls and in meetings every day. That's not the case anymore. When I have work calls now, I get a little nervously excited about them.

I'm not dry heaving into a paper bag, but there's a butterfly or two galivanting in my abdomen.

So, if you set up an intro call, ghost me, and cause this butterfly sensation to needlessly drag out while I wait for you to join, I will not like you.

Oh, and want to guess the origin of this introductory call request? A random LinkedIn connection. This time, it was a website/app developer that sent me a connection request and asked to chat. I deny these pointless call requests all the time because they just wind up being sales pitches.

But, for whatever reason, I set up a time. I guess their phrasing wasn't as salesy.

Our call was supposed to be at 11:30 am. I dropped at 11:36 am.

For in-person meetings, I'll wait 10-15 minutes. I'm even more inclined to wait if the person communicates that they'll be late. I hate when people are late *and* silent.

Anyway, rant over. Lesson of the day is don't waste people's time if you want to work with them.

Day 219: August 6, 2020 - 3:19 pm (Thursday)

I have zero insight into Substack's algorithms or how its search tool filters/prioritizes newsletters. BUT, if you search "freelance writing," you'll come across yours truly...

Showing results for **"freelance writing"**

The Write Brain by Shaunta Grimes
Launched a year ago
Daily Inspiration for Your Writing

One More Question by Britany Robinson
Launched 4 months ago
Inspiration and opportunities for freelance writers who want to make it wor...

Pitch Notes by Abigail Edge
Launched 3 months ago
A newsletter for freelance journalists, coming soon.

WordCount by Sara Meij
Launched a month ago
You're reading WordCount, a weekly newsletter with in-depth articles, tips ...

The Write Stuff by Eva & Kirstie
Launched 9 days ago
A roundup of everything you need to know to write the right stuff online.

Prose Agoge by Raj Chander
Launched a year ago
Discussing the business and mindset strategies required for successful free...

Slater Says by Slater Katz
Launched 2 months ago
Thoughts, tips, & tricks from a freelance writer

365 Days of Freelance Writing by Carter Kilmann
Launched 2 months ago
What's it like to be a freelance writer? Let me show you.

Waaaay down at the bottom.

Again, no clue if I just barely made the cut or if these are all of the publications related to freelance writing on Substack.

I like the simplicity of Substack's platform, but I wish they had more dynamic search or curation capabilities (like Medium). That would be a game-changer.

Day 220: August 7, 2020 - 5:22 pm (Friday)

Sometimes, when I finish writing a blog post I think, "Man, who's going to read this?"

From what I can tell, it's a common phenomenon in the writing world. I've touched on this in the past, and I'm sure it'll continue happening.

I experienced this form of self-doubt again yesterday after publishing my latest Bacon Bits post, "How to Protect Your Investments With Stop Losses."[56]

The title sounds like an excerpt from a finance textbook, so much so that I went ahead and accepted that it wouldn't do well. Honestly, I thought it was going to bomb. Like my lowest performing post yet.

Well, just like the other post I mentioned, I was incorrect.

How to Protect Your Investments With Stop L...

138	63	46%	7
views	reads	ratio	fans

These aren't crazy numbers, but it's not bad for only a day.

Self-doubt is dumb.

Day 221: August 8, 2020 - 2:12 pm (Saturday)

Kaileigh made a comment this morning that made me proud. She initially asked if I thought College Gameday, the college football pregame show every Saturday morning in the fall, would still take place this season. I hypothesized, "Yes, I think so. Just without the usual crowd of fans. Why?"

Her response: "I miss it."

You can call me a proud boyfriend.

This sequence got me thinking. It's pretty wild how fast time flies nowadays. The seven-ish months in between college football seasons used to feel like forever. I'd count down the days until football returned.

But not this offseason. Even with all the chaos 2020 unleashed, the year raced by.

I suppose that's the case when you're doing what you enjoy. I don't dread Mondays or the week ahead, so my perspective of the weekend shifted. Saturday and Sunday aren't my reprieves from the grind of Monday through Friday. Sure, they still serve as a break from working, but I don't wake up on Wednesday thinking "*Ugh*, only three more days till the weekend."

You can't put a price on that feeling.

Day 222: August 9, 2020 - 12:30 pm (Sunday)

No matter what stage of the writing journey you're on, you've either experimented with or heard of Upwork.[57] I briefly alluded to this freelance job sourcing platform one time earlier this year — but I haven't presented a firm opinion of it.

Before I do, let me provide some context. Much of my initial development as a freelance writer came through the teachings and writings of Elna Cain and Jorden Makelle. While I don't recall Elna having a hard opinion on the platform, I know Jorden loathes it. And she's not alone.

Most members of the writing community (that I've seen) tend to agree that it undercuts writers and creators alike. Writers share "horror stories" about overbearing clients that enforce tight turnaround times for massive projects. Like 4,000 words a day for a total of $10. That kind of thing.

My first impression took shape without ever trying the platform. I wanted nothing to do with Upwork if it undervalued writers. But, to be fair, I've heard success stories too.

To form an accurate and first-hand opinion, I'm going to peruse the platform and see if it's worthwhile. I mean, why not?

It sounds like it can be a fruitful marketplace with time and a little bit of luck. If it's bogus, I can check the box and move on.

Week 32 Lessons & Takeaways

#1: Far too many people abuse LinkedIn's networking capabilities. My DMs are overloaded with pushy salespeople that don't know how to cold pitch. Their intentions are quite clear when they're not interested in getting to know me.

#2: Bacon grease can be used to make explosives. Who knew?

#3: You know what grinds my gears? When people set up a call with you and then don't show up. That's such a bad look. Don't waste people's time.

#4: I enjoy Substack's platform, but — to create a successful newsletter — you'll need another source to drive traffic. Substack provides the tools, but you need to bring the audience. I've used Medium to generate signups, but I'm considering advertising too.

#5: It's impossible to predict a Medium post's performance. I swear, the posts I have the least confidence in always surpass expectations. Moral of the story: self-doubt is dumb.

#6: I'm experimenting with Upwork. I'm going into this trial run with a healthy dose of skepticism based on everything I've heard about the platform.

Day 223: August 10, 2020 - 10:45 am (Monday)

On Day 202, I highlighted the power of writing with emotion.

So, today, that's what I'm going to do.

Saturday night, a friend of mine, Joe Eynck, passed away. Joe was the kind of guy that lived life to its fullest, making this news even more tragic and unexpected.

I want to share a story that, in my opinion, captures the essence of Joe's being.

One weekend night several years ago, we were bar-hopping in Five Points, the college bar scene in Columbia, SC. As anyone familiar with the area will attest, Five Points after 9 pm is packed and boisterous. Streams of students flood the streets with little regard for traffic, making driving through the area quite a dangerous feat.

Well, as Joe crossed one particularly busy street, a Jeep Wrangler sped right past him, nearly separating him from his toes. The typical person would maybe shout some expletive and brush it off.

But Joe wasn't the typical type. He broke into a sprint after the Jeep (in flip-flops). His odds of catching the vehicle were low, but to his surprise, the Jeep's occupants saw him, stopped, and got out of the car. One of the passengers bluntly asked Joe whether he expected to fight all of them.

Joe, realizing how ridiculous that preconception was, expressed that he had no interest in fighting them, even though he chased them down. He laughed and eased the situation. Again, the typical person would probably move on at this point, scurrying away without any further escalation.

But not Joe.

After breaking the tension, Joe proceeded to grab drinks with and befriend these random guys who almost ran him over.

Joe was one of the most affable guys I've ever known. He never knew a stranger.

I'm not unfamiliar with death, but it's been a while since we've brushed shoulders. It elicits arguably the most intense and befuddling emotions. Like the concurrent and paradoxical feeling of heaviness and emptiness. Or the powerless frustration and yearning to alter the past.

The initial shock takes time to process. It's a form of denial — like an "I can't believe this happened" sensation. As reality soaks into fresh emotional wounds, denial passes the torch to sadness.

Today, anyone who had the pleasure of knowing Joe has to face and come to terms with this sadness. It won't be easy.

Rest in peace, my friend. You'll be missed.

Day 224: August 11, 2020 - 9:07 am (Tuesday)

I broke my routine of providing my weekly task list yesterday, but for good reason.

So, let's get Tuesday going with a review of last week's progress and a preview of this week.

This Week (8/2 - 8/8)

1. ~~365 Days of Freelance Writing (x7)~~
2. ~~Client B edits~~
3. Client E post
4. ~~Bits newsletter~~
5. Better Marketing post
6. ~~Bacon Bits post~~
7. Medium post

I never seem to complete every task...is the bar too high or is my approach handicapping my output?

I think it's the latter...

I'm starting to grasp how critical productivity and efficiency are to a successful freelance writing career. I still struggle with bouncing between tasks or getting distracted by emails. It's as if I need to retrain my brain to block out everything except the task at hand.

The Pomodoro technique has proven successful when I've implemented it, but I think I need to segment my days. Like, set separate blocks of time for writing, editing, and other admin/non-billable tasks.

I'll tinker with that this week...which is a busy one.

This Week (8/9 - 8/15)

1. 365 Days of Freelance Writing (x7)
2. Client B edits
3. Client B landing page
4. Client E post
5. Better Marketing post
6. Bacon Bits post
7. Medium post
8. Gaming Nexus review

12:59 pm

I just had a great call with a potential client, who's a startup in the FinTech space.

I know, I know. That didn't go so well last time. But their writing needs appear to be more structured. The guy I spoke with said they need a couple of landing pages ahead of their product launches — with the potential for steady blog content in the future.

This found me because a friend shared my freelance finances guest post. Coincidentally, the startup needs a writer. Funny how things work out sometimes.

Day 225: August 12, 2020 - 2:46 pm (Wednesday)

Well, I created an Upwork profile. *Braces for a barrage of expletives*

It felt wrong but remember it's just an experiment.

A few initial thoughts:

- It's an elaborate and dynamic platform. The interface is straightforward, and you can build a decent in-site profile. These guys must've pumped a lot of money into UX design.
- Since the platform has a lot of features and functionality, there's a good bit to digest.
- Applying to gigs is easy. A major plus.
- Holy Hemingway, does this site take a chunk of your pay or what? Upwork keeps 20% of every dollar you make. *To be fair, that percentage drops on a per-client basis as you deliver more and more work. But still.*

I applied to a couple of gigs, so we'll see how that goes. If I wanted to increase my odds and visibility, I could add more information to my profile. The only problem is that you can't share links — you can only upload certain file types (e.g. PDFs, Word documents, PowerPoints).

Of course, I can always save a webpage as a PDF, but the formatting usually looks scrambled.

I'm frustrated by the testimonials too. Considering Upwork offers to pull your LinkedIn page to build a base profile, I don't understand why it leaves out the testimonials. Upwork requires you to ask for **another** testimonial from past clients, which I'm not going to do.

Upwork feels like it could be a decent option if I'm ever short on client work. Otherwise, I'm not inclined to rely on it.

Day 226: August 13, 2020 - 1:51 pm (Thursday)

I just read an...*interesting*...story on Medium.

"Two Exes Wasted My Time. So I Sent Them Invoices."[58]

An enticing headline, no?

You can pretty much guess what it's about. The author feels wronged by past relationships, which still have an emotional impact today. So, she decided to bust out a couple of invoices, adding countless line items that specify "unpaid" services.

Considering the final bills were over $30,000, I'm not shocked they weren't paid — but I don't think she expected them to be. Instead, it sounds like she wanted her exes to acknowledge the emotional pain they allegedly caused. *I say allegedly since we only hear one side's perspective.*

The author doesn't seem to outright welcome debate, but the topic is a little controversial. As bizarre as it is to send two past partners invoices for abstract relationship stuff (which shouldn't be transactional in the slightest), I think the exercise was cathartic for her.

I'll let you read it and form your own opinion.

This got me thinking about the importance of relationships — not just in general but within the scope of entrepreneurship.

Starting and building a business takes a lot of time. It's kind of daunting when you think about it from a big-picture perspective. There are endless variables to consider and hurdles to overcome. It's thrilling — and I love it — but it's overwhelming too.

We can lose sight of what's important, like friends, family, personal well-being. In turn, it's easy to neglect relationships.

I thought about this before I quit my corporate job. I didn't want to look up one day and realize I pushed everyone aside to focus on my career. That's part of the reason why I don't embrace the hustle mindset or "all work, no play, every day."

My business is incredibly important to me. But, in the end, it's personal well-being (life satisfaction, physical and emotional health) and relationships that matter the most.

Day 227: August 14, 2020 - 10:16 am (Friday)

I saw the following question in the Writing Revolters Facebook group this morning.

> What is the best way to find out names and contact info for companies I want to cold email? I'm struggling...

Freelance writing has a lot of subtle obstacles. Finding the right contacts at the companies you want to work with is one of them. Fortunately, several apps and browser extensions can scan the internet for company email addresses.

I use Hunter, which has a convenient Chrome extension.[59]

It sort of looks like Swiper the Fox from Dora the Explorer.

Anyway, once I find a company that could be a good fit, I search their website and LinkedIn pages for the contact info of their Head of Marketing, Content Director, etc. If there isn't an email address, I'll simply click the hunter icon, which generates a list of email addresses tied to the site. Here's what that looks like for my website:

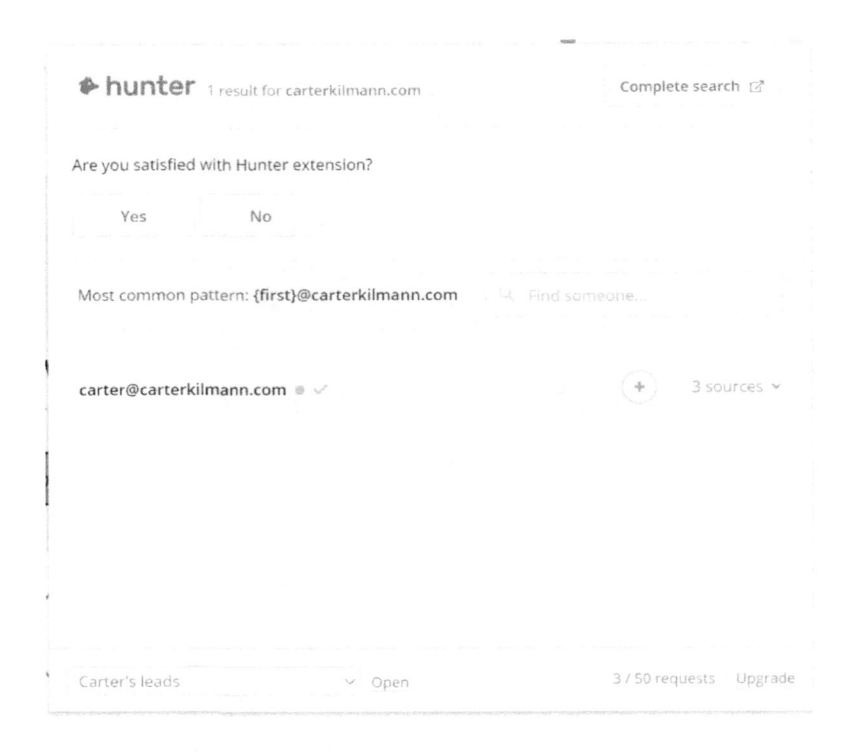

And it's free. I've never even come close to hitting my monthly request limit (i.e. how many sites I can scan for email addresses). There are paid options if you're a pitching monster though.

Day 228: August 15, 2020 - 9:17 am (Saturday)

Little did I know, while I slept this morning, I received the best pitch I've ever seen.

Brace yourself. You'll find yourself leaning toward the screen, unconsciously nodding in approval, unable to pull your eyes away from such magnetic, lyrical, poetic language.

Seriously, take a breath. Because it's going to take yours away.

Maybe grab a tissue too, the Notebook couldn't hold a candle to this email.

In fact, just grab a bath towel. The waterworks coming from your gaping eyes will require Hoover Dam-like reinforcement.

Okay, I won't keep you waiting any longer. Every second I gush, I'm robbing you of a truly life-altering experience.

Here it comes...

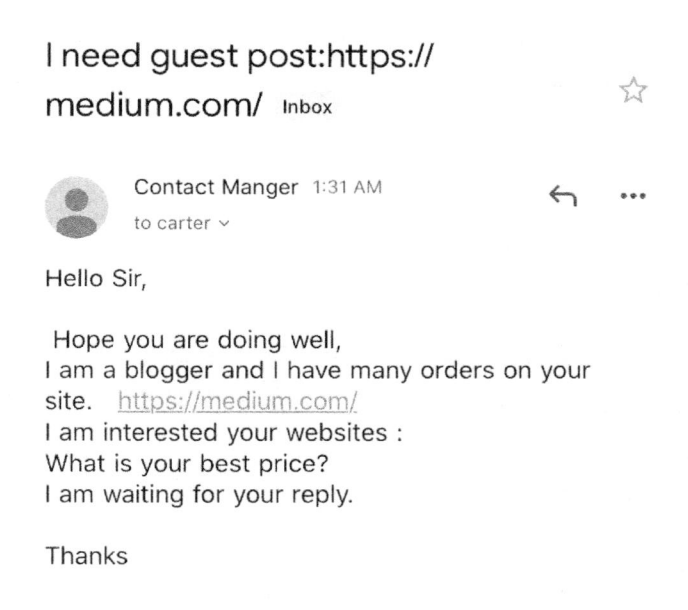

> **I need guest post:https:// medium.com/** Inbox
>
> **Contact Manger** 1:31 AM
> to carter
>
> Hello Sir,
>
> Hope you are doing well,
> I am a blogger and I have many orders on your site. https://medium.com/
> I am interested your websites :
> What is your best price?
> I am waiting for your reply.
>
> Thanks

See?

Poetry.

Do you feel it? The emotional and physical revolution coursing through your veins?

Me neither.

For a spammer, this person sucks at spamming.

The last time I checked, I'm not Evan Williams, the billionaire owner of Medium.

Day 229: August 16, 2020 - 11:30 am (Sunday)

Have you ever heard of the Baader-Meinhof Phenomenon?

Even if you haven't, you've probably experienced it. This phenomenon occurs when you notice something new or unfamiliar — like learning about a seemingly rare brand of clothing or discovering an unheralded actor. Then your encounters with this brand or actor become more frequent. Even though you'd never heard of it before, you learn of three friends that wear this brand. Or you notice that this actor seems to have roles in every other movie you watch.

The phenomenon applies to abstract things too. For instance, if you happen to hear about the Baader-Meinhof Phenomenon *again* in the coming weeks, you'll experience the Baader-Meinhof Phenomenon about the Baader-Meinhof Phenomenon.

It doesn't necessarily have to be unfamiliar to you either. As soon as you start to notice a lot of yellow cars on the highway, you'll start mentally noting every yellow car you see.

It's an uncanny feeling. One we have a hard time explaining when we feel it.

This phenomenon is a type of frequency bias. We tend to attribute significance to recurring events because we're pattern-oriented by nature. Our brains like patterns and they reward us when we recognize one.

Why do I mention any of this?

First, I love psychological concepts. Second, I experienced this phenomenon recently. I've noticed a lot of posts about flow in the last week-ish. *By flow, I mean that state of mind where you're totally in the zone. Razor-sharp focus.* Then, during a business call last week, the guy I spoke with had conducted research studies on flow states.

I knew there was a term for this, but I couldn't remember the name. So, I looked it up and decided to share.

In fact, I experienced this phenomenon **while looking it up**. I'm a nerd and like to expand my writing vocabulary. I don't force it, but I sort of file certain words away for when the need arrives. One of my current words is "cursory."

Guess what word was in one of the articles I read about Baader-Meinhof?

> Now if you've done a cursory search for Baader-Meinhof, you might be a little confused, because the

And there it is…

Baader-Meinhof strikes again.

Week 33 Lessons & Takeaways

#1: It's easy to lose sight of life's fragility. Don't forget to tell your friends and family that you care about them.

#2: I made an Upwork profile — despite the platform's negative reputation. So far, it seems like a decent source for gigs.* What's the asterisk? Well, Upwork takes 20% of your pay. It's like buying a Krispy Kreme donut, but the cashier gets the first bite.

#3: Entrepreneurship is time-consuming. But don't let that time commitment erode your relationships and personal well-being.

#4: If you're struggling to find the right contacts for your pitches, try using hunter. It's a chrome extension that's simple and convenient.

#5: When you run your own business, you will receive irrelevant cold pitches and spam with egregious formatting and spelling errors. Sometimes they're so bad, I honestly feel sorry for the spammer on the other end of the email. They probably think they're convincing enough to trick someone. Except they suck at writing.

Day 230: August 17, 2020 - 10:15 am (Monday)

New week, new me. Task list review time.

This Week (8/9 - 8/15)

1. ~~365 Days of Freelance Writing (x7)~~
2. ~~Client B edits~~
3. ~~Client B landing page~~
4. ~~Client E post~~
5. Better Marketing post
6. Bacon Bits post
7. Medium post
8. ~~Gaming Nexus review~~

I'm still chasing the elusive completed task list. As I mentioned a week ago, I started thinking about different ways to maximize my productivity. Pardon my pun, but optimizing time management takes time.

That said, I have an idea. I discovered my best writing output periods — early morning and late afternoon. When I wake up, my mind is free of inhibitions and distractions. I need about 30 minutes to shed my sleepy daze, but then I'm ready to roll.

And, weirdly enough, I found that my writing gains a bit of zest toward the end of the day. Maybe I'm just in good spirits as my workday comes to a close.

So, I think I'll dice up my schedule a few ways. I'll dedicate specific days to each stage of the creative process:

1. Brainstorming
2. Outlining
3. Writing
4. Editing

That's not a new concept, but I tend to drift away from an organized schedule. To solve for that, I'm designating each workday as a stage:

- **Sunday** - brainstorming and research
- **Monday** - outlining / writing (personal work)
- **Tuesday** - writing (personal work)
- **Wednesday** - outlining / writing (client work)
- **Thursday** - writing (mix)
- **Friday** - editing (mix)

But I need to make sure this accommodates my writing goals. For instance, I want to finish at least three personal projects per week — two Medium posts and a Bits newsletter or three Medium posts during the Bits off-week. So, my objective for Monday and Tuesday is to outline and write three rough drafts.

It's a work in progress and subject to change. I'll need to continuously adapt and tweak. Plus, I'll have occasional admin days.

This week, I'm aiming to complete four personal projects since I didn't finish any last week.

This Week (8/16 - 8/22)

1. 365 Days of Freelance Writing (x7)
2. Client B edits
3. Client B emails
4. Client E post
5. Better Marketing post
6. 365 DFW post
7. Bacon Bits post
8. Better Humans post
9. P.S. I Love You post

7:31 pm

Today was a good day. I had a good follow-up call with that FinTech startup I mentioned last week. I guess you could label it as a second interview, although it wasn't super structured like one. She asked me an interview-like question though.

"What makes good copy?"

Well, shit.

That was my initial thought. But I recovered and said that good copy provides value to the reader. No fluff or extraneous details. She seemed satisfied enough. Now I'm waiting for an NDA so that we can discuss their products.

In both of my intro calls, I asked if they had a rough estimate of a budget for this project, which will be two landing pages at first. Neither of them could give me an answer. Only the CEO knows this magical number.

I'm trying to get them to blink first, so to speak. Startups are tricky. They're cost-conscious, but I think they understand the value of quality copy. I don't want to underestimate or overestimate their budget — but I'd rather overestimate and come down a little.

Day 231: August 18, 2020 - 5:17 pm (Tuesday)

New schedule? So far so good. It's been a productive day. The segmented process makes it much easier to focus on the task at hand.

A bit of unfortunate news though. I finished writing a Medium post for Better Marketing, but they rejected it. *Bummer.*

I don't know if it's just me, but I continue to misread Medium's rejection emails. At first glance, I read them as: "Your story **was** accepted…"

See what you think. Here's what the email looks like in my inbox.

> Your submission to Better Marketing - Your story How NOT to Use LinkedIn to Market Your Business wasn't accepted into the publicati...

The rejection is a little clearer in the actual email, although they should adjust the spacing so that you don't see "accepted" hovering below when you start reading the paragraph.

Medium

> Your story **How NOT to Use LinkedIn to Market Your Business** wasn't accepted into the publication **Better Marketing**. However, your story is still published on Medium, and you can share it with your network.

It could be my self-serving bias that leads me to read what I want to see.

Anyway, I added the post to my 365 Days of Freelance Writing publication. So, it's not the end of the world. Plus, Medium curated it under "Marketing."

So, HA. I get the last laugh.

I'm kidding — I'm not bitter. Writing and rejection go hand-in-hand. It's like a hitter's batting average in baseball. Most at-bats don't produce hits, but that doesn't make you a bad hitter.

Most posts won't be huge successes, and that's okay.

Day 232: August 19, 2020 - 6:25 am (Wednesday)

I'm a morning person. Eight minutes into my day and I'm lucid and writing this. My secret? Eating.

Food gets me out of bed. Not a full-blown meal, that would be insane. I have a protein bar every morning right when I wake up. A Quest mint chocolate chip bar welcomes me to my day. This has been a staple in my routine for years.

The habit started when I learned the importance of eating before workouts. Again, I'm a morning person, so I go to the gym about 45 minutes after I wake up. But I didn't realize not eating leads to a sluggish workout until I tried eating beforehand.

It only just dawned on me that this little plastic-wrapped rectangle of protein is the reason I'm able to get up so easily. My body expects it. It's weird if I don't do it now.

There's your fun, unsolicited Carter fact of the day.

Day 233: August 20, 2020 - 10:13 am (Thursday)

Wait a minute. Hold on. How is this even possible? *Peep the follower counts.*

Brian Carter [Follow]

Digital Marketing Consultant with Carter Group. Keynote speaker. Author of The Like Economy, Facebook Marketing, LinkedIn For Business.

9.7K Following   10.6K Followers

Brian Carter hasn't been active on Medium yet. Check back later to see their stories, claps, and highlights.

Those follower numbers don't make sense at all. How can you have that large of a following without any Medium activity? Not even a clap?!

I'm losing my mind over this.

*Well, Carter, how did **you** find him then?*

Funny you should ask...I made an interesting discovery. I started typing the name of a writer, Sean Kernan, into Medium's search tool. I enjoy his writing and hope to emulate his success.

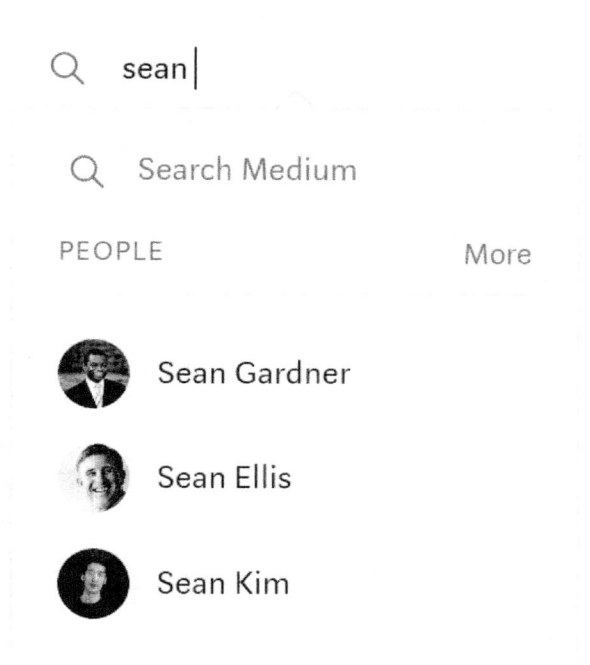

> 🔍 sean|
>
> 🔍 Search Medium
>
> PEOPLE   More
>
> 👤 Sean Gardner
>
> 👤 Sean Ellis
>
> 👤 Sean Kim

As you can see, the Sean I'm looking for didn't show up. This made me wonder...does that mean Sean Gardner is the most followed "Sean"?

Yep. He bests the other Seans with a following of 46,047.

And then it hit me, who's the most followed "Carter"?

Turns out, it's good ole Brian Carter, who's managed to claim the title of most-followed Carter on Medium without doing anything. I mean, just look at his profile picture.

It's like he's taunting me. Do you see that sideways look? That's not accidental. He knows what he did.

Damn you, Brian.

Day 234: August 21, 2020 - 4:22 pm (Friday)

What. A. Day.

I knocked out a couple of client assignments...*and landed a new client.*

It's a FinTech startup based here in Atlanta. On paper, it's a great fit. Right in my wheelhouse, exciting new venture, cool people.

Like most business arrangements, we had to agree to a rate for my services.

When I first started speaking with these guys, they only mentioned a need for two landings pages, which would have been fixed-price projects. Over the last couple of weeks, their writing needs have evolved, so they want a go-to writer for ongoing work.

The company suggested a tiered hourly rate structure with discounts between tiers. To be clear, this company wasn't pushy. It's just a structure they've used with other freelancers/consultants. Here's what it looks like:

> Aug 21
>
> Good Morning Carter - here are examples of the tier methods. Let me know if this method works for you and what your prices would be for the categories. Upon agreement of the pricing, I will have my team send the contract, and you can let us know your start date.
>
> Example: < 10hr = $0/hr (full rate)
> ≥ 10hr = $0/hr (10% discount)
> ≥ 20hr = $0/hr (15% discount)
> ≥ 30hr = $0/hr (20% discount)

But, as you're probably realizing, there are a few issues with this. First, what makes my 30th hour of work less valuable than the 9th? Why would I reduce my rate so significantly the more I work?

Second, there's already a little bit of natural tension with hourly rates; companies and writers can have different expectations for how long it'll take to finish a task. A tiered structure amplifies the subjectivity. Third, I'm more incentivized to charge less time in certain situations.

For example, 9.5 hours pays more than 10 hours due to the discount, which doesn't make any sense.

Instead, we're sticking to a flat rate of $75 per hour. Not too shabby.

Day 235: August 22, 2020 - 10:40 am (Saturday)

Man, I can't believe August is almost over.

I have friends on Facebook that have kids, so it's that time of year when back-to-school pictures start popping up. Seeing these pictures elicits a blend of concern and nostalgia.

Concern for teachers, who are likely more susceptible to the adverse effects of COVID-19. Concern for students, who have to try to learn and socialize in this weird, unnatural environment — one with masks and mandatory distancing.

But I also experience nostalgia.

As a kid, the calendar year elapsed much differently than it does as an adult. Kids think of time in terms of school schedules and sports seasons. Fall starts the year, winter has exams and holiday breaks, and the spring concludes. And then good ole summer, the season of freedom.

It's weird putting that in perspective. I remember how strange it felt to get a job and no longer be on a school schedule. The days blurred. The months are less identifiable. A corporate job amplified the disconnect. I spent most of my days in an interior cubicle, so I didn't have direct access to windows. It messed with my concept of time.

I miss elements of childhood, but I also couldn't imagine relinquishing my independence in exchange for no responsibilities.

There's no real lesson or moral of the story here. Getting older is just weird.

Day 236: August 23, 2020 - 11:35 am (Sunday)

I've started using a helpful organizational tool: **bookmarks**.

Not the little pieces of paper you use to remember the last page you read, but the toolbar function. It's far from a novel idea, but I didn't use this tool much in the past. *It was invented in 2003 if you're curious.*

Now, I save a bunch of pages — helpful copywriting forums, interesting topic ideas, potential leads, irresistible headlines. It's countered my tendency to have a bazillion tabs open.

For example, whenever I come across helpful copywriting tips, I add them to my "Copywriting" bookmark folder.

- How to Teach Yourself Copywriting
- How to get your first copywriting client (lesson for ALL marke...
- (1) Before You Ask: How To Get Started In Copywriting : copy...
- The Step-by-Step Guide To Writing Your ENTIRE Landing Pag...
- How to Write Landing Page Copy That Speaks to Your Audien...

Who said 2003 was out of style?

Week 34 Lessons & Takeaways

#1: I revamped my work schedule to boost productivity. I don't like too much structure, but I need some sort of schedule to keep me on track. Otherwise, I jump around too much. We'll see how it goes.

#2: Better Marketing rejected my post. Bummer. But that's the beauty of owning a publication. I can add relevant content to my publications when other publications aren't interested.

#3: I'm not the most popular Carter on Medium, and I'm a little salty about it. Just kidding (sort of). But I realized that Medium's search function ranks names and brands by follower counts. So, to unseat the top-ranked Carter, I need another 10,000 or so followers.

#4: I landed a new client! I almost agreed to a tiered rate structure, but then I came to my senses after talking it through with Kaileigh. They proposed a volume discount, and it sounded reasonable on the phone, but then I saw it on paper. No, thank you. Why would my 30th hour be worth any less than my 1st? Anyway, I'll make a flat rate of $75 an hour. Not too shabby.

#5: Getting older is weird.

#6: Seventeen years later, I jumped aboard the bookmark train. Maybe that's a little extreme. I've bookmarked web pages in the past. It's not like I'm just hearing about the concept of bookmarking. But, until recently, I hadn't used this function much for my business. Now I use it all the time. It's really helpful.

Day 237: August 24, 2020 - 6:07 pm (Monday)

Alrighty, it's been a busy day. Since I devised my new and improved routine last Monday, this week marks the first full-week trial.

At first glance, it won't look that much more productive. You also might wonder why the list grew. All valid thoughts.

This Week (8/16 - 8/22)

1. ~~365 Days of Freelance Writing (x7)~~
2. ~~Client B edits~~
3. ~~Client B emails~~
4. Client E post
5. Better Marketing post (rejected)
6. ~~365 DFW post~~
7. Bacon Bits post
8. Better Humans post
9. P.S. I Love You post
10. ~~Bits newsletter~~

Notes:

- First, I'll address the list's length. I accidentally left off "Bits newsletter" last Monday. On top of that, I submitted a post to Better Marketing, which they rejected. Instead, I published it on the 365 Days of Freelance Writing Medium page.
- Client E didn't provide an assignment, so I couldn't work on that by default.

- I pretty much wrapped up three other Medium posts — one for Bacon Bits, one for Better Humans (although I think I'll submit it to The Ascent instead, and another for P.S. I Love You). I'm branching out, as you can see.

This week should be a big one, I've got a lot of client work and personal projects to complete.

This Week (8/23 - 8/29)

1. 365 Days of Freelance Writing (x7)
2. Client B edits
3. Client B course
4. Client E post
5. Client J work
6. Better Marketing post (curation percentage)
7. Bacon Bits post (market concerns)
8. The Ascent post (supporting mourners)
9. P.S. I Love You post (emotional intelligence)

Let's get it.

Day 238: August 25, 2020 - 10:07 am (Tuesday)

Technology is the woooorst. I just had my first call with Client J (the latest FinTech startup) as their official copywriter and neither my audio nor my video worked on Zoom. Made for a pretty awkward sequence.

"Can you hear me? Can you hear me?"

opens Slack DM

"I can't hear you."

Pretty much that for 15 minutes.

3:01 pm

My schedule requires some tinkering.

The addition of Client J throws a wrench in my process. As a startup, they have time-sensitive needs and a lot of them, which they're being really cool about. And by cool I mean it doesn't seem like they're going to ride my ass until I complete everything. Nor will they message me at any and all times of the day.

So that's much appreciated.

But I need to reprioritize my schedule to ensure I deliver work to Client J in a timely fashion. I want to start on the right foot, especially after our Zoom debacle.

Day 239: August 26, 2020 - 7:04 am (Wednesday)

Time is such a funny concept. It's easy to get lost in the daily hustle and bustle. But it's humbling to see how life evolves over greater lengths of time. Like, day 1 of a journey versus day 100 or day 1,000. *Or, in my case, day 239.*

I'm drawn to stories about this concept. "What I would change if I could go back to day 1 of entrepreneurship." That sort of thing.

Part of my decision to become an entrepreneur was "there will never be a better time." Mid-twenties, no mortgage, no student loans, no pets, no kids, no major obligations or responsibilities. It made sense.

It helped to look at the job switch through a big picture lens. Take a calculated risk now, grind for a few years, and I can live the rest of my life doing something I control and enjoy. So long as I stay the course and impose a regimented schedule, I can look up in one year, five years, ten years, and so on and see the fruits of my labor.

Day 240: August 27, 2020 - 6:17 pm (Thursday)

Three days in, I'm enjoying my new client relationship. I know it's early, but it's much smoother than my previous FinTech startup gig.

As a refresher, I worked with a FinTech startup based out of San Francisco back in January. They have a viable product idea, a dedicated team, and plenty of vision. But there's a huge difference between that startup (Client C) and this new one (Client J).

Client J values and appreciates quality copywriting. Client C didn't.

Client C was hella focused on quantity. They wanted one person who could do everything — social media, advertisements, landing pages, blog content, guest posts, emails…

If it had anything to do with content, they expected me to do it immediately. The CEO would send me assignments at all hours of the day, across seven channels of communication. That's not hyperbole, I mean **seven**.

Personal email, work email, Slack, WhatsApp, texts, phone calls, and LinkedIn. It was impossible to juggle. At one point during my trial period, I had about five or six "urgent" tasks on my to-do list, so I asked him, "What should I prioritize?"

"Prioritize everything."

That was a bad sign.

They needed a diverse team of digital marketers and writers, but they weren't willing to pay for it. Well, you get what you pay for.

Anyway, rant over. Client J feels like a long-term relationship, which is exciting.

Day 241: August 28, 2020 - 1:58 pm (Friday)

I think everyone should write.

...a duck (mallard?) just grazed the top of my head...

For a brief, horrifying second, I thought it was a hawk. I prepared for talons. Then I locked eyes with an innocent, non-threatening duck (mallard?) before he waddled away. He/she underestimated his/her landing trajectory and nearly gave me a concussion/heart attack. Weird experience.

Anyway, as I was saying, I think everyone should write. Not necessarily from a professional or freelance standpoint, but just some form of writing — even if it's just self-reflection or jotting down ideas.

I think writing has a lot of personal benefits. It's a creative outlet. It's therapeutic to write out your emotions or struggles. It develops vocabulary and, believe it or not, speaking ability. I find it easier to verbally articulate my thoughts now that I've been writing for a while.

Your thoughts can run rampant, which can be hard to contain. *Sometimes, they disappear forever.* But writing puts structure and permanence to those thoughts.

Why not give it a try?

Day 242: August 29, 2020 - 10:12 am (Saturday)

I don't know if I could survive without coffee. I'm so accustomed to drinking it every morning. It's a staple.

I drink my coffee black. No sugar, no milk — just pure, bold, unadulterated coffee. It's an acquired taste, for sure.

I did **not** enjoy black coffee for a while. I didn't even start drinking it until I started my adult working career. But that wasn't for enjoyment, it was out of necessity.

I guess I came to love the taste over time. Isn't it weird how that works? It's like alcohol or particularly...hmm, what's the word...*pungent* foods and beverages.

You can't sit there and tell me you enjoyed your first beer or that you didn't gag at your first whiff of vodka or bourbon. Alcohol tastes terrible until your taste buds learn to appreciate it.

Some foods fall into this acquired taste category too. Olives are one example. Kaileigh couldn't stand olives — but she was determined to enjoy them. She incorporated olives into her snack routine. After *six* months, her taste buds got with the program once they realized olives were here to stay.

And I feel like most people hate vegetables growing up, but then magically start to enjoy them at an arbitrary age.

Taste buds are a hoot.

Day 243: August 30, 2020 - 11:49 am (Sunday)

Is there a consumer product that's messier than flour?

I've never successfully used flour in a recipe without initiating a mini-white explosion. Scooping it out is like disarming a bomb. One false move and **poof**.

Kaileigh made pancakes this morning.

9:45 pm

Does it terrify anyone else that work can invade your dreams?

I used to toss and turn at night as my mind danced around Excel spreadsheets, trying to build coherent models or balance financial statements.

I know there are worse nightmares — falling into shark-infested waters, running from a knife-wielding stalker, taking a Spanish test you didn't study for — but work dreams seem far more draining. I rarely have nightmares, but even when I do, I don't feel like I lost sleep over it. That wasn't the case for my work dreams. My brain worked to solve unsolvable problems instead of recuperating. I'd wake up exhausted like I never went to sleep.

Fortunately, writing dreams haven't plagued my mind in any way. I'm assuming that's because writing doesn't stress me out as much.

Week 35 Lessons & Takeaways

#1: Don't you just love when your audio doesn't work on your first conference call with a new client? *Ugh.*

#2: Time is funny. One day, you look up and realize how much time changes things. I think it's especially interesting from an entrepreneurial lens. There's a cloudy path between where you start and where you want to go, but when you put progress into perspective, it's wild to see. I can't wait to look up four or five years from now and thank my past-self for making the jump and working hard.

#3: I think everyone should write, at least in some capacity. Not for money, per se, but as an emotional or creative outlet.

#4: It's weird how certain foods and beverages have acquired tastes. Like, our taste buds reject something, but we can override them with time and repetition. It's crazy.

#5: I don't miss work nightmares. Back in my banking days, I'd have dreams in which my eyes would be inescapably glued to an excel spreadsheet, attempting to solve unsolvable problems. I'd wake up drained. It was awful.

Day 244: August 31, 2020 - 8:20 am (Monday)

I always forget that August has 31 days. Besides February, the black sheep of calendar months, August is a bit of a misfit too. The months rotate in a conveniently predictable fashion for most of the year — between 31 days and 30 days (again, unless you're February).

Except for July to August.

If you're curious, August has 31 days because good ole Julius Caesar added two days when he developed the Julian calendar in 45 BC.

Isn't the internet amazing? I found this answer from Wikipedia in seconds.[63] One second I'm typing, "Why does August have 31 days?" and then I'm reading about the Julian calendars, which were criticized for being off by 11-ish minutes and change from the earth's actual orbit of the sun. Here, you can be knowledgeable too.

Criticism

With the simple cycle, the length of the Julian year is exactly 365.25 days (365 days and 6 hours), but the actual time it takes for the Earth to go around the Sun once is closer to 365.2422 days (about 365 days, 5 hours, 48 minutes and 46 seconds). This difference is about 365.25 - 365.2422 = 0.0078 days (11 minutes and 14 seconds) each year, although Greek astronomers knew that.[3] This made the seasons get out of track, since the real first day of spring in western Europe (the equinox - day and night the same length) was happening earlier and earlier before the traditional 21 March as the centuries went by. By the 1500s, it was starting around 11 March, ten days 'too early' according to the calendar.

"Criticism." What an underrated section of Wikipedia pages. As if the Julian calendar was the 45 BC equivalent of some blockbuster movie.

9:09 am

In other news, we hit the 700 follower mark on Medium this morning.

Carter Kilmann
Member since Sep 2019
Freelance Writer & Editor | Personal Finance | Limitless Supplier of Spongebob & Family Guy quotes carter@carterkilmann.com

Editor of Bacon Bits and 365 Days of Freelance Writing

20	700
Following	Followers

I have four months to gain another 300 followers and accomplish my goal of reaching 1,000 followers in 2020.

Doable? Yes. Likely? Who knows.

AUGUST STATS

Don't call it a comeback. August introduced an exciting (and well-paying) new client, which helped get my income back on par with previous months after a shaky July. If Client A hadn't temporarily suspended my usual content delivery, August would have been even bigger.

Regardless, September looks like it'll set the record for 2020.

As a reminder, here's each client's description:

- Client A — Digital marketing agency
- Client B — Digital marketing agency (editing work)
- Client C — FinTech startup (no longer a client)
- Client D — Online finance publication (content freeze)
- Client E — Auto finance company
- Client F — ClearVoice assignments
- Client G — SaaS company (no longer a client, for now)
- Client H — Writing Revolt
- Client I — Consulting firm
- Client J — FinTech startup

365 Days of Freelancing - Monthly Stats	Jan	Feb	Mar	Apr	May	Jun	Jul	Aug
Income								
Client A	960	960	960	640	480	480	480	-
Client B	329	119	153	189	741	430	415	706
Client C	500	-	-	-	-	-	-	-
Client D	350	350	-	-	-	-	-	-
Client E	-	450	450	900	450	1,000	450	450
Client F	-	225	-	-	-	338	-	-
Client G	-	200	-	-	-	-	-	-
Client H	-	-	-	-	400	-	-	-
Client I	-	-	-	-	-	265	-	-
Client J	-	-	-	-	-	-	-	1,337
Medium	32	21	719	734	505	496	147	137
Total Income	**$2,171**	**$2,325**	**$2,282**	**$2,463**	**$2,576**	**$3,009**	**$1,492**	**$2,630**
Growth (%)	-	*7.1%*	*(1.9%)*	*7.9%*	*4.6%*	*16.8%*	*(50.4%)*	*76.2%*
Blog Posts (Paid)								
Client A	6	6	6	4	3	3	3	-
Client B	3	2	2	2	9	4	6	8
Client C	1	1	-	-	-	-	-	-
Client D	1	1	-	-	-	-	-	-
Client E	-	1	1	2	1	2	1	1
Client F	-	2	-	-	-	1	-	-
Client G	-	1	-	-	-	-	-	-
Client H	-	-	-	-	1	-	-	-
Client I	-	-	-	-	-	1	-	-
Total Paid Posts	**11**	**14**	**9**	**8**	**14**	**11**	**10**	**9**
Blog Posts (Unpaid)								
Medium	1	-	-	1	4	-	1	-
Bacon Bits	1	2	4	2	1	1	2	2
365	-	-	-	2	-	-	4	1
Total Unpaid Posts	**2**	**2**	**4**	**5**	**5**	**1**	**7**	**3**
Total Blog Posts	**13**	**16**	**13**	**13**	**19**	**12**	**17**	**12**
Copywriting Assignments								
Client C	5	-	-	-	-	-	-	-
Client J	-	-	-	-	-	-	-	3
Total Copywriting Asgns.	**5**	**-**	**-**	**-**	**-**	**-**	**-**	**3**
Total Assignments	**18**	**16**	**13**	**13**	**19**	**12**	**17**	**15**
Medium								
Views	1,151	1,352	19,466	11,052	15,778	8,562	4,552	4,945
Reads	439	468	7,413	4,220	6,320	3,651	1,947	2,055
Read Ratio	38%	35%	38%	38%	40%	43%	43%	42%
Existing Followers	54	63	80	238	371	530	595	645
New Followers	9	17	158	133	159	65	50	57
Total Followers	**63**	**80**	**238**	**371**	**530**	**595**	**645**	**702**
LinkedIn								
Existing Followers	458	465	493	526	570	590	599	613
New Followers	7	28	33	44	20	9	14	11
Total Followers	**465**	**493**	**526**	**570**	**590**	**599**	**613**	**624**

Highlights

- Client A temporarily suspended my content obligations in August. The firm we've been providing blog posts to hadn't paid them in three months. Totally out of my control. Fortunately, everything was settled, so our content schedule resumes in September.
- Client B offset most of the decline. She's launching a web design course in September, so she needed me to review and edit everything. It was a nice $300 fixed-rate project.
- I traded a couple of emails with Client D, so at least the relationship hasn't staled. But the content freeze continues.
- Despite agreeing to provide two assignments at a time, Client E has slacked a bit. Not the end of the world, but I'll remind them that I'd like two simultaneously.
- Client J injected my business with new life. In five days of work, I provided $1,337 worth of copywriting services.
- From a Medium output standpoint, I technically finished four posts, but I submitted one to The Ascent, which hasn't approved or denied it yet. I've also written the majority of two other posts.

SEPTEMBER

Day 245: September 1, 2020 - 6:47 am (Tuesday)

Yesterday was a doozy. Since it was the last day of the month, I tried to wrap up a few assignments. And Client J makes my new-and-improved schedule a little harder to follow. But they're providing a lot of work, which I can't complain about. In fact, I made $1,337 in five business days from Client J alone. *Not bad.*

Anyway, my task list review is a day late this week. *Oops.*

Last week was successful, especially from a client-work perspective. I didn't expect almost 20 hours of Client J work, so I didn't quite accomplish my Medium post goals — but that's the trade-off.

This Week (8/23 - 8/29)

1. ~~365 Days of Freelance Writing (x7)~~
2. ~~Client B edits~~
3. ~~Client B course~~
4. Client E post
5. ~~Client J work~~
6. Better Marketing post (curation percentage)
7. ~~Bacon Bits post (market concerns)~~
8. ~~The Ascent post (supporting mourners)~~
9. P.S. I Love You post (emotional intelligence)

The first week of September should look pretty similar to last week.

This Week (8/30 - 9/5)

1. 365 Days of Freelance Writing (x7)
2. Client E post
3. Client J work
4. Gaming Nexus review
5. Bits newsletter
6. Better Marketing post (curation percentage)
7. P.S. I Love You post (emotional intelligence)
8. Bacon Bits post

You can add a fantasy football draft to this list too. It's Kaileigh's work league (I'm serving as her "advisor").

Day 246: September 2, 2020 - 9:11 am (Wednesday)

You ever have those days where your head is just in a fog? It happens to me now and then.

I struggled to concentrate today. I finally flipped the switch on this afternoon and finished a couple of things. But, man, it took a while to shake the fogginess.

Total flexibility is nice, but there's also a constant sense that I need to work. A mini alarm pulses in the back of my head when I catch myself slacking. "You should be working." Pangs of guilt surge through my body.

It's hard to have unproductive days, but I guess it just comes with the territory.

Tomorrow is a new day.

Day 247: September 3, 2020 - 9:07 am (Thursday)

It's a new day! My mind feels much clearer.

While perusing my Facebook feed this morning, I came across an interesting post. A fellow writer posed a common question in the Writing Revolters Facebook group.

Looking for writers making $4k+ per month! What's your secret sauce?

I've been in the group for a while now, and I see this question pop up every month or two. Despite the frequency, it always attracts a bunch of attention and engagement.

Responses are always split between (a) people that comment "following" because they're curious too and (b) a variety of answers — most of which are vague or uninformative. To give you an example, this post's first comment was "Retainers!"

That's it.

Sometimes, a very dedicated and kind soul posts a multi-paragraph answer, detailing their exact process for earning money as a freelance writer. Those are real gems.

Quick aside: Even though I don't average $4,000 a month, in my mind I do. I know that sounds delusional, but I'm usually somewhere between $2,000 to $3,000. And I only commit about half of my time to client work. The other half is applied to personal projects, like 365 Days of Freelance Writing, Bacon Bits (and the Bits newsletter), occasional game reviews, and other Medium posts. Alone, this newsletter/future book is 60,000 words as of today.

So, I think it's reasonable to assume I could make $4,000 to $6,000 a month if I put all of my eggs in the client-work basket.

Before I share my two cents, let me make something clear: there's nothing wrong with this question. I think it's totally fair and necessary to ask. It's reassuring to see so many responses for a couple of reasons. First, it shows that other people are in the same boat wondering the same question; it's nice to see you're not alone. Second, the influx of writers who've achieved this monthly income proves freelancing is viable.

With that context out of the way, here's my problem with this question: **the path to entrepreneurial success is not linear — it's more like an intricate spider web**. There are countless approaches you can take, and the results will vary because everyone's situation is unique. One approach might work for you, but not for someone else. One writer might have an expansive network they can tap for referrals, while another writer doesn't and can't take that route.

My whole point is you can't expect to mimic the exact steps of someone else and produce identical results. It just doesn't work that way. Instead, based on my experiences thus far, I'd recommend treating it like a fluid process. Learn from successful writers, but play to your strengths. Figure out what works for you.

Day 248: September 4, 2020 - 9:47 am (Friday)

Happy Friday, ladies and gents. I've got a day of client work ahead of me, but I thought I'd share a helpful writing tool before I start grinding.

It's called Ludwig.[64]

If you're ever unsure about the correct way to use a word or phrase in a sentence, you can find the solution using Ludwig's search engine, which will scan the web for relevant and reliable examples. For example, let's assume you're trying to incorporate "chock full of" into a sentence — but you're unsure how.

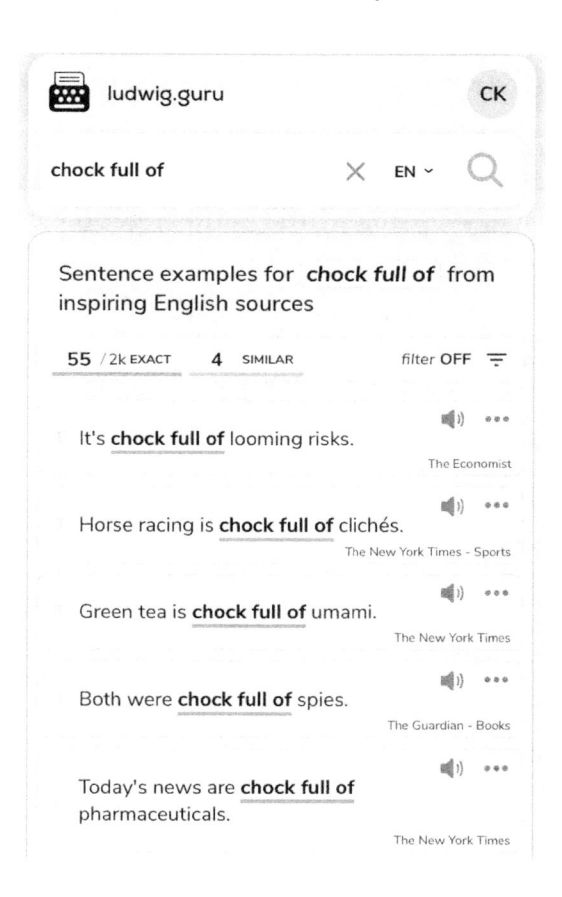

> **ludwig.guru**   CK
>
> chock full of   ✕   EN ⌄   🔍
>
> Sentence examples for **chock full of** from inspiring English sources
>
> 55 / 2k EXACT   4 SIMILAR   filter OFF
>
> It's **chock full of** looming risks.
> *The Economist*
>
> Horse racing is **chock full of** clichés.
> *The New York Times - Sports*
>
> Green tea is **chock full of** umami.
> *The New York Times*
>
> Both were **chock full of** spies.
> *The Guardian - Books*
>
> Today's news are **chock full of** pharmaceuticals.
> *The New York Times*

Ludwig pulls examples from prominent publications to demonstrate proper usage. It's helpful for uncommon words or adages you're used to saying aloud but not writing.

Day 249: September 5, 2020 - 10:43 am (Saturday)

I want to write fiction one day. I'm not an avid reader, but I enjoy getting lost in a good book. You see life and a particular society through a different lens. It's like riding shotgun on someone else's journey. Personally, I love dystopian novels. I'm already fascinated by psychology and sociology, and these books tend to tweak and exploit social norms for unique narratives.

I dabble with short story writing now and then, usually using Squibler — "the most dangerous writing app." I think I'll spend five minutes a day writing a little blurb to get the creative juices flowing.

Day 250: September 6, 2020 - 9:40 am (Sunday)

It's river day! I'll be casually floating down the Chattahoochee this afternoon.

My fellow river-floaters have tomorrow off for Labor Day, enabling a Sunday of festivities.

National holidays throw a wrench in my schedule. When you don't get PTO, it's hard to rationalize taking time off for a random holiday. Obviously, major family holidays like Thanksgiving and Christmas are different stories. But Labor Day, President's Day, Columbus Day? I'm still working.

Blame my boss.

But that won't be the case forever. Once I'm steadily making a certain amount of money, I'll adjust to a regular vacation schedule. Well, I'm actually taking vacation Friday — but I mean taking off general holidays too and not feeling guilty about it.

I've never set a milestone for this though...

Hmm.

Let's go with $5,000 per month, in three consecutive months. That feels like vacation-worthy income, and three months will prove it isn't a fluke.

Week 36 Lessons & Takeaways

#1: August has 31 days.

#2: The path to entrepreneurial success is not linear. It's a complex, entangled web with a bounty of traversable routes. And freelance writing is no different. Every writer's journey is different. Different styles, different niches, different opportunities, different networks, and so on. It's not formulaic. That doesn't mean you can't learn from other writers, but I think people have unrealistic expectations. Like, "If I do exactly what this writer does, I'll emulate their success." It just doesn't work that way. You have to forge your own path and figure out what works.

#3: Ludwig is great for accurately using terms and phrases.

#4: I want to write fiction one day. I've dabbled, but I haven't written anything of substance. The thought of designing a comprehensive story — with plot developments and in-depth characters — is daunting though. I need to work up to it.

#5: I'm hesitant to take vacations. It's easy to understand the importance of time away from work, but it's a harder argument when you are the sole catalyst behind your income. But that won't be the case forever. Once I make $5,000 per month for three consecutive months, I'll incorporate days off into my schedule.

Day 251: September 7, 2020 - 10:40 am (Monday)

Happy Labor Day, ladies and gents.

Yesterday's festivities extended into the early morning, so today got off to a slow start.

But another potential financial copywriting gig entered the picture.

> **Hi Carter!**
>
> Carter, I searched for financial copywriter and found you first on the list in LinkedIn!
>
> We're looking for a good writer for one of our financial products at ███ and we were wondering if you are taking on any additional work. Please let me know, Carter.

No clue if it's a good fit or worthwhile opportunity, but it's cool to see that my LinkedIn headline is appearing in searches.

I'm already thinking about tinkering with my schedule more. With client work picking up, I may need to commit entire mornings to assignments — no matter the day. At least it's a good problem to have...

Anyway, task list review time.

This Week (8/30 - 9/5)

1. ~~365 Days of Freelance Writing (x7)~~
2. ~~Client E post~~
3. ~~Client J work~~
4. ~~Gaming Nexus review~~
5. ~~Bits newsletter~~
6. Better Marketing post (curation percentage)
7. P.S. I Love You post (emotional intelligence)
8. Bacon Bits post

Unfortunately, Wednesday was pretty much a dud, so client work trickled into Friday. In turn, Medium content suffered. *Ugh.*

Since I'm taking a vacation on Friday, it's a short week, so I have less time to do quite a bit of client work. That doesn't bode well for Medium content this week either.

Double Ugh.

This Week (9/6 - 9/12)

1. 365 Days of Freelance Writing (x7)
2. Client A posts (x2)
3. Client E post
4. Client J work
5. Better Marketing post (curation percentage)
6. P.S. I Love You post (emotional intelligence)

Notes

- Client A sorted out its payment issues with its client, so the temporary content suspension was lifted.
- I should be able to deliver three Client E posts this month — even though they haven't been sending two assignments at once as I requested.
- I also have another fantasy football draft, which is extremely relevant and important.

Day 252: September 8, 2020 - 10:51 am (Tuesday)

It's a call-heavy day. I'm reminded of my corporate days and the excess number of meetings, which were absolute productivity killers.

Wish me luck.

2:03 pm

I'm not a political person. I'm also not the most informed when it comes to public policy. Oddly enough, I know about healthcare legislation more than anything else, but that's only because I did a white paper on this subject last year.

But this tweet caught my eye.

> If you're a freelancer, self-employed, contract worker, etc., think very carefully before voting for Biden, even if you agree with his other policies. Look at California and the ramifications of its disastrous AB5 policy, then imagine that and worse on a national scale. #NoToJoe

The AB5 sounded familiar, but I couldn't recall much detail. So, I dug into it a little more and realized it's incredibly relevant. Essentially, the California Assembly Bill 5 (AB5) tries to better regulate the gig economy by classifying **all workers** as employees unless they pass a three-pronged test. Here's Investopedia's simplified overview of the test:[65]

1. The worker is free to perform services without the control or direction of the company.
2. The worker is performing work tasks that are outside the usual course of the company's business activities.
3. The worker is customarily engaged in an independently established trade, occupation, or business of the same nature as that involved in the work performed.

If someone meets these qualifications, they can be treated as an independent contractor. Otherwise, they have to be treated as an employee, meaning entitlement to minimum wages, expense reimbursements, benefits, and so on.

It seems like the AB5 originated to counter massive companies like Uber and Lyft, which treat their employees as independent contractors. The intent seems righteous, but not all workers want to be treated as employees. It disincentivizes outsourcing certain tasks (like writing) if companies have to consider benefits and such, which are expensive.

I've read that legislators planned to include carve-outs for certain fields — like freelance writers — but I haven't read the law or seen any sources that confirmed that.

Getting back to the tweet: apparently, there's a push for a new law called the PRO Act, which is basically a federal law that mirrors California's AB5. From what I've read, the PRO Act would pave the way for gig workers to gain classification as employees and, ultimately, to unionize.

I'm sure it would benefit a lot of people, but it would do equal harm to many others. I'm not even a good example. Some people, like caretakers and handicapped individuals, need the flexibility and fluidity of the gig economy. Hopefully, lawmakers exercise some common sense with this.

But politicians and common sense don't exactly go hand in hand.

Day 253: September 9, 2020 - 8:03 am (Wednesday)

As expected, my calls from yesterday were productivity killers. The good news is I may have a trial run with a new client. The work would be direct-response copywriting, which could be quite lucrative down the road.

If you've ever read through a sales funnel, you've seen this kind of writing before. It's the language that highlights the needs for and benefits of certain products and services. The "direct response" portion of that title indicates the copy is tied to a specific action — usually making a purchase.

Sales funnels employ every psychological persuasion technique in the book: social proof, obedience to authority, consistency, reciprocity, scarcity, and liking.

From raving testimonials to limited time offers, these pages are designed to get you to buy immediately.

If it sounds like a total scheme, you're not wrong. In a way, it is — but if you're selling a viable and beneficial product or service, it's not. Persuasive writing simply leverages human psychology, and if that's wrong, then general marketing is wrong too.

For example, why do you think companies have limited time releases? *I'm looking at you and your nacho fries, Taco Bell.* We're more inclined to buy something if it's in limited supply or if there's overwhelming demand. But that's not the only tactic.

Did you know that retail stores hire "customers" to fabricate a perception of popularity? It's called mystery shopping. Seriously, look it up.

Marketing is questionable at times.

But, to uphold some sort of moral code, it's important to write for products and services that you believe in and trust.

8:17 pm

Today's been such a long day I convinced myself it was Thursday.

Oh, and I landed that new client at my desired rates, but I just have a funny feeling about the gig…

We'll see.

Day 254: September 10, 2020 - 9:00 am (Thursday)

One. More. Day.

This week has been exhausting. Mainly because I'm trying to get everything done before I'm on vacation tomorrow.

It's funny, vacation is actually stressing me out.

#entrepreneurprobz

The new client initially assigned me a project that would've been due Monday, which is a little concerning. But I told them about my vacation and they were very understanding, so it's not a red flag...*yet*. I'm still a little skeptical.

Anyway, I've got a bunch to do.

LET'S. KICK. SOME. ASS.

Day 255: September 11, 2020 - 4:44 pm (Friday)

Could you imagine living in a 250-room house? Or owning 125,000 acres of land?

Well, George W. Vanderbilt II did.

And it wasn't a "house," it was an estate. The Biltmore Estate.

We're touring the mammoth property in Asheville, NC today. I'm baffled that people lived here. Even by today's standards, this is excessive. But George moved into this place in 1895, after **six years** of construction.

We toured the house, and it feels endless — there are 33 freaking bedrooms. There's a ridiculously eloquent banquet hall for feasts AND a separate breakfast room because why not. The house even has an indoor pool and a bowling alley. *Keep in mind we're talking about the 1890s.*

You could play an epic game of hide-and-seek in this place.

The Vanderbilts were the richest family in the world at one point, playing prominent roles in the shipping and railroad industries. That title allows for opulent displays of wealth and influence.

I wouldn't even want to live here. It'd be like running a hotel, except even more work because there's excessive landscaping to worry about too.

I'll pass on the billion-dollar home, thanks.

Day 256: September 12, 2020 - 11:07 am (Saturday)

The second day of our vacation belongs to the mountains of Asheville, which would be excellent for creative inspiration. The views are enchanting.

While driving up the mountain, we saw three separate people painting the landscape. They'd simply pulled over, propped up an easel, and started painting.

Not a bad way to spend the day.

Day 257: September 13, 2020 - 8:13 pm

Man, I've missed football. Although crowdless games make for a weird dynamic, it's been utterly sublime watching the NFL's return.

Plus, my Packers dismantled the Vikings' defense. So that's fun.

I'll be honest, I'm a little anxious for the week ahead. I still have a lot of work to do. It's a good problem to have, I'm just worried about staying on schedule and delivering everything in a timely fashion.

I know you can't pick and choose when opportunities present themselves, but I kind of wish that direct-response copywriting opportunity would've popped up later this month instead of last week. I'm still trying to prioritize Client J's work since they have a lot of copy needs right now and I want to make a great impression.

Maybe I'll reach out and see if we can delay the initial trial a bit.

Week 37 Lessons & Takeaways

#1: I hate politics, but it's necessary to stay relatively informed. I recently learned about a potential bill that could significantly alter the gig economy, specifically the independent contractor employment classification. It's called the PRO Act, which I highly recommend looking into.

#2: Vacation is paradoxically stressful. On one hand, you need it to get away from work and relax. On the other hand, you have to strain to finish everything ahead of time. Otherwise, it's just work deferral.

#3: The Biltmore is a behemoth of a property. Can you imagine living in a 250-room house? I can't. That's just a silly number of rooms.

#4: Asheville's mountains are serene.

#5: My plate is overloaded with client work. Like a five-course meal stuffed onto one salad dish. I'm stressing a little.

Day 258: September 14, 2020 - 7:07 pm (Monday)

What. A. Day.

I finally finished two posts for Client A and another for Client E — plus I had a call with Client J. I elected not to message the direct response gig contact just yet. I wanted to finish the above assignments first. I still have another Client A post to finish and more copywriting work for Client J, so I'm not quite ready to open the door to more work.

Anyway, here's my task list progress for last week.

This Week (9/6 - 9/12)

1. ~~365 Days of Freelance Writing (x7)~~
2. Client A posts (x2)
3. Client E post
4. ~~Client J work~~
5. ~~Client K onboarding~~
6. Better Marketing post (curation percentage)
7. P.S. I Love You post (emotional intelligence)

The 3.5 day work week made for a stressful challenge. Plus, I didn't expect to onboard a new client, which takes a frustrating amount of time. Sitting through calls and emails with various people, reviewing legal documents, joining their workspace, and so on.

Medium content will have to wait. *Sigh*.

I'm still traversing a mountain of assignments, so this week looks similar.

This Week (9/13 - 9/19)

1. 365 Days of Freelance Writing (x7)
2. Client A posts (x3)
3. Client E post
4. Client J work
5. Client K assignment
6. Better Marketing post (curation percentage)
7. P.S. I Love You post (emotional intelligence)

Fortunately, as I mentioned, I finished three posts today. So… progress.

Day 259: September 15, 2020 - 2:20 pm (Tuesday)

I'm learning how to handle the stress of managing clients and their expectations. There's a natural inclination to treat clients as superiors and succumb to an intangible pressure to deliver assignments immediately. Or to drop everything you're doing when a client reaches out.

It's all about boundaries. I have to abide by my schedule or else I'll scramble back and forth, which isn't great for productivity.

There's a common expression for this: "Manage your clients or they'll manage you."

They're **clients**, not **bosses**.

Day 260: September 16, 2020 - 11:01 am (Wednesday)

I need to start tacking on an additional 20% whenever I provide my rates. My first assignment for Client K is a simple company bio for a trading software website. It'll be roughly three paragraphs MAX.

I figured it'd take me an hour or two at most, even with research. I don't know anything about this company, so I'll probably spend more time reading than writing. Assuming a healthy $100 per hour rate, that'd be $200. I quoted $250.

Their response: "Perfect."

They accepted on the spot. No hesitation or delayed response. What the hell? How much more could I have earned for roughly 100 words?

Entrepreneurship is wild, man.

1:13 pm

Well, that might be the easiest $250 I've ever earned.

Day 261: September 17, 2020 - 9:07 am (Thursday)

You know I can't resist reading Medium success stories and holistic performance analyses. Every writer's Medium approach is different, but it's nice to have points of comparison. It helps set realistic expectations.

Here's the latest one: Two Years, $30k, and 507 Articles on Medium. Here's What I've Learned.[66]

If you quickly connect the dots, you'll realize the author, Zulie Rane, wrote 507 posts in roughly 730 days — or about 0.7 posts per day. That's an insane output.

What's even crazier is that she wrote 383 of those posts in her first year. *That's actually an insane output.*

Zulie was kind enough to share an incredibly insightful graph of her time on Medium. It not only captures her statistical performance but also the emotional/personal journey.

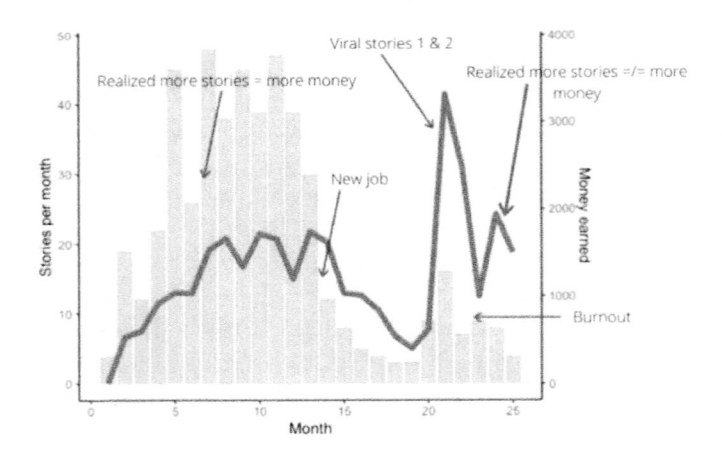

I love this chart because it perfectly encapsulates the quantity-versus-quality argument. Zulie pumped out 20 to 50 posts per month in her first year, and she made decent money. But she made even more when she switched her focus to quality.

Although it was somewhat out of necessity due to a new job, she started putting more time into each post, emphasizing value and an appealing headline. As you can see, this led to a pair of viral (and profitable) stories.

Zulie deserves major props for committing so much time and energy to Medium in her free time. A post per day isn't exactly sustainable, but she established herself with major publications and now has over 14,000 followers.

Day 262: September 18, 2020 - 3:56 pm (Friday)

I'm running on fumes to close the week. I've had a cold the last couple of days, so energy levels are low. That's also a consequence of taking NyQuil. It's great for sleeping through the night, but the NyQuil "hangover" is real. I'm just so sleepy the next day.

Fortunately, I had a very productive first few days, so I'm not stressing about it.

Day 263: September 19, 2020 - 11:10 am (Saturday)

I'm trying to get better at appreciating time away from my phone — and screens in general. *Of course, as I write this, I'm contradicting that sentence.*

I spend a lot of time looking at screens: my phone, computer, and TV. Honestly, it takes a toll. Sometimes, I'll look up at the end of the day and my vision is blurry. My eyes are fatigued. My brain's a little sore. It's not a good time.

I'm pretty disciplined when it comes to taking walks and getting exercise, but I still wind up transfixed on my phone. This job requires me to look at screens most of the day, but I need to incorporate screen breaks into my daily routine.

For the sake of my vision and sanity.

Day 264: September 20, 2020 - 12:53 pm (Sunday)

You know who's an amazing writer? Matthew Berry. He's a fantasy football expert that currently writes and produces for ESPN. He also has his own aptly-named show, The Fantasy Show.

Each week, he writes a "love/hate" fantasy football column, in which he shares a list of players he expects to either outperform or underperform. It's a nice blend of quantitative and qualitative analysis. But the list of players is only half of the picture. He leads with an entertaining story or personal narrative. It's always insightful and very well written, and I imagine it's time-consuming to write because it's quite lengthy.

This man is dedicated to providing as much value to the reader as possible. He has a genuine and affable tone/style. Plus, he's willing to write vulnerable content.

You might not think to emulate a writer known for fantasy sports content, but he's a great source for learning how to be a compelling storyteller and provide clear, transferable analysis.

Week 38 Lessons & Takeaways

#1: Manage clients or else they'll manage you. Words to live by.

#2: Setting rates is such a guessing game. I had my first assignment for Client K, the direct-response copywriting gig. All I had to do was write a company bio, which was roughly 100 words. I quoted $250, and my client didn't even blink. I have no idea how much more I could have charged. Entrepreneurship is bizarre.

#3: Are NyQuil hangovers a thing? It's a beautiful sleep potion, but it wrecks my next day.

#4: Take periodic breaks from screens. I spend a scary amount of time focused on my phone, computer, and TV. It can't be good for me.

#5: If you want to learn how to be a compelling storyteller, check out Matthew Berry. His writing is fluid and easy to read. He enlivens even somewhat benign stories.

Day 265: September 21, 2020 - 10:30 am (Monday)

Task list time.

I completed lots of client work last week (yay), but I failed to do any Medium writing (boo).

This Week (9/13 - 9/19)

1. ~~365 Days of Freelance Writing (x7)~~
2. ~~Client A posts (x3)~~
3. ~~Client E post~~
4. ~~Client J work~~
5. ~~Client K assignment~~
6. Better Marketing post (curation percentage)
7. P.S. I Love You post (emotional intelligence)

Maybe, *just maybe*, I'll finally get back to writing for Medium this week.

This Week (9/20 - 9/26)

1. 365 Days of Freelance Writing (x7)
2. Client B edits
3. Client E post
4. Client J work
5. Better Marketing post (curation percentage)
6. Bacon Bits post
7. P.S. I Love You post (emotional intelligence)

Day 266: September 22, 2020 - 10:03 am (Tuesday)

People and/or businesses that don't value writers make my blood boil. I received an inbound request for my services this morning.

> **writer needed** Inbox
>
> "Jifcast" 10:00 AM
> to carter
>
> Hi,
>
> I am looking for a writer to write well-research and detailed blog posts for me. All posts will be related to entrepreneurship, startups and marketing.
>
> I will give you full post outline with links so you can properly research and write a great post.
>
> Each post will be 5000+ words. Plan to spend 12-15 hours per article on detailed research.
> I will give you $150 per article.
>
> You will write 1 article every 2 weeks. If you agree, please reply to this email with links to articles you wrote.
>
> Thank you,
> Mary

Five thousand words for $150? That's $0.03 per word, which is an abysmal rate. On top of that, she explicitly states an expectation of 12-15 hours. If you want to pay a writer $10 per hour for "well researched and detailed blog posts," you might as well hire your six-year-old niece, Mary.

I wasn't going to dignify this email with a reply, but, you know what, I might as well.

Gimme a sec…

…

Alright, done.

> Mary,
>
> My typical rate for such long-form content is $0.50 per word, or roughly $2,500 based on your request. You'll receive minimal quality for $0.03 per word or $10 per hour, so I recommend bumping that offer up.
>
> Good luck with your search.

Now, I've never received anywhere near $2,500 for a single blog post. But, then again, I've never written a 5,000-word post either. I mainly said that to demonstrate how much she's underpricing her writing request.

Do better, Mary.

Day 267: September 23, 2020 - 11:50 am (Wednesday)

"Trust your gut."

Is it just me, or does that advice backfire 50% of the time?

Yesterday morning, the project manager from Client J reached out to set up a 4:30 pm call with her, a VP, and the CEO. The call was simply labeled copy feedback. I don't know why, but I read it with a negative connotation.

I spent my entire day expecting the worst-case scenario. Like they'd open up the call by telling me they hated my copy. "This is trash. We're not paying you."

Or something equally disastrous.

That didn't happen. Instead, they provided minor feedback and applauded most of my draft. I had no reason to suspect a barrage of complaints, but I did anyway.

Be skeptical of your gut.

Day 268: September 24, 2020 - 11:50 am (Thursday)

Sometimes, I wonder if my lifestyle is *too* balanced. I work hard, and my business is on my mind more hours of the day than it isn't. But, relative to some entrepreneurs and writers out there, my schedule incorporates plenty of breaks and leisure time.

I don't overload my schedule with client work. I'm not soliciting my services or promoting myself on social media every other hour. I don't pitch hundreds of companies per day.

I don't really "hustle." I'd say I walk at a brisk pace.

I read an interesting Medium post by Tom Kuegler, founder of the Post Grad Survival Guide, that got me on this thought train. Here's the post: I 'Wasted' 3 Years Hustling Like Gary Vee — Was It Worth It?[67]

He highlights the silver linings of hustling and burning through three years of his life to achieve entrepreneurial success. It's a worthwhile read.

I'm not arguing that hustling is bad. I get why people do it — I just don't want to sacrifice other aspects of my life.

At my pace, I have time to exercise and cook. I can hang out with Kaileigh or attend social events. I can spend my free time clearing my mind and doing something unaffiliated with work.

Collectively, I think those reasons outweigh the benefits of employing the hustle mentality.

I'm not sprinting the marathon to achieve success sooner. My route might be longer this way, but it'll still get me there.

Day 269: September 25, 2020 - 3:40 pm (Friday)

Woah. I just hit a massive mental wall. I was making good progress on a Medium post then BAM. Head-first collision with brain fatigue.

Kaileigh and I are in Charlotte visiting some friends, so we slept on an air mattress last night. We forgot pillows, so sleep quality was subpar.

A large Dunkin Donuts coffee got me through the day, but now I'm crashing.

I might have to call it a day soon, but I hate that my Medium content output is dropping off, so I'll probably push through the tiredness a little longer.

Day 270: September 26, 2020 - 11:45 am (Saturday)

We finally made it. SEC football is back, meaning my Gamecocks are back as well.

I have super low expectations, but I know as soon as kickoff occurs, I'll be wrapped up in Carolina football all over again. It's just what I do every year.

Unfortunately, that's led to a lot of disappointment over the last five-ish seasons. But that's what makes winning even sweeter.

We'll see if we can start the makeshift 2020 season on the right foot.

10:50 pm

Nope.

Day 271: September 27, 2020 - 6:30 pm (Sunday)

It took a lot of preparation to quit my banking job to pursue freelance writing. But the biggest preliminary step wasn't building a portfolio or landing my initial client. It wasn't even saving enough money to build a lengthy runway (although I'd say that was a close second).

The hardest part was — and still is — embracing the emotional volatility of entrepreneurship. It's so easy to be your own worst enemy. Self-doubt, worry, and uncertainty are massive roadblocks. They creep into your head unexpectedly and can cripple progress if you let them.

I just came across a fellow writer's Facebook post that illustrates this apprehension.

> This may sound strange but is there a limit to how far you can go as a freelance writer? It's a strange question but I'm in need of some serious motivation right now 😞

It's not strange at all. How do you prepare for an emotional rollercoaster you've never ridden?

What she's asking is a common question in the writing community. Even when you've been riding it for a while, it can still surprise you with a sudden turn. Although I'd posit that most writers are afraid to admit they're second-guessing themselves or struggling to see a future.

For me, the best I could do ahead of time was to have realistic, down-to-earth conversations with myself. It was like a little self-pep talk:

"Look, you're going to have irrational thoughts sometimes. You're going to doubt yourself. You're going to unnecessarily compare your progress to other writers. You're going to question the viability of this career. Just take a step back and remember why you're doing this. Remember that it's a long-term game, not a get-rich-quick scheme."

As crazy as that sounds, it helped me prepare. I still do this whenever I have doubts. Irrational thoughts are like fires that need to be doused with logic. Otherwise, they'll spread and incinerate your self-esteem.

Week 39 Lessons & Takeaways

#1: It's easy to spot a person/business that doesn't value writers. They're generally condescending and they have unrealistic expectations. Worst of all, they're not willing to match those expectations with a reasonable price.

#2: Is it just me, or is "trust your gut" a bad piece of advice? I feel like my gut is often wrong.

#3: I don't embrace the hustle mentality. I prefer to enjoy a balanced day-to-day life, even if that means delaying success.

#4: Sleep (and/or coffee) is essential. Otherwise, mental walls are inevitable.

#5: You are your biggest obstacle. I don't mean to sound like a cheesy self-help book, but you need to accept that assertion if you're going to succeed as an entrepreneur. The hardest aspect of freelance writing is facing spontaneous feelings of self-doubt. It's easy to lose sight of why you're doing what you're doing when you let irrational thoughts and concerns wear you down.

Day 272: September 28, 2020 - 11:00 am (Monday)

The best "happy Monday" gift to welcome us to the new week? A cacophony of hammering. I think our building is renovating the apartment above us, so it's a headphones kind of day.

Anyway, let's talk about last week's progress.

This Week (9/20 - 9/26)

1. ~~365 Days of Freelance Writing (x7)~~
2. ~~Client B edits~~
3. Client E post
4. ~~Client J work~~
5. Better Marketing post (curation percentage)
6. Bacon Bits post
7. Better Marketing post (writing tips)
8. Better Marketing post (writing ruts)

Overall, it was an okay week. I had some administrative tasks I had to take care of. Otherwise, I focused on Client J's work. *Client E never sent me an assignment. Sigh.*

I finally had time to focus on Medium writing, but I couldn't lock into any single post — I bounced around a bit.

Hopefully, I can finish a few this week.

This Week (9/27 - 10/3)

1. 365 Days of Freelance Writing (x7)
2. Client B edits
3. Client E post
4. Client J work
5. Better Marketing post (curation percentage)
6. Better Marketing post (writing rut)
7. Bacon Bits post
8. Bits newsletter
9. GN review

Day 273: September 29, 2020 - 1:00 pm (Tuesday)

My internet is shoddy today. So, I've worked from my phone, which I don't mind.

I had an odd realization this morning. I hardly leverage my website to generate traffic. I don't even actively promote it in pitches since it doesn't house my entire portfolio. I share my ClearVoice link instead.

It just takes too long to add my content to my site, and I'm not much of a website developer. So, I chose to use a separate platform for my portfolio.

Inbound leads probably review my site, so I think it's still a necessity. (I know Client J did, they said it was helpful.) But LinkedIn and personal referrals have been my best sources of work. It's just funny how much writing courses emphasize building a website, and now I rarely touch it.

I've seen plenty of writers succeed without websites. For example, Sarah Noel Block, a content marketing strategist and copywriter, took advantage of Medium's free publication feature to build a portfolio.[68] It's pretty genius, honestly.

That said, websites validate writers as professionals and business owners, so it's worth the annual domain renewal.

Day 274: September 30, 2020 - 3:28 pm (Wednesday)

Continuing with our website discussion, I was thinking back to when I first created my site — or "writer's platform" as several courses referred to it. Essentially, writer websites should promote you and your services, like a loyal salesperson.

There are a lot of routes you can take with website design, but I recall two early decisions that stuck out to me.

1. What should my domain name be?
2. Should my website include a blog?

First, there's the question of whether a writer's website domain should simply bear their name or a different moniker altogether. For example, Jorden Makelle's platform is under Writing

Revolt (writingrevolt.com), whereas mine is simply my name (carterkilmann.com). I think it's easier to promote a brand name rather than your personal name. Brands are catchier and more memorable.

But it also depends on what you're trying to do with your site. My site overviews my services. Nothing more. Jorden has an active blog and courses, plus it's tied to a large community of writers.

Second, should your writer platform have a blog? Mine does, but I don't write content for it anymore. That's mostly because I'd prefer to write on Medium, which has a massive audience and curation functionality.

If I offered courses or eBooks, I'd be more compelled to grow my site's visibility and traffic. In that case, I'd probably run an active blog and rename my site.

I still recommend running a blog or posting on Medium to create and grow your portfolio.

SEPTEMBER STATS

As expected, September was my best month thus far, as I pushed past $4,000 of income. A high-paying copywriting gig will do that. The downside? My Medium output suffered.

As a reminder, here's each client's description:

- Client A — Digital marketing agency
- Client B — Digital marketing agency (editing work)
- Client C — FinTech startup (no longer a client)
- Client D — Online finance publication (content freeze)
- Client E — Auto finance company
- Client F — ClearVoice assignments
- Client G — SaaS company (no longer a client, for now)
- Client H — Writing Revolt
- Client I — Consulting firm
- Client J — FinTech startup
- Client K — Digital marketing agency (copywriting)

CARTER KILMANN

365 Days of Freelancing - Monthly Stats									
	Jan	Feb	Mar	Apr	May	Jun	Jul	Aug	Sep
Income									
Client A	960	960	960	640	480	480	480	-	480
Client B	329	119	153	189	741	430	415	706	163
Client C	500	-	-	-	-	-	-	-	-
Client D	350	350	-	-	-	-	-	-	-
Client E	-	450	450	900	450	1,000	450	450	900
Client F	-	225	-	-	-	338	-	-	-
Client G	-	200	-	-	-	-	-	-	-
Client H	-	-	-	-	400	-	-	-	-
Client I	-	-	-	-	-	265	-	-	-
Client J	-	-	-	-	-	-	-	1,337	2,100
Client K	-	-	-	-	-	-	-	-	250
Medium	32	21	719	734	505	496	147	137	110
Total Income	**$2,171**	**$2,325**	**$2,282**	**$2,463**	**$2,576**	**$3,009**	**$1,492**	**$2,630**	**$4,003**
Growth (%)	-	7.1%	(1.9%)	7.9%	4.6%	16.8%	(50.4%)	76.2%	52.2%
Blog Posts (Paid)									
Client A	6	6	6	4	3	3	3	-	3
Client B	3	2	2	2	9	4	6	8	2
Client C	1	1	-	-	-	-	-	-	-
Client D	1	1	-	-	-	-	-	-	-
Client E	-	1	1	2	1	2	1	1	2
Client F	-	2	-	-	-	1	-	-	-
Client G	-	1	-	-	-	-	-	-	-
Client H	-	-	-	-	1	-	-	-	-
Client I	-	-	-	-	-	1	-	-	-
Total Paid Posts	**11**	**14**	**9**	**8**	**14**	**11**	**10**	**9**	**7**
Blog Posts (Unpaid)									
Medium	1	-	-	1	4	-	1	-	1
Bacon Bits	1	2	4	2	1	1	2	2	-
365	-	-	-	2	-	-	4	1	-
Total Unpaid Posts	**2**	**2**	**4**	**5**	**5**	**1**	**7**	**3**	**1**
Total Blog Posts	**13**	**16**	**13**	**13**	**19**	**12**	**17**	**12**	**8**
Copywriting Assignments									
Client C	5	-	-	-	-	-	-	-	-
Client J	-	-	-	-	-	-	-	3	2
Client K	-	-	-	-	-	-	-	-	1
Total Copywriting Asgns.	**5**	**-**	**-**	**-**	**-**	**-**	**-**	**3**	**3**
Total Assignments	**18**	**16**	**13**	**13**	**19**	**12**	**17**	**15**	**11**
Medium									
Views	1,151	1,352	19,466	11,052	15,778	8,562	4,552	4,945	3,522
Reads	439	468	7,413	4,220	6,320	3,651	1,947	2,055	1,438
Read Ratio	38%	35%	38%	38%	40%	43%	43%	42%	41%
Existing Followers	54	63	80	238	371	530	595	645	702
New Followers	9	17	158	133	159	65	50	57	31
Total Followers	**63**	**80**	**238**	**371**	**530**	**595**	**645**	**702**	**733**
LinkedIn									
Existing Followers	458	465	493	526	570	590	599	613	624
New Followers	7	28	33	44	20	9	14	11	13
Total Followers	**465**	**493**	**526**	**570**	**590**	**599**	**613**	**624**	**637**

Highlights

- After suspending content for August, Client A returned to business as usual in September.
- Client B's smaller workload offset the improvement. I knew it was coming though, she took a break from blog posts after launching her digital marketing course.
- The reminder to Client E worked — they sent me two assignments this month.
- Client J and Client K rejuvenated my income. If I can make these relationships last, I'll have a steady supply of high-paying work, which is a writer's dream.
- Despite having fewer assignments, my income increased by 52.2%. That's the beauty of copywriting gigs.
- The scales tipped in favor of client work, so my Medium output struggled. One post isn't going to cut it. Unsurprisingly, my Medium stats and earnings continued a gradual descent.

OCTOBER

Day 275: October 1, 2020 - 8:28 am (Thursday)

From out of the woodwork, writing opportunities flooded my inbox this morning.

Client K reached out with two article requests.

Then, shortly after, I received two LinkedIn messages, one for a copywriting gig and the other for a full-time position.

#1: Copywriting gig

> Hey Carter, how are you? I am looking for a second copywriter for my agency. I need a copywriter who has experience writing landing pages/sales funnels and Facebook ads. Our clients are US based and they are wealth managers, financial advisors, and alternative investment advisors.
>
> Let me know if you have experience in this field :) thank you!

#2: Full-time

> Hi Carter,
>
> I work at Clever Real Estate, A VC backed startup here in STL. We're hiring for our content team and I thought you might be a fit as a writer. We offer great pay / benefits, remote work, and the chance to make an impact at a rapidly growing startup.

I guess the LinkedIn optimization strategy is paying off. What's totally bizarre to me is that everyone's reaching out on the same day. I'm not going to complain about potential work, but — goodness gracious — can't these be spaced out a little bit more?

I'm not going to pursue the full-time job; I like doing my own thing too much. But it's nice to have options.

4:59 pm

Am I missing something? Did I unconsciously launch a marketing campaign recently?

To conclude this bizarre day of service requests, I received a text from an old acquaintance about writing recommendation letters.

> Hi. I▮ Hope you're well. I saw an update from you a while back that you are writing out on your own. Is that still true and are you open to work? I get inundated with letter of recommendations and need someone to help me write them. Is that something you'd consider?

Realistically, this will fall through — it's a bit too out of scope, and I don't think I have time anyway.

Day 276: October 2, 2020 - 8:00 am (Friday)

The second day of October is the hardest day of the year.

Fifteen years ago today, my mom passed away.

Man, time is hard to comprehend, isn't it?

Fifteen years. Just saying it makes me feel old.

This day always puts me in a pensive mood. I don't think about my mom too often. Not intentionally though. That tragic day oriented my mind to be present and forward-looking.

That's my way of coping I suppose.

So much has happened since then. I learned to drive. I had my first kiss. I lost my...err...car keys once. I finished high school. I made friends. I fell in love. I traveled abroad. I got a college degree. I joined society as an independent adult. I worked a corporate job. I quit a corporate job. I started a business.

And here we are, 15 eventful years later.

As sad as it is to say, my mom missed so much of my life. The fraction she saw only shrinks with each passing day. I wish I could've shared more with her.

Sometimes I wonder what my life would be like if she was still here. I like to think there's a parallel universe where she didn't have a premature exit.

It's funny how life events shape your perspective. Who knows if parallel-universe Carter would have gone to the University of South Carolina, or studied finance and worked in banking, or moved to Atlanta, or started a business.

Ever since that tragic day, I've been more determined to live a fulfilling life. Losing life makes you appreciate it more. And wondering "What if?" only leads to somber thoughts.

Day 277: October 3, 2020 - 4:21 pm (Saturday)

So, Medium launched a pretty big update to its platform yesterday.

Over the last few months, Medium rolled out several visual changes, which I was aware of but didn't give much attention to. Certain authors and publications could opt to use different profile designs. Honestly, I think I opted in but never changed any of my settings.

Then, Medium revamped their homepage:

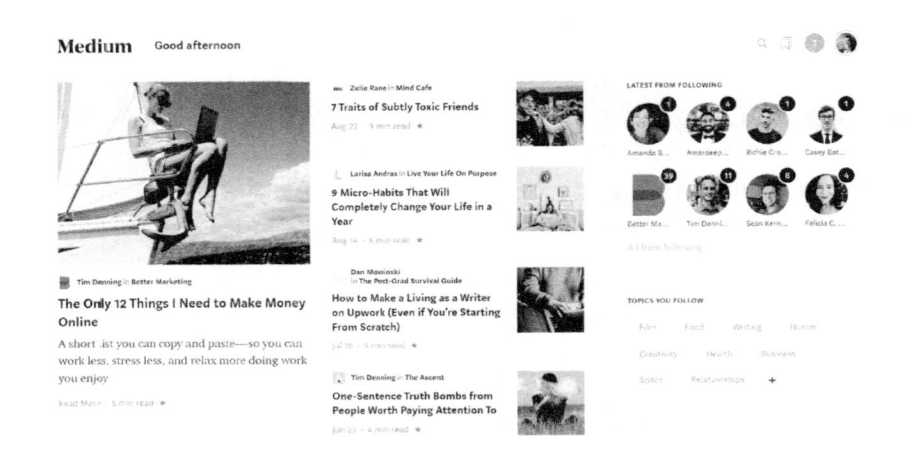

I don't recall when exactly that happened. It seems to emphasize publications, but at least a corner of the page shows the authors you follow.

Then Medium launched a pretty key feature change: the elimination of curation.

At first glance, I was worried. *Especially since I'm working on a post about increasing your curation percentage.* But after digging a little deeper, I think it's a positive update. Medium disabled curation under topics, but they aren't getting rid of widespread distribution. Here's what "curated" posts now state:

5 Empathetic Ways to Console Someone in Mourning

Chosen for further distribution.

I'm not sure how this will impact my personal stats, but it sounds positive overall.

Day 278: October 4, 2020 - 10:44 am (Sunday)

Being a professional stand-up comic has to be tough, right?

Can you imagine coming up with new material? Material that can rouse an entire room of diverse people and inspire them to laugh?

That sounds so daunting.

What does the average day of a stand-up comic look like? Do they literally sit around their living rooms or random spots in public and conjure up odd perspectives that can be manipulated into a story or joke?

Hmmm...makes me wonder...

stares at a collection of cork wine-stoppers on the kitchen counter

Isn't it weird how "cork" became a decorative style?

As you can tell, my material would ignite a crowd…

They say funny things happen to funny people. I believe that, in a sense. I think funny things happen to everyone, but funny people know how to interpret and spin them in such a way that you're like, "Damn, that's relatable and hilarious."

Also, the thought of bombing in front of a room of people sounds like a torture technique in a ring of hell. I've seen amateur comedy, and when it's bad, it's *bad*. It's painful to watch. I can't imagine living it.

Kudos to the comedians out there. I respect what you do.

Week 40 Lessons & Takeaways

#1: If you don't want to build a website just to house your portfolio, you could use a combination of ClearVoice and Medium.

#2: Choosing a domain name can be tricky. While there are a few routes you can take, I decided to launch a website under my own name — as opposed to something cleverly linked to writing or a business name. Since I don't actively add content to my site, that seems like the right decision. If I did and I wanted to rank on Google's first SERP, I probably would change my domain name to something more fitting.

#3: Continuing with that same thought, I'd also regularly post to my website's blog if I cared about ranking.

#4: Death has a funny way of making you think about life.

#5: Being a professional comedian sounds equally cool and terrifying. I'll stick to occasionally injecting humor in my writing.

Day 279: October 5, 2020 - 8:42 am (Monday)

Monday already? The weekend flew by. Kaileigh and I had a Harry Potter movie marathon yesterday. We powered through the Chamber of Secrets all the way through Order of the Phoenix.

I love the Harry Potter series. Every time I watch it, I'm overwhelmed with a yearning to create my own story universe.

Maybe one day…

But, for now, task time:

This Week (9/27 - 10/3)

1. ~~365 Days of Freelance Writing (x7)~~
2. ~~Client B edits~~
3. Client E post

4. ~~Client J work~~
5. Better Marketing post (curation percentage)
6. ~~Better Marketing post (writing rut)~~
7. Bacon Bits post
8. The Ascent post
9. ~~Bits newsletter~~
10. GN review

Yet again, I struggled to concentrate on a particular Medium post, so I bounced around. I'm holding off on my Medium curation piece, as I need one more curated post to have a curation percentage of 70%.

Yet again, *again*, still nada from Client E. They sounded a little short-staffed in their last email, so I think they're just behind.

Otherwise, I closed out September with a bang, delivering $4,000 worth of work.

This Week (10/4 - 10/10)

1. 365 Days of Freelance Writing (x7)
2. Client A posts (x2)
3. Client B edits
4. Client J work
5. Client K post
6. Better Marketing post (writing tips)
7. Bacon Bits post
8. GN review
9. Q3 Taxes

Plenty of client work this week. I pitched a couple of article ideas to Client K on Friday, so I should hear from them soon.

I might take a break from game reviews for a bit. It's cutting into client/Medium time.

Day 280: October 6, 2020 - 5:00 pm (Tuesday)

Client K tasked me with writing the following article:

> "How This 26-Year Old Went From Overworked and Underpaid To Building A 7-Figure Digital Agency Working Only 5 Hours A Day and 10 Client Max"

The only problem with this assignment is that I have zero insight into how this guy built his business. The purpose of the article is to drive traffic to one of his many online courses, except the specifics of his success story seem to live behind the paywalls of those courses. All I have to go off of is a few vague landing pages and sales-oriented inspirational videos.

The dearth of information makes me skeptical. How am I supposed to write a full-fledged article on a veiled success story?

This is a rewrite by the way — the previous writer asked the same question and didn't get a helpful response. I reached out to Client K's Head of Copywriting for more information, so we'll see...

Day 281: October 7, 2020 - 6:27 am (Wednesday)

Another Medium earnings analysis found its way to my feed this morning, courtesy of Itxy Lopez. In her post, Itxy provides a month-by-month breakdown of her earnings progress. Like Zulie Rane, another Medium author I mentioned recently, she pumps out an extraordinary amount of content each month. To date, she's published over 400 articles.

Here's her story: A Breakdown of My Earnings From the Past 14 Months[69]

I love when dedicated Medium writers share their perspectives. Despite her publishing consistency, Itxy hasn't had a viral article yet. That said, she earns approximately $200 per month from Medium, which is well within the top ~6% of active Medium writers.

8:30 pm

Surprisingly enough, Client K is working on getting me the proper information. I'm not sure why the previous writer was expected to write a success story without any background.

In the meantime, I've been tasked with writing YouTube scripts for an assortment of financial topics. Does anyone know how that process works? Because I don't.

Should be interesting.

Day 282: October 8, 2020 - 3:30 pm (Thursday)

I just received an AWESOME email.

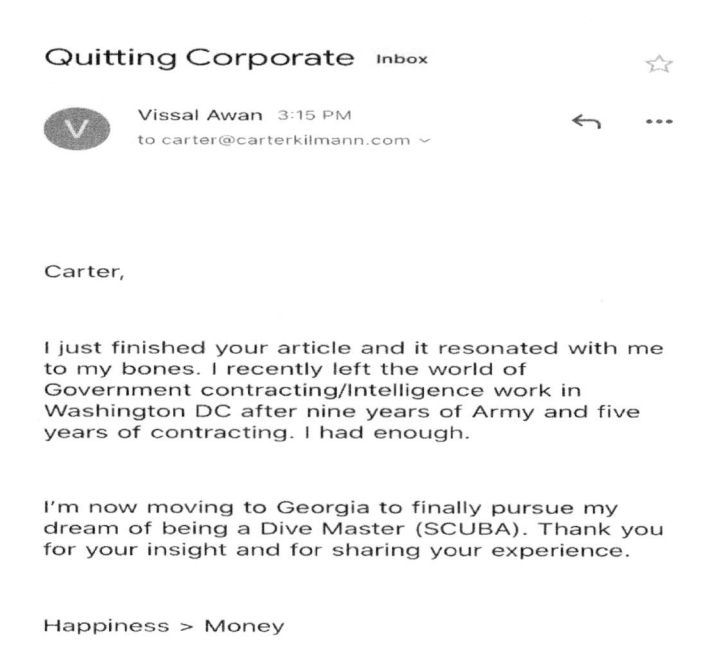

>
> **Quitting Corporate** Inbox
>
> **Vissal Awan** 3:15 PM
> to carter@carterkilmann.com
>
> Carter,
>
> I just finished your article and it resonated with me to my bones. I recently left the world of Government contracting/Intelligence work in Washington DC after nine years of Army and five years of contracting. I had enough.
>
> I'm now moving to Georgia to finally pursue my dream of being a Dive Master (SCUBA). Thank you for your insight and for sharing your experience.
>
> Happiness > Money

That's what I LOVE to see. Plus, scuba diving? What a cool dream job.

That "enough is enough" point is very real. It takes a while to reach it, but it provides a jolt of conviction.

Power to you, Vissal.

This random email exemplifies the power of writing. You can lose your mind concentrating on views and reads, but you won't find an "Inspired" counter anywhere. That stat trumps all the others.

Day 283: October 9, 2020 - 11:03 am (Friday)

AHA, I figured it out. For the last day, I've tried to determine why I recognized someone's name.

Quick context: Medium sends you an email anytime a reader highlights your stories. I rarely pay attention to these alerts, but one caught my eye yesterday.

Medium

Matt Lillywhite highlighted your stories.

Matt Lillywhite highlighted How to Climb Out of Your Writing Rut
Some days, I can't resist looking at my phone. It's the ultimate productivity disruptor. Other days, even when I have the will power to escape mindlessly scrolling through social media, I still can't muster an ounce of creativity. Like a dead battery, my creativity runs out of juice.

That name, Matt Lillywhite, seemed so familiar. But I couldn't place it.

I checked out his Medium profile, and he has over 15,000 followers. Maybe I read one of his posts? So, I scanned my reading history. No dice.

Then it hit me this morning. Itxy mentioned him in her 14-month earnings review post (the one I shared two days ago).

Want to See Other People's Earnings?

Fourteen months. As I said, that's how long I've been writing on Medium. Fourteen months, and I've never had one of my 441 articles go viral. I've never made more than $219 in a month.

After 14 months, Matt Lillywhite made $6,513.13. This was in July of this year. I could rip myself apart in a hundred ways because my achievements are nowhere near his, but what's the point? Where's it gonna get me?

So, by sheer coincidence, I read Itxy's story, which happened to mention Matt, and then he read/highlighted my post the next day.

That's pretty neat.

Day 284: October 10, 2020 - 11:31 am (Saturday)

One of the obvious perks of freelancing is the ability to work remotely. In theory, freelancers can work from wherever, which opens the door for seemingly endless travel. For me, freelancing translated to mainly working from home.

Which makes me wonder...

Would I have survived working from home this long without Kaileigh?

If I didn't have social stimulation as a result of having a roommate, would I feel isolated and lonely?

I'm introverted, but zero human interaction would be debilitating.

I guess I would work from a coffee shop or something to simulate some human connectivity, but a pandemic doesn't exactly spur people to be friendly and talkative.

Well, thank the heavens for Kaileigh then.

Day 285: October 11, 2020 - 4:39 pm (Sunday)

I'm starting to rethink my newsletter approach. First, I don't think a daily newsletter is a viable long-term activity. Uploading these posts every day is a time-consuming process. Second, who wants to read a daily email containing a random tidbit of my life as an entrepreneur?

I always intended 365 Days of Freelance Writing to be a book, and that's not going to change. I just don't think it makes sense to send each daily entry as an email.

I'd rather build an email list of people who simply appreciate my writing or perspective, and I think I have a better chance of doing that with less writing-specific content and more abstract thoughts and open-ended questions.

Editor's note: If it wasn't abundantly clear, I uploaded each of these daily entries to Patreon to simulate a daily newsletter. I decided that Patreon's platform wasn't the best place for my content, so I uploaded everything to Substack — a much better newsletter platform. However, the concept of sharing each day as an individual newsletter just didn't pan out.

Week 41 Lessons & Takeaways

#1: You can't write about someone's success story when you don't know the story. Communicate questions and concerns to editors upfront, if you can. Otherwise, you'll find yourself in a content bind.

#2: Views and claps are cool metrics, but receiving genuine, appreciative feedback from inspired readers is invaluable.

#3: I'm thankful for Kaileigh's existence for many reasons, one of which is that I'd probably be driven to insanity if I didn't live with someone during the pandemic.

#4: Substack was an interesting and worthwhile experiment for 365 Days of Freelance Writing entries, but I don't think it's the best use of my time — unless I started paying for advertising to drive traffic.

Day 286: October 12, 2020 - 9:21 am (Monday)

Copywriting can seem daunting, but you don't need to reinvent the wheel. It goes without saying that plagiarism is off the table, but you can learn a lot from successful copy.

Swipe-Worthy is an excellent source for studying said material.[70] I stumbled across it today, and it seems like a huge find. It's a compilation of landing pages, ads, emails, and anything that can be considered copywriting.

Anyway, it's task time.

The theme continues: client work prevails, personal work languishes. At least I worked on a couple of Medium posts.

The only client task I didn't complete was a post for Client K because I need more information to write it.

This Week (10/4 - 10/10)

1. ~~365 Days of Freelance Writing (x7)~~
2. ~~Client A posts (x2)~~
3. ~~Client B edits~~
4. ~~Client J work~~
5. Client K post
6. Better Marketing post (writing tips)

7. Bacon Bits post
8. ~~GN review~~
9. ~~Q3 Taxes~~

The week ahead:

This Week (10/11 - 10/17)

1. 365 Days of Freelance Writing (x7)
2. Client A post
3. Client B edits
4. Client J work
5. Client K scripts (x3)
6. Better Marketing post (writing tips)
7. Bacon Bits post
8. Bits newsletter

Based on Client K's communications, it sounds like I'll be handling a host of YouTube Scripts instead of an article. So, there's a good chance client work will consume my time again...

Day 287: October 13, 2020 - 6:59 pm (Tuesday)

My heart just wasn't in it today. I couldn't get going. Productivity was at an all-time low.

And, of course, I crack open Medium, looking for a nice dose of inspiration, a little boost to get me going...and the *first* post in my feed imparts this gem of wisdom:

"The tough days are the most important days."

Why? Because if you skip the tough days (the days when you're struggling to write for whatever reason) you make tomorrow harder. And the next day. And the day after that.

I needed this like 10 hours ago.

Day 288: October 14, 2020 - 8:34 am (Wednesday)

One of the purest writing moments I've had was when I earned my first dollar. It was surreal. I just remember thinking, "Wow, I can get paid to do this."

I didn't need to interview, put on a suit, commute to work, sit through a meeting that could've been an email. Nope, none of the corporate monotony.

I'll never forget my first paid piece. I wrote about the benefits of mindful spending and submitted it to the Quill blog. I was absolutely thrilled when it was accepted. I donned an unshakable smile for days. And I earned a crisp $100, which only stoked the fire more. Earning money made writing a viable option.

I still get a nice confidence boost whenever my writing is accepted, but nothing can top your first time.

Day 289: October 15, 2020 - 7:07 pm (Thursday)

Three clients — Client E, Client J, and Client K — messaged me today with more work...while I was grinding through assignments from Client A and Client B. If there were any doubts that content demand would return after the pandemic struck, they've been vanquished.

I'm trying something that probably isn't advisable, but I think it will work. Remember how Client K didn't even flinch at $250 for a 90-word company bio?

Well, I'm just going to assume $350 for a YouTube script is appropriate.

And now that I actually type that dollar figure, I'm wondering if I'm short-changing myself again.

Okay, so here was the thought process. Client K provided an SOP when I joined their team, which included a section on copywriting fees. They usually pay between $60 and $80 per YouTube script — at least according to the document.

Which makes zero sense to me. It's the equivalent of a short blog post. So, I'm going to charge based on the rate I gave for short blog posts — $350.

Again, maybe I'm leaving money on the table again. Oh well. It's still solid income, considering there are **20** scripts in total.

Day 290: October 16, 2020 - 7:34 am (Friday)

What makes a writer's content worth reading?

Here's what prompted this question:

> **Katie | Dream Scribe**
> @dreamscribeuk
>
> Question: what do you think makes a good blogger or why do you follow certain bloggers? For me, they have to be helpful, friendly and relatable. 🙂
>
> 7:45 AM · 10/15/20 · Hootsuite Inc.

I like Katie's answer, which encapsulates the attributes of good content.

I think style and perspective are so important. A lifeless writing style is so off-putting — it's like reading a textbook. And I love unique perspectives. Some people have a real knack for shedding new light on the most saturated topics.

Anyway, today's a vacation day. We're celebrating Kaileigh's birthday.

Happy birthday, Kaileigh! I love you!

Day 291: October 17, 2020 - 10:23 am (Saturday)

Even though my Gamecocks are struggling this year, I can't help but love every second of football season.

I like doing my own thing and having diverse clients, but I wouldn't mind being a college or pro football writer/journalist. I can talk about sports for hours and hours and hours.

It's a gift and a curse because when my teams lose I'm totally deflated. But I wouldn't trade my fan spirit away for anything.

Day 292: October 18, 2020 - 11:10 am (Sunday)

I can't wait to have three-day weekends. That extra day makes all the difference. I feel so refreshed today.

Back in college, I had the most beautiful class schedule every semester. The business school had the most course flexibility, so I successfully avoided Friday classes seven out of eight semesters.

I know, I've got a lot of hard work between me and that point in time, but it's a nice little motivator.

Week 42 Lessons & Takeaways

#1: Should you power through the tough days or give yourself a break? You know the days, the ones where you can't seem to spark an ounce of creativity or productivity. I'm not immune to them. In the past, I've posited that it's okay to take a day off here and there, and I still believe that — but I read a post that made a valid point: when you don't push through the tough days and get work done, you set yourself back. This is true, unfortunately. That's the tricky part about being the sole driver of your success. If you're not working, you're not progressing (at least until you establish passive income streams). I guess the answer is "it depends."

#2: Everyone remembers their first time — the first time you earn money writing that is.

#3: Does anyone know how much money to charge for a YouTube script? Because I'm winging it. I'm just going to assume $350 is a fair price, but I could be undercutting my earnings.

#4: What makes content worth reading? Personally, I love affable writing styles and unique perspectives.

Day 293: October 19, 2020 - 9:10 am (Monday)

You know what time it is.

Task time.

This Week (10/11 - 10/17)

1. ~~365 Days of Freelance Writing (x7)~~
2. Client A post
3. ~~Client B edits~~
4. ~~Client J work~~
5. ~~Client K scripts (x3)~~
6. ~~Better Marketing post (writing tips)~~
7. Bacon Bits post
8. Bits newsletter

Plenty of money-making activity last week. And I finally wrote a Medium post (yay!)...but an upswing in client work led me to miss a Bits newsletter (boo!). That's disappointing.

I feel like I let my readers down, although if we're being realistic, they probably didn't notice.

The week ahead promises to be loaded with client work again, so I'm not sure if I'll get to the next installment of Bits by Friday.

This Week (10/18 - 10/24)

1. 365 Days of Freelance Writing (x7)
2. Client A post
3. Client B edits
4. Client J work
5. Client K scripts (x4)
6. Bacon Bits post
7. Bits newsletter

5:45 pm

Don't be afraid to set due dates that accommodate your schedule.

I'm not gonna lie, a little anxiety bubble forms in my stomach when a new client asks when I can deliver an assignment to them. I want to make a good impression and provide timely services, but I don't want to overload my plate.

Which is silly, right? There's no reason to bear the burden of an expedited content turnaround, especially when the client doesn't indicate it's urgent.

I encountered this scenario just now with Client K. They asked when I'd be able to deliver another 16 YouTube scripts. In this situation, it's easy to assume the client is impatient. However, unless they specify that the project is urgent or has a tight deadline, there's no reason to over-promise anything.

In my response, I gave myself plenty of cushion:

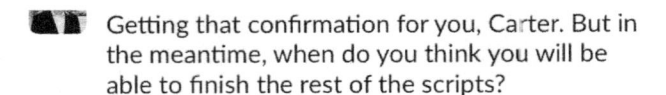

> Getting that confirmation for you, Carter. But in the meantime, when do you think you will be able to finish the rest of the scripts?
>
> **Carter Kilmann** 5:32 PM
> Thanks, Chris. I'll have another one for you shortly. I'm aiming to knock out one or two a day, I'd estimate about two or three weeks. That said, a few of these topics seem duplicative. For example, "Investing For Beginners: How Do Stocks Make Money?" and "How Does a Stock Make You Money?" are nearly identical. Thoughts?

He immediately agreed to my timeline. Now I can work without unnecessary pressure.

Day 294: October 20, 2020 - 8:07 am (Tuesday)

Email etiquette is absolutely a thing. There are (straightforward) rules to follow, especially for professional emails like client pitches.

Don't misspell the recipient's name (you'd think that'd be obvious — see Day 49).

Write in complete sentences and use proper grammar.

Don't use an excessive amount of exclamation points!!!

And don't send a prospect **four** consecutive emails.

Here's a fellow writer's Facebook post and inquiry:

> It's okay to follow up 3 times, right? It's for a cold email. How many times do guys follow up?
>
> Hello,
>
> I don't want to be rude, but 4 emails is excessive. Thank you
>
> On Tue, Oct 13, 2020 at 10:00 AM Shubham

Welp. When you don't know, you don't know.

For some context, this writer pitched several prospects and continued following up every two weeks until they responded. Of course, after four consecutive emails, the above prospect was a bit irked — naturally so.

Sure, it'd be easier if every prospect replied, even if it was a blunt "no." But you can't rely on that. People are busy, and they usually don't like to be cold pitched.

Being ignored comes with the territory.

In most cases, I only send one follow-up email. But, every now and then, I'll send two. And that's the most a writer should ever send unless a significant amount of time has passed. If it's been six months and you want to check in with a prospect to see if their needs have changed, that's reasonable.

Here's a standard timeline writers can follow:

Day 1: Writer sends an email pitch to the prospect.

Day 8: One week later, writer sends a follow-up email to the prospect.

Day 15: At this point, if the prospect hasn't responded, it's safe to assume they're not interested.

If the writer thinks the prospect is a perfect fit, they could try sending one last email — but it should be worded carefully.

Here's an example of an initial follow-up email, but you could use this as a second follow up too.

> Hi Keran - how was your weekend?
>
> I just wanted to follow up on my previous email. If I don't hear from you, I'll assume you are not interested in expanding your content output and will look elsewhere!
>
> Best,
>
> **Carter Kilmann**

The only times I've ever sent two were when the prospects initially responded and indicated interest, but then went radio silent. Otherwise, I leave it alone after one follow-up email.

Day 295: October 21, 2020 - 6:34 pm (Wednesday)

Aaaaand Client E sent me two assignments.

Which, of course, I asked them to do — I just have so much client work in my pipeline right now. I still have 15 YouTube scripts to write and a couple of landing pages to write/edit.

I've never juggled this much client work at one time; I'm actually turning work down (politely, of course).

I guess if you freelance long enough and optimize your website or a social media platform for inbound work solicitations, you'll eventually receive plenty of gigs. You just have to stick with your strategy and keep delivering outstanding content.

Day 296: October 22, 2020 - 8:45 am (Thursday)

Well, that schedule I devised a couple of weeks ago hasn't panned out. It was great for a week or so, but then clients inundated me with assignments.

It's been great from an income perspective, but not so great for personal projects. My Medium output and viewership plummeted,

I missed a Bits newsletter deadline, and I stopped uploading these entries to Substack.

I keep telling myself to carve an hour out of my day to focus on Medium content, but I can't bring myself to pick a time and stick to it.

It's hard to focus on personal stuff when I know I have client work to do.

Day 297: October 23, 2020 - 8:46 am (Friday)

Well, nothing sparks motivation like competition.

> Also, I think cause Dan wants a quicker turnaround for these, I will assign another copywriter to help out with the workload, @Carter Kilmann.
>
> I can see the ones you've already done and shared in the card. But are you currently working on other ones that I am not aware about? That way there's no duplicating work or any mix ups

If the payout was meager, I wouldn't mind. But I'm getting $350 per script (hopefully), and each script is about 400-600 words. Considering the request is 20 scripts in total, that's a healthy $7,000 (hopefully).

So, yeah, these scripts just took priority.

Day 298: October 24, 2020 - 7:12 pm (Saturday)

Guess whose invoice was approved? Miiiiiiiiine.

I anxiously submitted my invoice to Client K yesterday, which included six YouTube scripts at $350 a pop — for a total of

$2,100. We never agreed to a price for each script, but I assumed $350 would be appropriate.

Thankfully, it was approved.

Hell. Yes.

Day 299: October 25, 2020 - 8:45 am (Sunday)

Do you think there are freelance ghostwriters that specialize in song lyrics?

I mean, there has to be right? I know ghostwriters are a thing in the music industry, I just never equated that career path to my own. I would imagine it looks somewhat similar: networking, pitching artists, compiling a portfolio, maybe running a site with samples or something.

Googles lyric ghostwriter

Yep, it's a thing.

SoundBetter

Top Lyric Songwriters for Hire

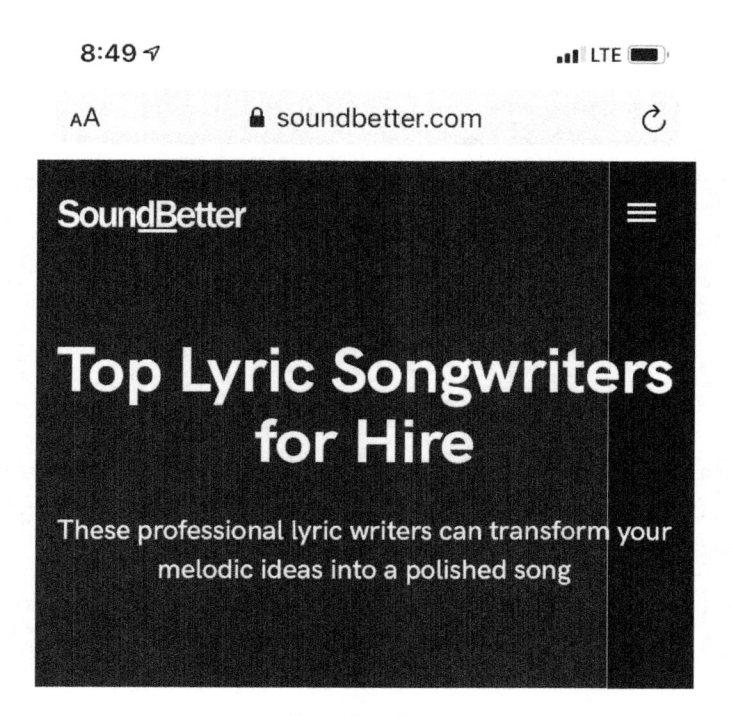

These professional lyric writers can transform your melodic ideas into a polished song

Filters Results ▼

Songwriter, Lyricist, Vocalist
Mariami , Los Angeles
★ ★ ★ ★ ★ (338)

I have a decade of experience in recording & songwriting, I write for my own catalog and for Top 40 Artists! My collaborations and partnerships

Ghostwriter/Singer/Rapper
Merty Shango , New York
★ ★ ★ ★ ★ (322)

Week 43 Lessons & Takeaways

#1: Don't compromise your sleep schedule and sanity just to deliver content. Set boundaries and reasonable expectations. It's always better to underpromise and overdeliver.

#2: Email etiquette is a necessity. For everyone's sake, don't send a prospect four consecutive emails. One follow-up email is enough.

#3: Inbound leads will come. You just have to be patient — and optimize a platform like LinkedIn.

#4: Balancing client work and personal projects seems impossible, mostly because I prioritize income. At the end of the day, money matters.

#5: Competition is a big motivator. Client K assigned another writer to my assignment to expedite the process.

#6: Copywriting is a lucrative service. I billed Client K for six YouTube scripts, which totaled $2,100. Reminder: these scripts were 400-600 words.

#7: If you're musically inclined, you could try to break into the lyric ghostwriting business. Who knows, maybe you'll write the next Drake hit.

Day 300: October 26, 2020 - 9:11 am (Monday)

Wow.

300 days.

That's...

That's.....

Wild.

Day 1 seems like it was just yesterday. I had my feet propped up in a beach chair, wondering what 2020 would entail. For starters, I couldn't have predicted that global pandemonium was on the horizon, but I also couldn't have imagined everything that's happened in my little writing sphere. It still feels like I have such a long way to go until Day 366, but it's really only a handful of weeks away.

I'm not exaggerating when I say I can mentally teleport back to my first day as a full-time freelance writer. I mainly dealt with administrative stuff, but I also published announcement posts detailing my career transition on Facebook and LinkedIn. Those posts ultimately led me to my first few clients.

I didn't make much money my first few months. From August until the end of 2019, I earned $8,114. Don't get me wrong, I was thrilled at the time. Earning thousands of dollars from my own business? Unbeatable. I wasn't expecting to break even for quite some time anyway.

That said, my expectations are totally different now. If I don't break even in a particular month, I'm disappointed.

It's just so humbling to compare where I was 15 months ago and where I am now.

Hopefully, I'll feel the same way again this time next year.

Day 301: October 27, 2020 - 8:50 am (Tuesday)

I know I said this already, but there's nothing quite like competition to give you a swift kick in the fanny.

Remember how another writer was assigned to my YouTube scripts project? Well, the other writer just shared three drafts.

Guess who's about to press the pedal to the floor and crank out some scripts today?

Day 302: October 28, 2020 - 7:03 am (Wednesday)

Okay, this might seem ridiculous, but the other writer assigned to this YouTube scripts project is pissing me off. *We'll call her Lynn.*

First, some context.

I haven't said anything because I didn't want to jinx it, but I'm on pace to deliver a hair under $7,100 this month. Of course, I'm thrilled at the prospect of clearing $7,000 — but that dollar figure means even more because it was my monthly banking salary. It's been my goal since day one of freelance writing to match my old monthly income.

But that's in jeopardy because "Lynn" keeps snagging two YouTube scripts at a time.

▇▇▇▇ commented: Yesterday at 3:05 pm
@Carter Kilmann great, I'll do 7 and 8 next 😊

You commented: Yesterday at 6:40 pm
Sounds good - I've also started #20 FYI

▇▇▇▇ commented: 1 hour ago
@Carter Kilmann great! I'll work on #13 and #18 today!

C'mon. She's calling dibs on scripts before turning in her current ones.

Again, I know it's immature, but I can't help but have a "I was here first, stop taking my scripts" mindset.

8:27 am

Update: I claimed another script to ensure I hit my income goal.

Day 303: October 29, 2020 - 8:27 am (Thursday)

Two more days. I've been grinding to get all my client work finished before month-end. *I'm so close.*

And then, starting Monday, I'm going to try to write at least 30 minutes a day for Medium. I'm also not fixating on long-form posts anymore. If I can explain a story, perspective, or lesson in three or four minutes of reading time, so be it.

That's how Medium writers manage to pump out multiple posts per day. I knew this, but, for whatever reason, it took writing YouTube scripts to come to this realization.

I've written 12 scripts in the last 10ish days, and they range from 450 to 700 words. But a YouTube script is practically a blog post. So, nothing is preventing me from writing a Medium post every day.

1:20 pm

Except another high volume copywriting assignment. *I swear I didn't stage this.*

> We need to create an Email Sequence to follow up with the people who opts in to Digital Agency Launch Pad.
>
> First 7 days we will send 1 email Daily [7 emails]
> - First 7 emails will be to promote Consumption. Video 1, Video 2 etc.
>
> After that we will continue to send emails every 3 days switching between the Jeremy emails and a testimonial/success story email. Can be any of the following categories listed below: [24 Emails]
> - Case Studies
> - Testimonials
> - Social Proof Emails
>
> The main purpose is to drive people to HTA.

Client K assigned me an email sequence project, consisting of 31 emails in total. Based on what I can gather, these emails are roughly 200-300 words. Considering I quoted them $300 per email, that's a potential $9,300 payday.

Hard to take a break from client work when they keep throwing money at you.

Day 304: October 30, 2020 - 9:05 am (Friday)

One more day, one more assignment (for this month).

At this point, it's just to say I surpassed my monthly banking salary. The assignment is for Client E, and it's not due until November 4 — but it's a major goal I didn't expect to even sniff until sometime next year.

So, I'm gunning for it.

6:45 pm

Finished. I officially eclipsed my monthly banking salary ($7,083.33) this month based on delivered client work ($7,149.92).

Who knows if that's sustainable, but I'm ecstatic regardless. What a way to enter the weekend.

Day 305: October 31, 2020 - 10:09 am (Saturday)

Happy Halloween! I imagine trick-or-treating will be at an all-time low this year, but I'm sure kids will figure out a way to get their hands on some candy.

You know what I'm more excited about? An extra hour of sleep tonight.

It's been a long week, and going out last night to celebrate wasn't exactly rejuvenating.

OCTOBER STATS

September's reign as my top-earning month was short-lived. October said, "Hold my keyboard."

Thanks to my budding relationships with Client J and Client K, I surpassed my monthly banking income. Only time will tell if these earnings are replicable, but I'm thrilled to accomplish this goal.

As a reminder, here's each client's description:

- Client A — Digital marketing agency
- Client B — Digital marketing agency (editing work)
- Client C — FinTech startup (no longer a client)
- Client D — Online finance publication (content freeze)
- Client E — Auto finance company
- Client F — ClearVoice assignments
- Client G — SaaS company (no longer a client, for now)
- Client H — Writing Revolt
- Client I — Consulting firm
- Client J — FinTech startup
- Client K — Digital marketing agency (copywriting)

OCTOBER

365 Days of Freelancing - Monthly Stats

	Jan	Feb	Mar	Apr	May	Jun	Jul	Aug	Sep	Oct
Income										
Client A	960	960	960	640	480	480	480	-	480	480
Client B	329	119	153	189	741	430	415	706	163	283
Client C	500	-	-	-	-	-	-	-	-	-
Client D	350	350	-	-	-	-	-	-	-	-
Client E	-	450	450	900	450	1,000	450	450	900	1,050
Client F	-	225	-	-	-	338	-	-	-	-
Client G	-	200	-	-	-	-	-	-	-	-
Client H	-	-	-	-	400	-	-	-	-	-
Client I	-	-	-	-	-	265	-	-	-	-
Client J	-	-	-	-	-	-	-	1,337	2,100	1,088
Client K	-	-	-	-	-	-	-	-	250	4,200
Client L	-	-	-	-	-	-	-	-	-	-
Client M	-	-	-	-	-	-	-	-	-	-
Medium	32	21	719	734	505	496	147	137	110	49
Total Income	**$2,171**	**$2,325**	**$2,282**	**$2,463**	**$2,576**	**$3,009**	**$1,492**	**$2,630**	**$4,003**	**$7,150**
Growth (%)	-	7.1%	(1.9%)	7.9%	4.6%	16.8%	(50.4%)	76.2%	52.2%	78.6%
Blog Posts (Paid)										
Client A	6	6	6	4	3	3	3	-	3	3
Client B	3	2	2	2	9	4	6	8	2	4
Client C	1	1	-	-	-	-	-	-	-	-
Client D	1	1	-	-	-	-	-	-	-	-
Client E	-	1	1	2	1	2	1	1	2	2
Client F	-	2	-	-	-	1	-	-	-	-
Client G	-	1	-	-	-	-	-	-	-	-
Client H	-	-	-	-	1	-	-	-	-	-
Client I	-	-	-	-	-	1	-	-	-	-
Client L	-	-	-	-	-	-	-	-	-	-
Total Paid Posts	**11**	**14**	**9**	**8**	**14**	**11**	**10**	**9**	**7**	**9**
Blog Posts (Unpaid)										
Medium	1	-	-	1	4	-	1	-	1	2
Bacon Bits	1	2	4	2	1	1	2	2	-	-
365	-	-	-	2	-	-	4	1	-	-
Total Unpaid Posts	**2**	**2**	**4**	**5**	**5**	**1**	**7**	**3**	**1**	**2**
Total Blog Posts	**13**	**16**	**13**	**13**	**19**	**12**	**17**	**12**	**8**	**11**
Copywriting Assignments										
Client C	5	-	-	-	-	-	-	-	-	-
Client J	-	-	-	-	-	-	-	3	2	2
Client K	-	-	-	-	-	-	-	-	1	12
Total Copywriting Asgns.	**5**	**-**	**-**	**-**	**-**	**-**	**-**	**3**	**3**	**14**
Total Assignments	**18**	**16**	**13**	**13**	**19**	**12**	**17**	**15**	**11**	**25**
Medium										
Views	1,151	1,352	19,466	11,052	15,778	8,562	4,552	4,945	3,522	1,906
Reads	439	468	7,413	4,220	6,320	3,651	1,947	2,055	1,438	776
Read Ratio	38%	35%	38%	38%	40%	43%	43%	42%	41%	41%
Existing Followers	54	63	80	238	371	530	595	645	702	733
New Followers	9	17	158	133	159	65	50	57	31	12
Total Followers	**63**	**80**	**238**	**371**	**530**	**595**	**645**	**702**	**733**	**745**
LinkedIn										
Existing Followers	458	465	493	526	570	590	599	613	624	637
New Followers	7	28	33	44	20	9	14	11	13	5
Total Followers	**465**	**493**	**526**	**570**	**590**	**599**	**613**	**624**	**637**	**642**

Highlights

- The obvious problem with hourly work: the more efficient you are, the less you get paid. This is becoming apparent with Client B.
- My 78.6% income increase can be attributed to Client K and the 12 YouTube scripts I delivered. My work for them alone earned more than all of my assignments did in September. Crazy.
- To be frank, I don't care if my Medium output suffers if I can make $7,000 a month from writing. That said, my Reads dipped below 1,000 for the first time since February, and I only added 12 new Followers (a measly 1.6% growth rate).

NOVEMBER

Day 306: November 1, 2020 - 12:12 pm (Sunday)

The final stretch is on the horizon. Two more months until we can wave goodbye to a wild year.

Now feels like a good time to review my 2020 goals progress.

2020	Goal	Actual	% Complete
Medium followers	1,000	745	75%
Bits subscribers	100	74	74%
365 DFW subscribers	100	10	10%
Daily entries	366	305	83%
Monthly income	$5,000	$7,150	143%
Annual income	$40,000	$30,102	75%

Some thoughts:

- Less content = less viewership. Thus, my Medium follower count's growth rate has diminished. If I prioritize Medium writing, I think I can still get to 1,000 followers by year-end though.
- It's even harder to land email subscribers (doesn't help when I neglect to publish content on my only traffic source, oops). Honestly, I don't expect to reach my subscriber goals, especially for this book since I'm not publishing my daily entries anymore.
- Somehow, I still find things to write about on a daily basis. So long as that continues, I'll finish this book.
- My income goals were far-fetched a month ago, but not anymore. The latest Client K assignment will get me pretty close by itself, assuming they don't assign another writer again.

Even if I don't hit my goals, I'm still happy with my 2020 progress — so far, at least. I think my primary goal for 2021 is to adopt an effective daily and weekly schedule. It's too much of a crapshoot at times.

Week 44 Lessons & Takeaways

#1: Excuse my language, but time fucking flies. We hit Day 300 this past week. It's humbling to see where I was back then and where I am now. It's even crazier to think of where I'll be a year from now.

#2: If you can write a 400-600 word YouTube script in a day, you can write daily blog posts. No more excuses.

#3: I eclipsed an income goal, which was to exceed my monthly banking salary. On Friday, I turned in my final assignment for October, bringing my delivered earnings to a hair under $7,150.

#4: Two months to go on this year-long journey, so I revisited my goal progress. I already know I won't reach a few milestones, but that's okay.

Day 307: November 2, 2020 - 8:59 am (Monday)

So, as you've probably noticed, I didn't bother creating a task list last week. Instead, I buckled down and powered through my client assignments.

Here's what I completed:

1. 365 Days of Freelance Writing (x7)
2. Client B edits
3. Client E posts (x2)
4. Client K scripts (x6)

This month, I'm focusing on Medium content. To accommodate that prioritization, I'm getting all of Client A's deliverables out of the way this week. I also plan to finish six emails for Client K, alongside some edits.

This Week (11/1 - 11/7)

1. 365 Days of Freelance Writing (x7)
2. Client A post (x3)
3. Client B edits
4. Client E edits
5. Client K emails (x6)
6. Bacon Bits post (x2)

2:39 pm

I don't use Quora very often, but I have an account and receive "Quora Digest" emails, which flaunt random — yet incredibly tantalizing — questions.

The latest:

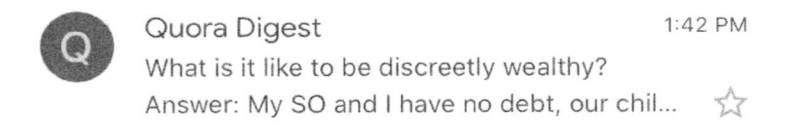

> **Quora Digest** — 1:42 PM
> What is it like to be discreetly wealthy?
> Answer: My SO and I have no debt, our chil...

I'll admit it, Quora is a limitless source of killer headlines.

Within this particular answer, one line really stood out to me:

"Having money doesn't create happiness — strong relationships does that — but it reduces stress immeasurably."

I spoke about this on Day 205, but studies prove extravagant wealth isn't the key to happiness. Emotional fulfillment stems from relationships. That said, as this person suggests, *smart* money will limit your stress. And, yes, I added the "smart."

Living within your means is integral to achieving stress-free wealth. If you let your lifestyle override your income, you're screwed — even if you have significant wealth.

Day 308: November 3, 2020 - 12:15 pm (Tuesday)

In business news, Client K decided to handle that email sequence, rather than assign it to me.

> I think we are good on this, Carter. Not cause of you, but we thought about it and since Jeremy knows his product the best, we should have him write these emails since it is so heavily dependent on his content. (edited)

Glass half full: now I should have plenty of time for Medium content.

Glass half empty: there goes a *very* lucrative project.

Day 309: November 4, 2020 - 3:20 pm (Wednesday)

Writing about dull topics can be so painful. I like reading and learning about new things, but certain topics just lose my attention after a while, making it difficult to power through blog assignments.

The latest topics for Client A:

1. Open enrollment for Medicare
2. Sustainability in the print and mail industry
3. Cybersecurity best practices

Woof.

At least I'll be done with Client A's deliverables earlier than usual this month.

Day 310: November 5, 2020 - 2:36 pm (Thursday)

I'm *way* too into fantasy football. I just wrote a detailed analysis of a self-assembled lineup for a weekly FanDuel league.

And it's not even my league.

It's Kaileigh's uncle's league.

…

It was a superb analysis though.

Day 311: November 6, 2020 - 9:47 am (Friday)

You know what's weird? I have to start thinking about publishing this book.

I happen to know a guy who launched a publishing company, so I have that sorted out already. But I have to review and edit this beast.

Did you know this document got so long I had to create a second version? The original is around 61,000 words, but it kept freezing my computer…and that was only through 8.5 months.

I'll hire an editor, but I still need to read this from start to finish.

Which is daunting…

Kaileigh gets to be my first beta reader.

Day 312: November 7, 2020 - 11:19 am (Saturday)

For the first time in a while, I'm writing on a Saturday. *That's excluding these entries, of course.*

I want to make more progress on Medium. As a whole, I've experienced tremendous growth on the platform this year, but a lot of that is attributed to one post.

So, I'm writing for 20-30 minutes this morning before I watch hours of college football.

Go Gamecocks.

Day 313: November 8, 2020 - 10:12 am (Sunday)

WOOF. My health care premium will be hefty in 2021. I took advantage of a $100 tax credit in 2020, so my premium has been $185 instead of $285.

But I'm not eligible for another tax credit based on my estimated annual income for next year.

Prices went up too.

So, $295 will flow out of my bank account every month, even though the coverage is terrible, the deductible is high, and I'm a healthy 26-year-old who doesn't smoke.

What a system.

Week 45 Lessons & Takeaways

#1: Quora is a surprisingly bountiful source for post titles and topics.

#2: Canceled projects are bittersweet. Client K no longer needs assistance with that massive email sequence, which is a bummer since it would've been lucrative. But at least I get to focus on Medium.

#3: Pick a niche you'll enjoy. Client A's topics can be quite dry, so they take longer to write. Originally, I just needed experience and a steady income. Now, they don't pay as well relative to my other assignments. I should raise my rates in January.

#4: I'm far too invested in fantasy football.

#5: Editing this book is going to be a marathon.

#6: One major downside to freelancing: health care premiums. I'm looking at an uncool $295 monthly premium next year.

Day 314: November 9, 2020 - 3:10 pm (Monday)

I miss paid time off, but the flexibility to take Kaileigh to the doctor and work from my phone is quite nice.

Speaking of work, let's take a look at my tasks.

Last week, I got my deliverables for Client A out of the way. I also finished a round of edits for Client B and Client E. I finally got to write some Medium content too, which I plan to wrap up this upcoming week.

This Week (11/1 - 11/7)

1. ~~365 Days of Freelance Writing (x7)~~
2. ~~Client A post (x3)~~
3. ~~Client B edits~~
4. ~~Client E edits~~
5. Client K emails (x6)
6. Bacon Bits post (x2)

I also have a wave of Client B work on my plate now, but that shouldn't take too long. I don't know if I'll have any requests from Client J, but I'm being preemptive since I haven't heard from them in a while.

This Week (11/8 - 11/14)

1. 365 Days of Freelance Writing (x7)
2. Client B edits
3. Client B website edits
4. Client B client report edits
5. Client J work
6. Bacon Bits post (x3)
7. Medium posts (x2)
8. Bits newsletter

Yep, I know what you're thinking. *Five Medium posts?*

I think it's doable. I have to compensate for the recent content lapse.

Day 315: November 10, 2020 - 8:40 am (Tuesday)

If you can't tell, I'm growing tired of random LinkedIn solicitations.

> • 11:45 am
> Hi Carter, I noticed your role at Kilmann Media LLC, hoping we can add value to each other's network. Let me know if you'd like to connect sometime. Take care!

TODAY

> • 8:29 am
> Hi Carter, have you ever experienced this issue - being overwhelmed with all the business operations needs and handling employees?

> **Carter Kilmann** · 8:36 am
> Nope, not really

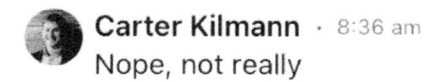

Day 316: November 11, 2020 - 2:47 pm (Wednesday)

You know what's sort of annoying? Submitting a draft to a client, mentally checking it off the task list, and then receiving feedback weeks later.

It feels like backtracking. I want to focus on producing more content, not revising something I finished a while ago.

What makes it worse? When this is the feedback:

6. How Risky Is The Stock Market in 2020?
    a. FLUFF. Not useful info at all.
7. Understanding Stocks - The Importance of Financial Literacy
    a. TOTAL FLUFF. WASTE OF THE AUDIENCE'S TIME. We need to explain what stocks are. WHATEVER promise we make in the headline, we need to deliver.

Client K finally reviewed those YouTube scripts, and they weren't delicate.

The good news: #7 wasn't my submission.

The better news: out of 12 submissions, only 2 of mine require extensive changes.

The client ripped the other writer on this assignment to shreds. None of her submissions were approved. To be fair, this client is ridiculously vague and blunt. It's not conducive to productivity or quality writing at all.

But, hey, they pay well.

Day 317: November 12, 2020 - 10:47 am (Thursday)

In case you didn't know, when you get health insurance from open marketplaces, you have to reassess your plan and reapply every year. If you're already enrolled in a plan, it'll renew automatically — but coverage and rates are subject to change, so it's prudent to revisit available plans.

In my case, as I mentioned last weekend, my premium will be significantly higher in 2021 due to my expected earnings increase.

I can't rely on a tax credit anymore. Plus, I had to change plans to keep dental and vision coverage under a single policy.

Health insurance is complicated, but I hope that tidbit helps.

Day 318: November 13, 2020 - 4:01 pm (Friday)

It's been nice to get some Medium momentum back this week. After a lackluster couple of months, I published three stories over the last few days. Three obviously isn't five, but I'll take it.

This needs to become a weekly habit. Publishing three posts isn't a ridiculous feat, especially if I write succinct stories and lessons.

Day 319: November 14, 2020 - 11:51 am (Saturday)

Earlier this week, I expanded on Wednesday's entry and published a Medium post about frustrating editors. I specifically referenced Client K's feedback of "fluff" and shared how I think lack of detail is counterproductive.

And one particular reader decided to be an asshat.

> Frustrated with your editor's feedback? You h... 260 3
> Carter Kilmann
>
> Fluff article.
>
> Make up your mind if you are writing an article on how to deal with and utilize your editor's feedback. OR, you're writing an article about how to communicate with your clients. By doing both under the guise of doing one, you haven't served your readers.
>
> I editorially suggest you take this article down. Pull it apart into two articles and add additional information to both. Then post both with appropriate headlines.

Debra, I say this with the utmost respect and sincerity, **kindly fuck off**.

And I say that not because of the actionable criticism, but because of your public mockery.

Do you really think *your* feedback will be well received if you open with "fluff" — the same grievance I aired within my post's introduction?

I see how that's rudely clever, but seriously, **fuck off**.

To be fair, I tried to take her criticism objectively. But I'm having a hard time understanding why she thinks handling an editor's feedback and communicating a response are two different things.

Yes, I used editor and client interchangeably — because, as is often the case, writers deal with "editors." Whether it's a publication's editor or the CEO or a Head of Content, they each serve in an editorial capacity when they review your work.

As I've stated in the past, I'm not going to stoop to someone's level by engaging in back-and-forth mudslinging in the comment section of a Medium article.

But on Day 319 of my own book? Absolutely.

Debra, I editorially suggest you do some soul searching.

Day 320: November 15, 2020 - 8:43 am (Sunday)

Despite one annoying reader's opinion, my Medium posts are performing well.

Frustrated with your editor's feedback? You have...

262	114	44%	25
views	reads	ratio	fans

You Don't Have to Love Writing to Be a Writer

43	20	47%	8
views	reads	ratio	fans

How Quickly Can You Make $1,000,000 by Investi...

510	308	60%	20
views	reads	ratio	fans

I should post in Bacon Bits more often — like every few days. Money-related subjects do so much better than anything else I write about.

Week 46 Lessons & Takeaways

#1: LinkedIn solicitors are the worst.

#2: Completing revisions for client work can be frustrating. I have a tendency to mentally move on from submitted work, so it feels like I'm backtracking when I have to spend time making updates instead of writing new content.

#3: Assuming you don't benefit from being on your parents' or partner's insurance, you'll need to reassess/renew your health care plan each year if your coverage is from an open marketplace. Otherwise, you could get stuck in a renewed plan with a worse premium and less coverage.

#4: I need to speak this into existence: three Medium posts per week is achievable. Now, I just need to do it consistently.

#5: Negative criticism comes with the territory of being a writer. One particular reader left a less-than-stellar comment on one of my Medium posts. I'll be honest, I let it get to me. But, taking a step back, there's really no need to take anything personally. I can't control other people's opinions. It's a waste of time to think otherwise.

#6: Money talks. And I suppose money reads well too. My money-related posts seem to attract many more eyeballs than my other content.

Day 321: November 16, 2020 - 9:15 am (Monday)

Aaaaaaaand we're back.

Another weekend in the books, another week of writing lies ahead.

I won't keep you waiting, let's jump into task time.

It goes without saying, but last week was a good one for Medium content. There was some client work peppered in, but I concentrated on writing desirable Medium posts. Thus far, the stats indicate success.

As I predicted, Client J continued its stretch of radio silence. I'm not too concerned though. I think they're focused on the actual visual designs of the landing pages rather than the copy at the moment.

Also, don't ask me why I keep adding the Bits newsletter to my task list despite weekly neglect. I think part of me wants to reestablish a Medium writing routine before I get back to sharing biweekly newsletters. Is that the best mentality or approach? Probably not. But it is what it is.

This Week (11/8 - 11/14)

1. ~~365 Days of Freelance Writing (x7)~~

2. ~~Client B edits~~
3. ~~Client B website edits~~
4. ~~Client B client report edits~~
5. Client J work
6. ~~Client K revised post~~
7. Bacon Bits post (x3)
8. ~~Medium posts (x2)~~
9. Bits newsletter

The week ahead includes much of the same. *Even the ever-elusive Bits newsletter.*

This Week (11/15 - 11/21)

1. 365 Days of Freelance Writing (x7)
2. Client B edits
3. Client B client report edits (x2)
4. Client K revisions (x5)
5. Bacon Bits post (x2)
6. Medium post
7. Bits newsletter

Day 322: November 17, 2020 - 3:20 pm (Tuesday)

Why on earth did I ever stop writing Medium content?

After weeks of minimal views due to, well, a lack of producing something for people to view, my content is gaining traction again.

Let this be a lesson on consistency.

Day 323: November 18, 2020 - 11:07 am (Wednesday)

I think I'm pretty good at responding to negative Medium comments.

Here's the latest salty comment on one of my Medium posts. At least, it sort of feels that way. It's hard to gauge the tone, but word choice seems to suggest moderate disapproval.

> How Quickly Can You Make $1,000,000 by Inv... 👏 325 💬 2
> Carter Kilmann
>
> The headline, like many on Medium, makes me feel that I could invest, and perhaps, make income quickly. The article then, rightly so, talks about the long-term grind of investing (with a lot space wasted on the old 'if you had seen/invested in Netflix, you'd be a millionaire'...or Apple, Amazon or...). I got it, start early, invest as much as you can afford, be frugal...and enjoy your riches in 50 years. No problem...just get disciplined! (No life stuff should get in the way of your $1 million...like medical, college, elder care, emergencies).

While it's far from calling my work "fluff," it does sprinkle some sarcasm in at the end.

I like to think that my response politely addressed his criticisms.

Carter Kilmann
30 min ago · 1 min read

Thanks for reading, Kevin. I appreciate you taking the time.

My hope was to discourage the belief that investing leads to immediate riches. To that point, I included the Netflix example to do the opposite of what you're suggesting - that you would NOT be a millionaire even if you invested in Netflix's IPO and that it's unreasonable to expect one stock to catapult you to wealth.

You're right, certain life events/expenses can get in the way of saving. That said, I did mention the importance of establishing an emergency fund first in the event you incur a major, unexpected cost.

On top of that, everyone's financial situation is unique, and personal finance is such a broad topic that it's impossible to cover all bases or share universal advice in 1,000 words. The purpose of this post was to merely clear a mental path for readers to see how compound interest can lead to generous returns when you commit to saving.

If you're curious about a more detailed overview of investing or saving, I've written plenty of other posts here: https://medium.com/bacon-bits?

Day 324: November 19, 2020 - 8:18 am (Thursday)

Well, this was a pleasant surprise.

How Quickly Can You Make $1,000,000 by Investi…

3.8K	2.2K	58%	56
views	reads	ratio	fans

9:05 am

Remember when I mentioned that I was growing tired of the random LinkedIn solicitations?

Remember when I said not to send someone four consecutive emails?

Well, one particular LinkedIn connection — the one who missed an introductory phone call back in August (see Day 218) — has sent me EIGHT consecutive messages without a response on my end.

Six through LinkedIn. Two emails.

I'd share all of them, but that seems extensive. I will share the first few and the last two though.

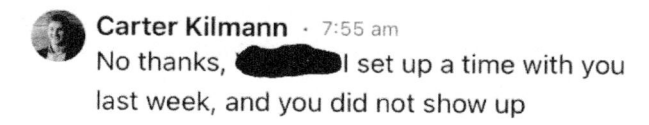

> **Carter Kilmann** · 7:55 am
> No thanks, ▓▓▓ I set up a time with you last week, and you did not show up
>
> ▓▓▓▓▓▓▓ · 3:58 pm
> I did't receive invitation from you last week. 😔 Did you really enter a date and time in my calendar?..
>
> AUG 18
>
> **Carter Kilmann** · 11:50 am
> I misspoke, it was two weeks ago on August 5
>
> AUG 19
>
> ▓▓▓▓▓▓▓ · 5:51 am
> Please accept my sincerest apologies. I am sorry for bothering you.
> It won't happen again.
>
> SEP 1
>
> ▓▓▓▓▓▓▓ · 7:02 am
> Hi Carter !
> I have previously contacted you and would like to gather information about whether you are doing any software development within the company and, if so, how.
> Mostly I receive answers:
> 1. We hire developers at the headquarters. Despite the fact that it is expensive, it is a

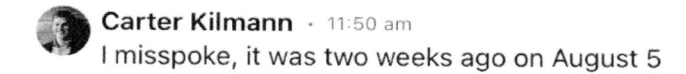

Looking back, maybe I was overly harsh — I just hate being stood up. On top of that, this was around the time I started receiving **tons** of irrelevant sales pitches. It clicked that this call would likely be a waste of time, so I lost all interest in speaking.

She also outright said she wouldn't bother me anymore and then proceeded to launch into a sales pitch two weeks later.

After another five follow-up messages, she moved to email.

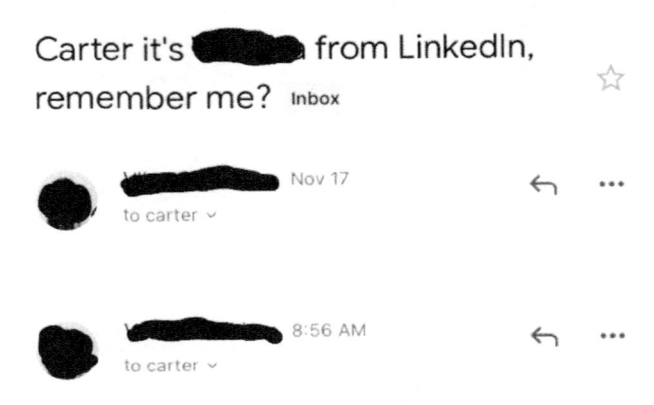

Her resolve is unparalleled, I'll give her that.

First, she used an email as a quasi-text message and reminder. It's just a blank email with a subject. Even better, her follow-up email was merely a resend of the first email.

I know, I could easily put an end to this if I just blocked her or told her to stop contacting me. But, at this point, I'm curious if she'll continue.

She's really embracing "don't take no for an answer."

Day 325: November 20, 2020 - 4:43 pm (Friday)

If you commit enough time to writing about a certain topic, you'll figure out a unique angle.

I spent way more time on a Bacon Bits post today than I anticipated, but I'm not upset about it. The story evolved into something far more interesting than what I initially pictured.

Well, the meat and substance of the post stayed the same, but the headline and introduction sound much more appealing — in my opinion.

My temporary title was "Why you need to invest during downturns," which is an okay title but nothing special. I would've introduced the subject, admitting that retrospective analysis is an oversaturated topic, before arguing that it can be helpful to promote and appreciate long-term outlooks. Then I would dive into the S&P 500's return since the housing market crisis.

However, after contemplating the idea for a bit, I had a better idea: ask readers to rethink the "buy low, sell high" adage in the intro; then, in the body, compare long-term capital appreciation from two points in time: (1) if you would have invested in an S&P 500 index fund at the market's **peak** before the housing crisis crash and (2) if you would have invested in the same fund at the market's **trough** during the crisis.

Not only is it more unique, but it's also more entertaining to write.

Day 326: November 21, 2020 - 4:32 pm (Saturday)

Well, it took longer than I expected, but I hit 800 followers on Medium.

Carter Kilmann

Member since Sep 2020

Freelance Writer & Editor | Personal Finance | Limitless Supplier of Spongebob & Family Guy quotes carter@carterkilmann.com

Editor of Bacon Bits and 365 Days of Freelance Writing

20	800
Following	Followers

What's crazy is I wasn't even that close 10 days ago. My post — How Quickly Can You Make $1,000,000 by Investing — spurred roughly 50 people to follow me.[71]

Day 327: November 22, 2020 - 1:33 pm (Sunday)

Hmm, today's Quora question is intriguing.

Quora

Carter's Digest

TOP STORIES FOR YOU

You can add a zero to any number in your life. Which number do you choose?

The immediate, obvious answer would be a bank account balance — but that seems too easy, right? I want to think of a better one.

Any number is so broad too. Like you could loosely justify *any* response. I guess that's the point.

Here are a few other ideas that come to mind.

1. My IQ (does that entitle me to telekinesis or telepathy?)
2. My squat max
3. My vertical (does that count as flying?)

Boosting my IQ by a full digit is sort of terrifying. That's too much mind power.

I'm not sure if there's much practical value to having inhuman strength in my legs. Plus, jumping over buildings probably isn't good for the ankles.

Ohhhh wait, what about boosting my hourly word output? For instance, if I can write 1,000 words per hour, I'd be able to up that to 10,000.

Man, that'd be nice.

Week 47 Lessons & Takeaways

#1: Why do I let my Medium output lapse? After a long absence, I ramped up my content — and the views are following suit.

#2: Public criticism doesn't matter, your response does. You can choose to ignore someone's negative comments, and that's a respectable decision. But, if you want to settle the matter, you can address the criticism in a polite, yet direct manner. To date, I haven't failed to quash a complaint.

#3: The "never take no for an answer" mentality might not be worth the time and energy at some point. It's hard to draw the line, but I'd say eight consecutive unanswered messages is a fair starting point.

#4: Creativity can be spontaneous at times and deliberate at others. Don't get discouraged if a unique angle doesn't immediately pop into your mind when you're outlining a particular post.

#5: Sure, one post can boost your Medium following, but you still need to consistently publish content. You can't predict virality. Quality always takes precedence, but it's still a numbers game.

Day 328: November 23, 2020 - 9:21 am (Monday)

I don't know whether to be concerned or grateful.

Two high-paying clients, Client J and Client K, have been radio silent. I'm not sure if it's a holiday thing so they're off for a while or something else.

On one hand, I want to continue my income momentum. Without them, I'm back in the $2,000ish per month range. On the other hand, I'm happy to focus on building my Medium following.

What a conflict.

Editor's note: Client J's business went in an entirely different direction, which drove my contacts at the company to leave. I only found out because I messaged them on LinkedIn in January 2021. So, I no longer work with Client J.

Anyway, task time.

This Week (11/15 - 11/21)

1. ~~365 Days of Freelance Writing (x7)~~
2. ~~Client B edits~~
3. ~~Client B client report edits (x2)~~
4. ~~Client K revisions (x5)~~
5. ~~Bacon Bits post~~
6. Bacon Bits post
7. Medium post
8. Bits newsletter

It was a frustrating week in a sense because I had to allocate a lot of my time to Client K revisions. I've already been paid for these scripts, so it didn't feel productive. Otherwise, I made solid headway on Medium content.

Dare I even comment on the newsletter anymore? It's safe to say I'm not prioritizing it, but it's not dead. It's just...sleeping.

This Week (11/22 - 11/28)

1. 365 Days of Freelance Writing (x7)
2. Client B edits
3. Client E post
4. Bacon Bits post
5. Medium post

It's a short work week. I'm taking Thursday and Friday off, so I don't anticipate completing much if I'm being honest.

Day 329: November 24, 2020 - 10:01 pm (Tuesday)

Well, I could have one solution to my income concern. From the sound of it, I think this guy stumbled across my writing for Client E, who (reminder) is in the auto refinance space.

> Hi Carter,
>
> Thanks for responding. I hope you're doing well.
>
> I am looking for a byline author to contribute about once every two weeks or so. The first type of content I need are reviews of existing personal loan programs. A large amount of RV loans are personal loans, and I want content that will educate my readers about the pros and cons of individual loan programs. Take a look at the attachment and let me know if you have questions.
>
> The rate is $0.35 per word. I can send you some programs to cover if you're interested.

I'll take an uncapped $0.35 per word rate. It's not as lucrative as copywriting, but it's certainly not bad.

Day 330: November 25, 2020 - 9:01 am (Wednesday)

Since I don't religiously post on Medium, I never expected to become a top writer under any topic tags.

Well, I am now.

GREAT WORK, CARTER KILMANN

Congratulations! You are now a top writer in Investing.

This milestone will appear on your profile and on the Investing tag page. Learn more about how top writers are selected.

To retain your status, just keep publishing great stories tagged Investing.

[Tweet]   [Share]

STORIES THAT HELPED YOU REACH THIS MILESTONE:

1. **How Quickly Can You Make $1,000,000 by Investing?**
   105 fans · 6.8K views

2. **6 Investing Mistakes to Avoid so You Don't Cripple Your Finances**
   6 fans · 59 views

3. **Buy Low, Buy High...Sell Higher?**
   2 fans · 21 views

You don't need to be Neil deGrasse Tyson to figure out what led to this status. The first investing post garnered a lot of attention. The second and third posts just checked the "frequency" box.

What's also interesting is that distribution doesn't matter. Medium only distributed the first post — if you can't tell from the pitiful view counts.

From what I've read, it's pretty easy to lose your tag if you stop writing. So, I'm setting the bar low now; I don't expect to retain my status forever.

Editor's note: As of July 2021, I'm still a top writer in "Investing."

Day 331: November 26, 2020 - 9:46 am (Thursday)

Happy Thanksgiving, my dear readers.

In light of the holiday, I'm keeping today's entry short.

I just want to express how thankful I am to have such life satisfaction. Of course, some days as an entrepreneur are hard. The uncertainty of it all can induce anxiety and tax my emotions. But the upsides outweigh the downsides like an elephant does a church mouse.

Mostly because I have an incredible support system of friends and family — especially my head cheerleader, Kaileigh.

It's easy to get swept up in the madness of running your own business and being the sole driver of your success, but don't forget to take a step back and appreciate what the madness allows you to do.

Day 332: November 27, 2020 - 11:22 am (Friday)

While I don't think it's a requirement, writers can take online courses to achieve certifications in relevant business areas, such as social media marketing or email marketing. Then you can display your certifications on your website or LinkedIn profile, which provides credibility. It can be particularly helpful if you're totally new to writing and don't have a portfolio.

Your portfolio will always trump anything else in terms of proving your worth as a writer, but specialty certifications can help bridge the gap if your portfolio is still a work in progress.

From what I've seen, HubSpot is the most popular and recognizable platform to take digital marketing courses on.[72] So, I recommend starting there.

Day 333: November 28, 2020 - 9:29 am (Saturday)

Even though it's work in a sense, I like having this daily writing requirement. It's something I hope to continue next year in the form of Medium posts.

Not that I anticipate 365 Medium posts next year. That would be exhausting.

But I think I can at least contribute 300-500 words a day to blog posts, which would bump up my typical output by a considerable amount.

Day 334: November 29, 2020 - 10:03 am (Sunday)

As I mentioned a week ago, Client K has been radio silent — and it's making me uncomfortable.

Thankfully, they weren't silent when it came to my invoice, which was just approved.

At least I'm getting paid.

Editor's note: Client K decided to handle all copywriting projects internally, so I don't work with them anymore.

In other news, I'm headed back to Atlanta to resume my usual work and life routine. I'll miss the spaciousness of a house, but there'll be less temptation to lounge or do something unrelated to work.

Week 48 Lessons & Takeaways

#1: Radio silence is not rare...which, yeah, kind of sucks. When clients disappear for weeks or even months at a time, it's frustrating. Freelancing is volatile enough as it is, uncommunicative clients don't help foster a sense of stability. The best you can do is impress upon your point of contact that you appreciate open lines of communication.

#2: The more content you write, the greater the chance of inbound work requests. My work for Client E (I'm assuming) appealed to someone enough that they decided to reach out and offer work.

#3: Hey, here's a surprise: I'm a top writer in "Investing." My recipe for success? Frequency and luck.

#4: Freelance writing is a grind. Don't forget to look up and appreciate what you have.

#5: From an optics standpoint, certifications can offset a small portfolio — at least, to an extent. Check out HubSpot's certifications, their programs are popular and their brand is recognizable.

#6: Daily writing requirements pay off in the long term. Who knows, maybe I'll write another book next year using the same formula.

Day 335: November 30, 2020 - 9:31 am (Monday)

An interesting opportunity popped up in my inbox this morning.

> Hi Carter,
>
> I saw your Medium profile, wanted to ask - are you also open to advertising? I am interested to promote my investing game. Let me know if you are open for that,

Sounds like an advertorial. I'm not opposed if the product and payment are solid. We'll see what she says.

In the meantime, *task* time.

Weekly Tasks (11/22 - 11/28)

1. ~~365 Days of Freelance Writing (x7)~~
2. ~~Client B edits~~
3. Client E post
4. Bacon Bits post
5. Medium post
6. Medium post

It's about as much as I could expect. I took Thursday and Friday off — for the most part — but I still got a decent amount of writing in.

Weekly Tasks (11/29 - 12/5)

1. 365 Days of Freelance Writing (x7)
2. Client B edits
3. Client E post
4. Client K revision
5. Client L post
6. Bacon Bits post
7. Medium post
8. Medium advertorial outline
9. November invoices

This week, I'm ramping up expectations. Beyond the usual names, you'll see an assignment for a new client, Client L. It's a review of an RV financing company, so nothing too crazy.

NOVEMBER STATS

A lot of good things happened in November. My Medium views skyrocketed, which helped me become a top writer in "Investing." Two potential clients reached out about working together. The Packers demolished the Bears.

But there was a major downer — Client J and Client K disappeared. As far as I know, nothing of my doing spurred the radio silence, so I'm quite perplexed. In turn, my income plummeted in November as quickly as it surged in October.

As a reminder, here's each client's description:

- Client A — Digital marketing agency
- Client B — Digital marketing agency (editing work)
- Client C — FinTech startup (no longer a client)
- Client D — Online finance publication (content freeze)
- Client E — Auto finance company
- Client F — ClearVoice assignments
- Client G — SaaS company (no longer a client, for now)
- Client H — Writing Revolt
- Client I — Consulting firm

- Client J — FinTech startup
- Client K — Digital marketing agency (copywriting)
- Client L — RV finance site
- Client M — Medium advertorial

365 Days of Freelancing - Monthly Stats

	Jan	Feb	Mar	Apr	May	Jun	Jul	Aug	Sep	Oct	Nov
Income											
Client A	960	960	960	640	480	480	480	-	480	480	480
Client B	329	119	153	189	741	430	415	706	163	283	468
Client C	500	-	-	-	-	-	-	-	-	-	-
Client D	350	350	-	-	-	-	-	-	-	-	-
Client E	-	450	450	900	450	1,000	450	450	900	1,050	500
Client F	-	225	-	-	-	338	-	-	-	-	-
Client G	-	200	-	-	-	-	-	-	-	-	-
Client H	-	-	-	-	400	-	-	-	-	-	-
Client I	-	-	-	-	-	265	-	-	-	-	-
Client J	-	-	-	-	-	-	-	1,337	2,100	1,088	-
Client K	-	-	-	-	-	-	-	-	250	4,200	-
Client L	-	-	-	-	-	-	-	-	-	-	-
Client M	-	-	-	-	-	-	-	-	-	-	-
Medium	32	21	719	734	505	496	147	137	110	49	282
Total Income	$2,171	$2,325	$2,282	$2,463	$2,576	$3,009	$1,492	$2,630	$4,003	$7,150	$1,730
Growth (%)	-	7.1%	(1.9%)	7.9%	4.6%	16.8%	(50.4%)	76.2%	52.2%	78.6%	(75.8%)
Blog Posts (Paid)											
Client A	6	6	6	4	3	3	3	-	3	3	3
Client B	3	2	2	2	9	4	6	8	2	4	7
Client C	1	1	-	-	-	-	-	-	-	-	-
Client D	1	1	-	-	-	-	-	-	-	-	-
Client E	-	1	1	2	1	2	1	1	2	2	1
Client F	-	2	-	-	-	1	-	-	-	-	-
Client G	-	1	-	-	-	-	-	-	-	-	-
Client H	-	-	-	-	1	-	-	-	-	-	-
Client I	-	-	-	-	-	1	-	-	-	-	-
Client L	-	-	-	-	-	-	-	-	-	-	-
Total Paid Posts	11	14	9	8	14	11	10	9	7	9	11
Blog Posts (Unpaid)											
Medium	1	-	-	1	4	-	1	-	1	2	1
Bacon Bits	1	2	4	2	1	1	2	2	-	-	3
365	-	-	-	2	-	-	4	1	-	-	1
Total Unpaid Posts	2	2	4	5	5	1	7	3	1	2	5
Total Blog Posts	13	16	13	13	19	12	17	12	8	11	16
Copywriting Assignments											
Client C	5	-	-	-	-	-	-	-	-	-	-
Client J	-	-	-	-	-	-	-	3	2	2	-
Client K	-	-	-	-	-	-	-	-	1	12	-
Total Copywriting Asgns.	5	-	-	-	-	-	-	3	3	14	-
Total Assignments	18	16	13	13	19	12	17	15	11	25	16
Medium											
Views	1,151	1,352	19,466	11,052	15,778	8,562	4,552	4,945	3,522	1,906	10,705
Reads	439	468	7,413	4,220	6,320	3,651	1,947	2,055	1,438	776	6,077
Read Ratio	38%	35%	38%	38%	40%	43%	43%	42%	41%	41%	57%
Existing Followers	54	63	80	238	371	530	595	645	702	733	745
New Followers	9	17	158	133	159	65	50	57	31	12	86
Total Followers	63	80	238	371	530	595	645	702	733	745	831
LinkedIn											
Existing Followers	458	465	493	526	570	590	599	613	624	637	642
New Followers	7	28	33	44	20	9	14	11	13	5	11
Total Followers	465	493	526	570	590	599	613	624	637	642	653

Highlights

- It was almost another record-setting month — the bad kind though. I put forth my second-lowest income total ($1,730). My usual regulars (Clients A, B, and E) kept things afloat, but less than $2,000 a month won't cut it.
- Paging Clients J and K….can you hear me?
- The good news is that my Medium output and stats rebounded. I published five points and have several drafts in progress. My views popped back, crossing 10,000 again. On top of that, my read ratio was the highest it's ever been at 57%.

DECEMBER

Day 336: December 1, 2020 - 9:10 am (Tuesday)

So, about that Client L assignment...

Client L seems to be a newish company, so they don't have a well-established content marketing system. As a result, I'm writing this review without much direction.

The polar opposite approach compared to Client E, who provides a detailed assignment brief that includes keywords, key questions, a style guide, etc.

It's fine — I don't mean to quibble — but my review will require more upfront research. That $0.35 rate is a little less appealing when you factor in reading through a lender's website and financing terms.

Day 337: December 2, 2020 - 2:03 pm (Wednesday)

Here are my most successful Medium titles. Do you see a pattern?

- How I Cut My Monthly Expenses by 32%
- How Quickly Can You Make $1,000,000 by Investing?
- How I Landed 3 Clients in My First Week of Self-Employment
- How to Take Advantage of the Down Market Before It Rebounds
- Quitting Corporate: Why I Chose Happiness Over Money

Explaining "how" seems to be what gets the most attention. If you were to break these down into a simple, replicable formula, it's pretty much this: How X can Y.

I think I'll write a blog post about this.

Day 338: December 3, 2020 - 5:14 pm (Thursday)

Is it just me, or is Facebook messenger a creepy app?

I received a random friend request from this person at some point last night. At 8:35 am, I accepted, assuming it could be a business inquiry. Seconds later — and I'm not exaggerating when I say *seconds* — I received a solemn "Hello" from Maria. Mirroring her formal fashion, I responded with a "Good morning." Then this stranger hit me with two trivial questions.

> Hello
>
> Good morning
>
> Morning
>
> How are you doing
>
> My name is Maria from Texas and you?
>
> 9:22 AM
>
> I'm doing well, is there something I can help you with?

Considering my name and location are staring her in the face, I elected to answer the first question alone and then accelerate past the unwanted pleasantries.

Then...nothing.

Here we are, eight hours later, and she left me on read.

Who does this?

Look, if you're going to market on Facebook or reach out to strangers, get to the point immediately.

Day 339: December 4, 2020 - 11:23 am (Friday)

Woooooof.

I was quoted $2,500 to $3,000 for editing my book. I knew this would be an investment, but sweet peanuts that price range seems high.

Is it unheard of to have another writer do it for cheaper? I'll have to shop around and report back.

Wish me (and my wallet) luck.

Editor's note: I decided to do most of the heavy lifting myself. It saved money, but it's a time-consuming process. I also had a couple of generous friends serve as beta readers.

Day 340: December 5, 2020 - 10:22 am (Saturday)

As you know, I love reading about other writers' performance assessments. It can introduce new angles on business analytics and writing approaches. The latest comes from Zulie Rane, who I mentioned a while back (Day 260).

Zulie isn't just a writer, she's a business owner. She knows the importance of developing and maintaining multiple income streams — the path to stability and wealth.

In her latest Medium post, she shared her November income report, which includes implied hourly rates for each income stream.[73]

Client	Project	Money	Hours	Hourly Rate
Self	Medium	$3,187.92	11.55	276.01
	YouTube	$259.08	19.85	13.05
	Website (zuliewrites.com)	$0.00	1.32	0.00
	Profile	$0.00	0.91	0.00
	Newsletter (ConvertKit)	$0.00	0.32	0.00
	Patreon	$197.00	6.55	30.08
	Sum	$3,447.00	40.50	85.12
Client 1	Writing	$600.00	4.15	144.58
	Meetings	$0.00	0.00	0.00
	Sum	$600.00	4.15	144.58
Client 2	Writing	$2,077.50	10.57	196.61
Client 3	Writing	$250.00	1.78	140.19
	Meeting	$0.00	0.12	0.00
	Sum	$250.00	1.90	131.35

Zulie's keen business instincts are further exemplified by her hourly breakdown. She knows the importance of billable time too.

Tracking time can open your eyes. It's something I should implement into my routine. I track my assignments when they pay hourly rates, but that's about it. I don't measure how long it takes to complete a Medium post, for instance.

Also, how nuts is that implied Medium rate? $276 per hour?!

My goodness.

Day 341: December 6, 2020 - 12:12 pm (Sunday)

For someone that's attuned to personal finance, I have a disappointing statement to make.

I forgot I had a SEP-IRA with Wealthfront.

Well, maybe "forgot" isn't the right word. I know I have one, but I haven't checked my account in months. I've been making contributions to my Fidelity accounts instead.

Tomorrow is my monthly "finance day," during which I'll shift savings to my brokerage accounts and make sure everything is on track. So, I'll be sure to make a contribution to my SEP-IRA too.

Considering I write about finance **a lot**, is it strange that I don't write about it here much?

Week 49 Lessons & Takeaways

#1: Medium advertorials can be another route to making money on the platform.

#2: When calculating an appropriate rate for an assignment, don't forget about upfront research.

#3: My most successful Medium posts answer "how-to" questions.

#4: Facebook Messenger is a creepy place.

#5: Damn, book editing is expensive. I was quoted $2,500 to $3,000.

#6: If you want to maximize your time, track it. I've been bad about tracking and analyzing how I spend my time, but I'm going to work on it.

#7: If you run your own business, you should have a SEP-IRA for your retirement savings. Your annual contribution cap is much higher in a SEP than it is in a normal IRA. For 2020, the maximum contribution is the lesser of (a) 25% of your compensation or (b) $57,000.[74]

Editor's note: ***This isn't financial advice*** So, I would eventually learn that it's smarter to make retirement contributions once you know your final income for the year. Otherwise, you risk contributing more *than you're permitted to and incurring a penalty. The contribution I make tomorrow wound up pushing me over that limit. I had to go through an annoying process to have my contribution amount corrected. Long story short, hire an accountant.*

Day 342: December 7, 2020 - 11:05 am (Monday)

Jeez, we're already a week into December. Not only is Christmas less than three weeks away, but this book's conclusion is also on the horizon.

There's so much to do ahead of my union-mandated vacation time. WOOF.

Obviously, I'm joking — but I plan to take time off at the tail end of the month, so I need productivity to be at an all-time high.

With that in mind, task time.

This Week (11/29 - 12/5)

1. ~~365 Days of Freelance Writing (x7)~~
2. ~~Client B edits~~
3. ~~Client E post~~
4. Client K revision
5. ~~Client L post~~
6. Bacon Bits post
7. Medium post
8. Medium post
9. ~~Medium advertorial outline~~
10. ~~November invoices~~

It was a decent week overall. I need to push a few medium posts across the finish line though; I have like seven posts that are well into development.

This Week (12/6 - 12/12)

1. 365 Days of Freelance Writing (x7)
2. Client A posts (x2)
3. Client B edits
4. Client E post edits
5. Client K revision
6. Bacon Bits post
7. Medium post
8. Medium post
9. GN review

After reading Zulie's income report and time-tracking sheet, I'm going to follow suit and track my hours as well.

I already know this is going to expose some productivity flaws in my schedule...

5:11 pm

Here's how my first day of time-tracking went. I didn't get started until 11 am, so it's been an abbreviated workday. I cleaned the apartment this morning, did laundry, worked out, and made breakfast.

So, keep that in mind...

Task	Time
Task List	9 minutes
Finance Day	38 minutes
365 Days of Freelance Writing	20 minutes
Game Review	1 hour 16 minutes
Total	**2 hours 24 minutes**

That's telling.

Shane Beamer was also introduced as the Gamecocks' new head coach, so that press conference cut into my afternoon a bit.

Yeah, I know — that's unacceptable.

I need to do better.

Day 343: December 8, 2020 - 9:48 am (Tuesday)

Alright, I put an end to my enduring, one-sided conversation with that LinkedIn solicitor.

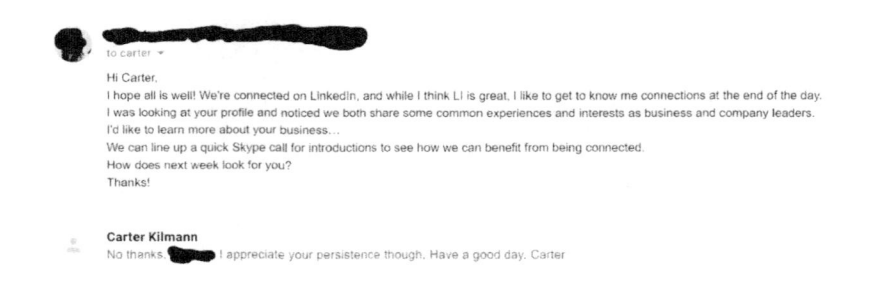

> to carter
>
> Hi Carter,
> I hope all is well! We're connected on LinkedIn, and while I think LI is great, I like to get to know me connections at the end of the day. I was looking at your profile and noticed we both share some common experiences and interests as business and company leaders. I'd like to learn more about your business...
> We can line up a quick Skype call for introductions to see how we can benefit from being connected.
> How does next week look for you?
> Thanks!
>
> **Carter Kilmann**
> No thanks. ▇▇▇ I appreciate your persistence though. Have a good day. Carter

6:00 pm

My second day of time-tracking was almost twice as productive, but I still have room for improvement. I think banking rewired my brain to correlate work ethic with urgency. When I'm up against multiple impending deadlines, I can **grind**. But I tend to take my foot off the gas when that urgency dissipates.

At my old job, I had tight turnaround times every week. The urgency never waned. Nowadays, it's intermittent.

I need to rewire my brain again.

Task	Time
Client A Outlines & Research	1 hour 12 minutes
Medium Advertorial	10 minutes
365 Days of Freelance Writing	21 minutes
Game Review	2 hours 31 minutes
Total	**4 hours 15 minutes**

Editor's note: I highly recommend tracking your time. I've tracked my time ever since these entries, and my productivity and efficiency have improved exponentially.

Day 344: December 9, 2020 - 2:22 pm (Wednesday)

What makes a good freelance writer?

It's not writing ability — or even a keen eye for detail. Of course, those traits help writing quality, but to be a good *freelance* writer, you need two abilities.

Time management and work ethic.

If you can't be productive with your time, you'll struggle.

Am I a good freelance writer?

I'm a good writer, but I'm still working on the freelance part. You've had a first-hand account of my efforts to live and work by a weekly schedule. I've mentioned I need to instill a sense of urgency even when assignments aren't urgent. It's not an overnight process, but I think I'm getting there.

Day 345: December 10, 2020 - 8:23 am (Thursday)

If I haven't sold you on freelance writing by now, you're probably not pursuing this career path. But there's a benefit of this career that's sometimes lacking in the corporate world: you're learning something new every day. New concepts, beliefs, methods, ideas, and so on.

I'm currently writing that Medium advertorial about forex, which is a topic I hadn't explored much before. Meanwhile, if I were still in my banking role, I'd be learning a TON about the same topic each and every day.

Freelancing empowers you with the independence to explore diverse subjects and expand your knowledge.

Day 346: December 11, 2020 - 1:35 pm (Friday)

I compiled an overview of my implied hourly rates thus far:

Client	Project	Completed	Payment	Hours	Implied Hourly Rate
Client A	Blog Post	12/10/2020	160.00	2.35	68.09
Client A	Blog Post	12/10/2020	160.00	1.82	88.07
Client L	Blog Post	12/4/2020	584.85	9.07	64.51
Client B	Edits	12/3/2020	79.17	1.58	50.00
			$984.02	14.82	$66.41

Not too shabby. I wrote my assignment for Client L before this time-tracking experiment, so my hourly input is a rough approximation (I aggregated the Google Document's revision history hours). I'd like to make at least $75 an hour, but my goal is to exceed $100 an hour.

Also, Client B has a fixed hourly rate of $50, so that'll weigh down my overall implied rate.

I still have a few client assignments left, so I'll revisit this table at the end of the month to see if I've improved.

Day 347: December 12, 2020 - 10:30 am (Saturday)

I just finished reading a Medium post, and I liked a particular sentence.

"Perfectionism" is just another fancy word for procrastination.

It's a painful truth to accept and overcome. I struggle with it every time I write.

Day 348: December 13, 2020 - 4:33 pm (Sunday)

It's easy to slip into this "I need to" mindset when you're self-employed.

I need to connect with more writers.

I need to write a newsletter.

I need to update my website.

I need to be more active on social media.

I need to organize my finances.

I need to figure out my health insurance.

I need to hire an accountant.

It's a lot for one person to manage. The way I see it, you have two options:

1. Outsource responsibilities
2. Organize your time, set realistic expectations, and prioritize these tasks

If personal finance isn't your thing, you can hire an accountant for bookkeeping and taxes. If social media isn't your thing, you can hire a digital marketer. These services come at a price, but you have to think in terms of dollars **and** time — not just dollars. More time means more billable hours or personal projects.

Or, if you're committed to the DIY-approach, you'll need to incorporate structure into your routine to ensure you accomplish as much as possible. You might need to table certain "want to" projects to make time for "need to" projects.

Week 50 Lessons & Takeaways

#1: Track your time. I'm late to the game, but it's worth it.

#2: I need to rewire my brain. Banking caused me to correlate work ethic with urgency. I know how to grind when I need to, but it's the slow periods that kill my productivity.

#3: Time management and work ethic are the primary traits of a good freelance writer.

#4: You can use freelance writing to explore a bunch of diverse topics. I never imagined learning so much about healthcare, auto financing, and digital marketing.

#5: It's helpful to track and assess your implied hourly rate. Money is great, but time is the ultimate currency. If you can do more with less, you'll have far more flexibility and freedom. A $200 assignment sounds appealing, but what if it takes 10 hours to complete? Not as enticing anymore. A measly $20 hourly rate limits your capacity and earning potential. But if you can complete a $200 assignment in 30 minutes, your implied rate is a stratospheric $400 per hour. A much different story.

#6: Perfectionism is a fancier word for procrastination.

#7: If you're feeling overwhelmed by your business responsibilities, it might be time to outsource.

Day 349: December 14, 2020 - 10:30 am (Monday)

We're nearing the end of our weekly task time sessions.

Even though completing this book won't stop me from tracking tasks, it'll feel strange to not share them here anymore.

Last week was a little slow from a client work standpoint. I expected work from Clients B and E, but nothing appeared in my inbox. Instead, I focused on a pair of Client A posts, Medium, and a game review — which tend to take longer than I'd like them to. *I need to fix that.*

Last Week (12/6 - 12/12)

1. 365 Days of Freelance Writing (x7)
2. ~~Client A posts (x2)~~
3. Client B edits
4. Client E post edits
5. Client K revision
6. ~~Bacon Bits post~~
7. Medium post
8. ~~Medium post~~
9. ~~GN review~~

I've got plenty to do before my Christmas vacation (specific days are TBD).

Let's go.

This Week (12/13 - 12/19)

1. 365 Days of Freelance Writing (x7)
2. Client A post
3. Client B edits
4. Client K revision
5. Client L review
6. Bacon Bits post
7. Bacon Bits post
8. 365 DFW post

2:22 pm

Reinvesting in your business is hard.

I know, I know — yesterday's post literally suggested outsourcing responsibilities, which is a form of business reinvestment. But it's still easier said than done.

My domain registration just auto-renewed for another three years, which is a chunky $600 flowing out of my bank account. Happy three-year anniversary to my website, I guess.

On top of that, I'm considering a marketing campaign for my book, which is looking pricey too.

It just feels weird to front money that's not guaranteed to be recouped. I'm well aware of the premise of paid advertising — spending money to make money — but I've never experienced it firsthand. Outside of a website, I haven't relied on paid marketing whatsoever.

Day 350: December 15, 2020 - 2:21 pm (Tuesday)

To be a successful freelance writer, you need thick skin.

Of course, I'm not saying you can't feel down or that you should ignore your emotions. But the self-esteem of a freelance writer is bound to endure a few blows from time to time.

Rejection is discouraging. Comparing your progress to more prominent and successful writers is discouraging. Criticism from a new client is discouraging. Animosity from a complete stranger who seems to have a baseless vendetta against you is discouraging.

But these things happen. You'll be rejected more than accepted. Whether you intend to or not, you'll compare yourself to other writers. You'll have clients who dislike your work. You'll have random readers hate you for no good reason.

It comes with the territory.

Day 351: December 16, 2020 - 10:38 am (Wednesday)

How many hours a day does a freelance writer work? With my time charts, I've provided some insight into that already, but I think it's important to shed more light on the topic.

While my workdays start sometime between 9:00 and 10:00 am and end around 5:00 or 6:00 pm, that doesn't mean I get in a full eight or nine-hour workday. Making food, taking breaks, and managing other life responsibilities all detract from that time.

On top of that, a freelancer's schedule will vary depending on workload and general desire to work more or less. That's the beauty of it.

While I haven't been the best about tracking my time up until now, I'm sure I've worked plenty of legitimate 40 "billable" hour weeks in the past year. October was a prime example. I had TONS of client work, and I was determined to power through it, starting work early and ending later.

On top of THAT, it's also a different story if you're talking about someone who's new to freelancing compared to someone who's established. I'm by no means a veteran, but my infrastructure is in place. I have a portfolio, a website, clients, business accounts, financial spreadsheets, creative processes, and a general work routine.

You don't start down this career path with any of those things. You have to establish them, which requires a lot more upfront time.

Day 352: December 17, 2020 - 7:52 am (Thursday)

I feel targeted.

Two of Medium's suggested daily reads were on the nose:

1. "How to Overcome Perfectionism and Just Write the Thing"[75]

2. "Your Blog Posts Don't Always Need to Be That Long, Okay?"[76]

Medium knows my writing vices. I'm a perfectionist writer, which means I can't help but edit and fine-tune as I go. *I'm working on it though, and I'm getting better.* I also have a tendency to lengthen my Medium posts without realizing it. Sometimes it's necessary content, sometimes it's unnecessary fluff.

In the first piece, Shaunta Grimes offers a few solutions, but one is unique to me: write a "zero draft." It's a pre-draft that you use to tell yourself the story you're about to write about. It sheds the structure and formality of a polished product and adopts a conversational flow. Even though she's speaking about novel writing, it can still apply to shorter forms of content.

In the second post, Tom Kuegler's solution is simple: just accept it. Normalize short blog posts. In fact, your readers might appreciate it more since it'll take them less time to read. He stresses the importance of "less is more" even in a time where long-form content is the norm.

Perfectionism and overly lengthy blog posts are common issues for writers, myself included.

Day 353: December 18, 2020 - 2:00 pm (Friday)

An invaluable benefit of tracking your time: becoming a more efficient worker. I feel like I'm getting a lot more done in less time. Since I know I'm against the clock, in a way, I'm more determined to crank through my tasks.

Day 354: December 19, 2020 - 11:02 am (Saturday)

Could you imagine trying to explain social media to someone from the early 20th century?

One hundred years ago, back when people rolled around in Model Ts, jazz was all the rage, the economy boomed after the First World War, the Roaring Twenties were just getting underway...

Imagine handpicking a stranger from a crowd in 1920 — someone who has no concept of a television much less a computer and internet connectivity — and explaining Twitter.

How would you even go about that?

It's a byproduct of several technologies, so I guess I'd first explain computers, the Internet, smartphones, and apps. Only then could I start educating the stranger about the prevalence and interconnectivity of social media — except, by now, they'd likely be distraught. Imagine their face once I shared how millions of people mindlessly scroll through mostly irrelevant quips, trivial nonsense, and — of course — memes.

They'd report me. I'd be institutionalized. They'd be institutionalized. Both of us would be lobotomized.

Day 355: December 20, 2020 - 11:39 am (Sunday)

In 2020, PayPal kept $177.55 of my hard-earned dough in exchange for processing said dough.

It's not a backbreaking amount of money, but I still don't like paying for a service with cheaper alternatives. I use Veem when I can (since it's free), but one-off clients typically haven't heard of it and aren't willing to sign up for a new payment processor just to pay one bill.

You might be stuck with PayPal at times. The trick is to work with a client for a month or two, prove your worth, and then ask about their willingness to try a platform like Veem. I plan to do this for Client L in the next month or so.

Editor's note: If you're reading the eBook version of 365 Days of Freelance Writing, that link to Veem's website is an affiliate link. I receive a commission if you sign up using that link.

Week 51 Lessons & Takeaways

#1: Paying for marketing can be tough to wrap your head around. It's a necessary cost, but the benefits aren't always immediate — results can take a while.

#2: Freelance writing isn't all rainbows and butterflies. Rejection is common. People are rude and, sometimes, downright hateful. You need thick skin to survive.

#3: How many hours does a freelance writer work? It depends on their income wants/needs and where they are in their freelancing career.

#4: Perfectionism and fluff content are two common writing vices. If you're a perfectionist, try a zero draft, which is more like a laidback conversation about what you plan to write. If you tend to write fluff, recognize this issue and accept that longer doesn't mean better. You can also try stricter editing. Shorten lengthy sentences that have a bunch of clauses. Delete valueless paragraphs that appeal to you more than they appeal to the reader.

#5: Tracking your time will help you be more productive. In about two weeks, I've already noticed a significant improvement.

#6: PayPal fees add up. To date, I've paid $177.55 to PayPal for processing invoices. If you can, try free platforms like Veem to lessen this cost burden.

Day 356: December 21, 2020 - 12:33 pm (Monday)

Guess which one of my Medium articles ranks on the second page of Google?

"Idioms Are Weird. Why Did Curiosity Kill the Cat?"

If you guessed it, I'm in awe.

I wrote this a while back just to try something different. It was fun to write, and I hope it attracted a few chuckles, but it didn't fare too well in terms of viewership. In its first month, it only garnered 52 views. I expected this minimal interest to fizzle out and die.

Nope. This post continues to attract a handful of readers each month.

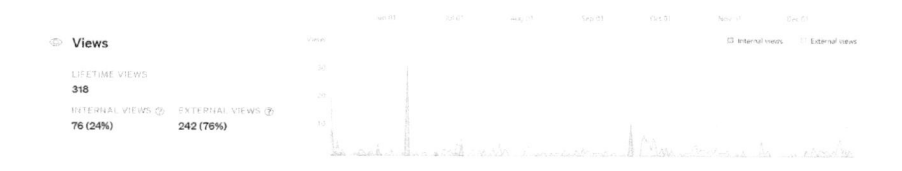

And, as you can see, they're mostly external views. Since Medium lists external sources of traffic, I can see that Google is responsible for 122 of those views.

VIEWS BY TRAFFIC SOURCE	317
Internal	24%
External referrals	76%
google.com	122
email, IM, and direct	103
www.bing.com	9
search.yahoo.com	4
duckduckgo.com	2
ecosia.org	1

Funny enough, I'm on the second SERP for the following keyword phrases:

1. "curiosity killed the cat"
2. "why did curiosity kill the cat?"
3. "the origin of curiosity killed the cat"

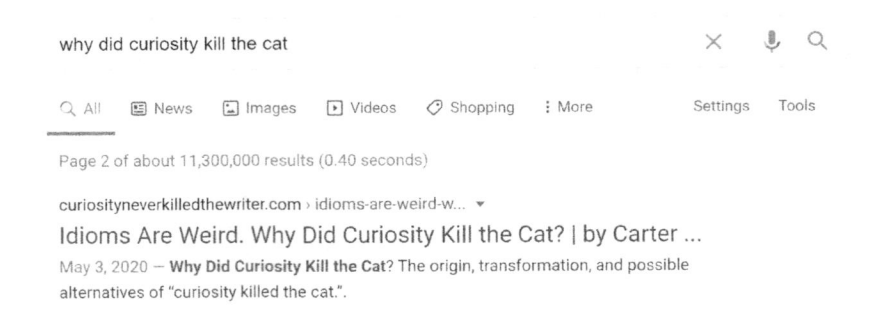

why did curiosity kill the cat	× 🎤 🔍
🔍 All 📰 News 🖼 Images ▶ Videos 🛍 Shopping ⋮ More	Settings Tools

Page 2 of about 11,300,000 results (0.40 seconds)

curiosityneverkilledthewriter.com › idioms-are-weird-w... ▾
Idioms Are Weird. Why Did Curiosity Kill the Cat? | by Carter ...
May 3, 2020 — **Why Did Curiosity Kill the Cat**? The origin, transformation, and possible alternatives of "curiosity killed the cat.".

I don't try to optimize my Medium articles for SEO. The Medium Partner Program doesn't pay you for external views. Then again, if you're promoting a product or service, Google traffic is super valuable because you can direct traffic to another page.

Day 357: December 22, 2020 - 1:04 pm (Tuesday)

I'm jittery. Can't focus for prolonged periods. Productivity waning.

Too much coffee.

Day 358: December 23, 2020 - 2:39 pm (Wednesday)

I'm hustling to finish two Client E assignments by the end of the day so that I can take tomorrow and Friday off.

I also started looking into the book publishing process. Man, there's a lot to do.

I still have to…

1. Finish writing it (obviously)
2. Proofread

3. Hire an editor
4. Format
5. Design a book cover

And that's just to produce a finished product. Marketing is another time-intensive story.

Day 359: December 24, 2020 - 8:07 am (Thursday)

Oh no.

My stomach dropped at the thought of this tweet by A Purple Life:

"This is a friendly reminder to check what you and your loved ones are invested in (if they invest). Just discovered a friend in their 60s thought they invested their 401K in the stock market...turns out it was in a money market (aka savings) account the whole time. Fuuuuuuuck."

I can't imagine the shock, embarrassment, frustration, and disappointment all blurred into one horrible amalgam of human sensation.

I hope this person had investments beyond their 401k and that they weren't banking on this for retirement.

If you're a hands-off investor, check on your investments to ensure they're aligned with your needs and goals. If you're still in the corporate world, reevaluate your 401k allocations for the same purpose — and make sure you're maximizing your employer's matching benefit. Why leave money on the table that you're entitled to?

Man, the thought of this kills me. I'm distraught for this person.

1:15 pm

Finished. My client work for 2020 is complete and delivered.

Now I can relax, dabble with some Medium writing from time to time, and enjoy a break. It's a pleasant relief.

Day 360: December 25, 2020 - 10:03 am (Friday)

Merry Christmas!

You know what I've always found bizarre? Christmas Day itself is a bit of a downer. I guess that's because the festivity concludes and we begin looking ahead to 2021.

Anyway, Tuesday's Google ranking discovery got me thinking about the rest of my portfolio. I'm not sure if any of my other Medium posts rank on Google, but I optimize my Client E assignments for search engines. I should say "we" because my editor does all the upfront SEO analysis.

As it turns out, **a lot** of my articles rank on the first page for the keywords we focused on.

I feel like I should include this on my LinkedIn page or something.

Day 361: December 26, 2020 - 9:28 am (Saturday)

I had an interesting call this past week, which I forgot to mention.

I spoke with Nick Rimsa, a product designer at Tortoise Labs who reached out to ask me about my Medium strategy. After questioning the "whats" and "whys" of my Medium process and goals, he asked if I'd ever heard of Buy Me a Coffee, which implements a unique spin on article CTAs. It lessens the blunt greediness of asking readers for monetary tips. Instead, readers can donate under the guise of "buying you a coffee."

Does it make or break a writer's month? No, probably not. But an extra $50 to $100 adds up over time.

Nick's trying something similar but without the java. He's targeting the finance-focused demographic by changing the CTA to "buy me a stock."[77]

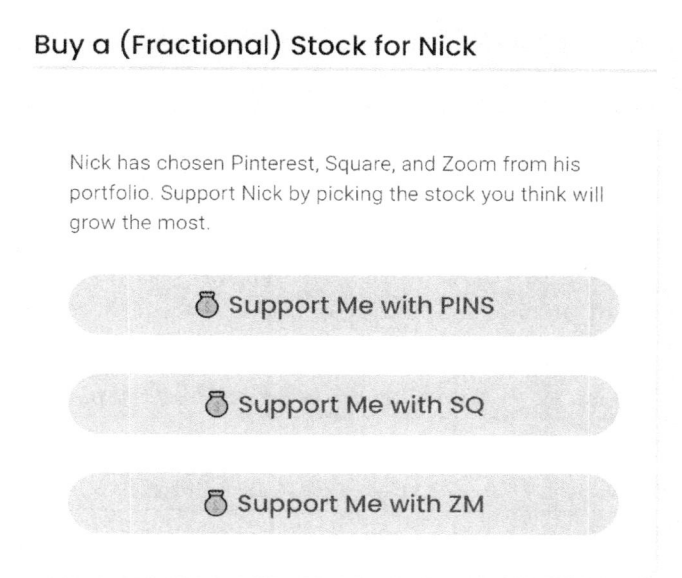

> **Buy a (Fractional) Stock for Nick**
>
> Nick has chosen Pinterest, Square, and Zoom from his portfolio. Support Nick by picking the stock you think will grow the most.
>
> 💰 Support Me with PINS
>
> 💰 Support Me with SQ
>
> 💰 Support Me with ZM

Creative, right?

The way I see it, this idea achieves two major accomplishments. First, it opens up another revenue stream for writers. Second, it targets the finance community, which is a highly profitable niche.

He says it's had success so far, which I don't doubt. If I've learned anything about marketing, it's that targeted content performs well.

Day 362: December 27, 2020 - 6:07 am (Sunday)

I got to the airport way too early. My flight departs…*sarcastically checks watch*…two hours from now.

I'm already at the gate.

By myself.

Well, that's not totally true. There's a security guard FaceTiming a friend, discussing Wendy's burgers at six in the morning.

Oh, and there's a dude draped by an arctic parka passed out in the corner.

I suppose now is a good time to talk about something I read yesterday that's been on my mind. The post outlined a particular writer's typical workday.

By now, I hope my daily routine is evident; however, in case it isn't, I've laid out a quick synopsis:

6:45 - 7:15 am	Wake up (a critical first step)
7:30 - 9:00 am	Exercise
9:00 - 10:00 am	Eat breakfast and shower
10:00 - 11:30 am	Work
11:30 - 12:00 pm	Snack break (I'm always hungry, it's a curse)
12:00 - 2:00 pm	Work
2:00 - 3:00 pm	Eat lunch and take a walk
3:00 pm - EOD*	Work

*My typical workday ends a little after 5:00 pm, but it's not uncommon for me to work until 6:00 or 6:30 pm.

No day is the exact same though. Sometimes I get started as early as 8:30 or 9:00 am. Other days I end at 4:00 pm if I'm happy with my progress.

Week 52 Lessons & Takeaways

#1: Publishing a book is a helluva process.

#2: Monitor. Your. Investments. Or else you could wind up like the poor sucker who didn't realize their 401k was 100% allocated to money market funds. Yikes.

#3: I have several articles on Google's first SERP. Who knew?

#4: When thinking of tipping people for a service, I doubt writers come to mind. Yet, there are ways writers can earn this form of income. While I'd heard of Buy Me a Coffee, I recently discovered another creative CTA for tips: Buy Me a Stock.

#5: No day is the same as a writer, but it's still good to have a routine.

Day 363: December 28, 2020 - 9:45 am (Monday)

Hmmm, I knew this name sounded familiar. John Gruber has appeared under my Top Recent Followers quite a few times.

◐	Medium Stats for your stories: Dec 18–Dec 25 followers: John Gruber (https://medium.com...	Dec 25
◐	Medium Stats for your stories: Nov 6–Nov 13 followers: John Gruber (https://medium.com...	Nov 13
◐	Medium Stats for your stories: Jul 17–Jul 24 followers: John Gruber (https://medium.com...	Jul 24
◐	Medium Stats for your stories: Apr 17–Apr 24 -writer_stats John Gruber (https://medium.c...	Apr 24
◐	Medium Bel Neo, Elharym Abdelkebir, and 5 others s... .users_following_you John Gruber (https://...	Apr 24

Does that indicate he's following and unfollowing? It's hard to say for sure because Medium isn't sending new follower pushes for him. But he keeps showing up in my weekly stats report.

The follow-unfollow strategy can work, it just feels deceptive. It's not an approach I ever plan to implement — or yield to. I follow writers that provide relevant and valuable content. If I think I can learn something from a writer, I follow them.

As a writer, I have to earn your follow — just as other writers have to earn mine.

Day 364: December 29, 2020 - 2:17 pm (Tuesday)

Just kidding, I haven't completed client work for the year. Client B has one last assignment for me.

I don't mind though. This assignment and a Medium resurgence will push my income past $3,000 for December. Considering I worked fewer hours and days, I'm happy with that figure.

I appreciate this time of year because it's become a regular vacation period, dating back to my time in banking. It's the most detached I feel from writing and my business, which is a strange feeling, but I think total detachment is beneficial. I can relax, turn my brain "off" for a while, and return revitalized.

11:39 pm

My goal of 1,000 Medium followers by year-end is a long shot, but at least I eclipsed 900.

Carter Kilmann

Member since Sep 2020

Freelance Writer & Editor | Personal Finance | Limitless Supplier of Spongebob & Family Guy quotes carter@carterkilmann.com

Editor of Bacon Bits and 365 Days of Freelance Writing

Top writer in Investing

21	900
Following	Followers

Day 365: December 30, 2020 - 12:07 pm (Wednesday)

It's been 365 days. A freaking YEAR. And we've got a bonus day tomorrow since 2020 is a leap year.

How on earth am I supposed to conclude my journey journal?

I think it's fitting to review my goals, right? I'll save the heartfelt sentiment for tomorrow.

2020	Goal	Actual	% Complete
Medium followers	1,000	915	91.5%
Bits subscribers	100	83	83.0%
365 DFW subscribers	100	10	10.0%
Daily entries	366	365	99.7%
Monthly income	$5,000	$7,150	143.0%
Annual income	$40,000	$34,980	87.5%

As the hours wind down, it looks like I'll only accomplish two of my writing goals for 2020: writing this book and earning more than $5,000 in one month. Thanks to one Medium post's late surge, I came close to hitting 1,000 Medium followers and

100 Bits subscribers — which is crazy since I haven't published a Bits newsletter in a couple of months — but I'm going to come up short.

Last but not least, I was a crisp Jackson short of $35,000 of income for the year. While $5,020 isn't exactly a slim margin, I'm pretty pleased considering I had only earned $18,949 through August. My last quarter was huge — I almost doubled my first eight months of income in the last four.

What about next year?

An excellent question. Here's what I'm thinking:

1. **5,000 Medium followers.** I'll have more time for Medium now that I've "finished" this book.
2. **2,000 email subscribers.** This might be far-fetched, but I plan to pay for marketing next year, which should help boost these numbers.
3. **Breakeven book sales.** I don't know how many copies I'll need to sell to break even, but I think it's a realistic goal.
4. **An eBook.** I mentioned this back on Day 212, but I have enough blog content to make an eBook.
5. **$48,000 annual income.** That would equate to $4,000 per month in 2021. If you annualize my Q4 income, I'd make $48,093...so it's doable.

Day 366: December 31, 2020 - 5:12 pm (Thursday)

Is it time for the inevitable, obligatory, and sentimental recap? I think so.

We've come full circle. My feet are back in the sand, except this time I'm sipping on a Michelob Ultra instead of a Corona. To celebrate the occasion, I decided to reread the first few days of this year-long journey. And, as you'd expect, nostalgia swept me away as I reminisced about the early days. It feels so recent, yet so much time has passed.

The thought of writing 366 entries was daunting.

I remember thinking, "How am I going to write something unique every single day?" You would know better than I would, but I think I refrained from being too repetitive.

But, funny enough, I also cringed while I went back through those first entries. My writing has come a long way in 2020. I suppose 80,000+ words (in this book alone) will do that, so shuddering at my old writing shouldn't come as too much of a surprise.

Looking back at the year, a few memories stick out. There was my first viral Medium post (Day 84). I was elated...and obsessed. I couldn't stop checking my stats, which probably wasn't good for productivity.

There were also a few instances of validation. Like the time when the CEO of Client E complimented my work (Day 161) or when a total stranger reached out just to say that my writing resonated with them (Day 282). I also became a "top writer" on Medium for the "Investing" tag — something I honestly never expected to accomplish (Day 330).

My proudest achievement? Easy. Surpassing my monthly banking salary in October (Day 304). That was a goal from the very beginning, and it's a milestone I'll never forget. It proved I can make a decent living doing something I enjoy.

Of course, there were tough times too. I experienced imposter syndrome (Day 33, Day 108, and Day 186). I broke up with a client (Day 35). I wrestled with my perfectionism and lost (Day 59). Clients dropped me due to the pandemic's economic fallout (Day 91 and Day 96). I dealt with hostile Medium responses (Day 145). I was rejected and ignored (too many to count).

But, all in all, the tough times were still worth it.

You know, it's funny — today doesn't feel like New Year's Eve or the final day of this book.

I mean, damn, I just wrote a **book**. *How bananas is that?*

I've said it before, but even if this venture totally bombs, I won't regret a thing. It's one of the cooler things I've done in my lifetime.

Hell, at the very least, when my future kids learn about the craziness of 2020 and ask what it was like, I can show them.

Now you know my story. Is it time to start yours?

DECEMBER STATS

2020 is in the books. My stat totals are locked in. *How exciting.*

December was a good month. I started being more productive with my time, which helped me take a vacation without feeling guilty or stressed. Oh, and the Packers went undefeated this month and secured the #1 seed in the NFC. That's tough to beat.

As a reminder, here's each client's description:

- Client A — Digital marketing agency
- Client B — Digital marketing agency (editing work)
- Client C — FinTech startup (no longer a client)
- Client D — Online finance publication (content freeze)
- Client E — Auto finance company
- Client F — ClearVoice assignments
- Client G — SaaS company (no longer a client, for now)
- Client H — Writing Revolt
- Client I — Consulting firm
- Client J — FinTech startup
- Client K — Digital marketing agency (copywriting)
- Client L — RV finance site
- Client M — Medium advertorial

365 Days of Freelancing - Monthly Stats

	Jan	Feb	Mar	Apr	May	Jun	Jul	Aug	Sep	Oct	Nov	Dec	Total
Income													
Client A	960	960	960	640	480	480	480	-	480	480	480	480	6,880
Client B	329	119	153	189	741	430	415	706	163	283	468	140	4,137
Client C	500	-	-	-	-	-	-	-	-	-	-	-	500
Client D	350	350	-	-	-	-	-	-	-	-	-	-	700
Client E	-	450	450	900	450	1,000	450	450	900	1,050	500	900	7,500
Client F	-	225	-	-	-	338	-	-	-	-	-	-	563
Client G	-	200	-	-	-	-	-	-	-	-	-	-	200
Client H	-	-	-	-	400	-	-	-	-	-	-	-	400
Client I	-	-	-	-	-	265	-	-	-	-	-	-	265
Client J	-	-	-	-	-	-	-	1,337	2,100	1,088	-	-	4,525
Client K	-	-	-	-	-	-	-	-	250	4,200	-	-	4,450
Client L	-	-	-	-	-	-	-	-	-	-	1,107	-	1,107
Client M	-	-	-	-	-	-	-	-	-	-	-	116	116
Medium	32	21	719	734	505	496	147	137	110	49	282	405	3,638
Total Income	**$2,171**	**$2,325**	**$2,282**	**$2,463**	**$2,576**	**$3,009**	**$1,492**	**$2,630**	**$4,003**	**$7,150**	**$1,730**	**$3,148**	**$34,980**
Growth (%)	-	7.1%	(1.9%)	7.9%	4.6%	16.8%	(50.4%)	76.2%	52.2%	78.6%	(75.8%)	81.9%	
Blog Posts (Paid)													
Client A	6	6	6	4	3	3	3	-	3	3	3	3	43
Client B	3	2	2	2	9	4	6	8	2	4	7	2	51
Client C	1	1	-	-	-	-	-	-	-	-	-	-	2
Client D	1	1	-	-	-	-	-	-	-	-	-	-	2
Client E	-	1	1	2	1	2	1	1	2	2	1	2	16
Client F	-	2	-	-	-	1	-	-	-	-	-	-	3
Client G	-	1	-	-	-	-	-	-	-	-	-	-	1
Client H	-	-	-	-	1	-	-	-	-	-	-	1	2
Client I	-	-	-	-	-	1	-	-	-	-	-	-	1
Client L	-	-	-	-	-	-	-	-	-	-	-	2	2
Total Paid Posts	**11**	**14**	**9**	**8**	**14**	**11**	**10**	**9**	**7**	**9**	**11**	**10**	**123**
Blog Posts (Unpaid)													
Medium	1	-	-	1	4	-	1	-	1	2	1	-	11
Bacon Bits	1	2	4	2	1	1	2	2	-	-	3	2	20
365	-	-	-	2	-	-	4	1	-	-	1	2	10
Total Unpaid Posts	**2**	**2**	**4**	**5**	**5**	**1**	**7**	**3**	**1**	**2**	**5**	**4**	**41**
Total Blog Posts	**13**	**16**	**13**	**13**	**19**	**12**	**17**	**12**	**8**	**11**	**16**	**14**	**164**
Copywriting Assignments													
Client C	5	-	-	-	-	-	-	-	-	-	-	-	5
Client J	-	-	-	-	-	-	-	3	2	2	-	-	7
Client K	-	-	-	-	-	-	-	-	1	12	-	-	13
Total Copywriting Asgns.	**5**	**-**	**-**	**-**	**-**	**-**	**-**	**3**	**3**	**14**	**-**	**-**	**25**
Total Assignments	**18**	**16**	**13**	**13**	**19**	**12**	**17**	**15**	**11**	**25**	**16**	**14**	**189**
Medium													
Views	1,151	1,352	19,466	11,052	15,778	8,562	4,552	4,945	3,522	1,906	10,705	10,714	93,705
Reads	439	468	7,413	4,220	6,320	3,651	1,947	2,055	1,438	776	6,077	5,710	40,514
Read Ratio	38%	35%	38%	38%	40%	43%	43%	42%	41%	41%	57%	53%	43%
Existing Followers	54	63	80	238	371	530	595	645	702	733	745	831	54
New Followers	9	17	158	133	159	65	50	57	31	12	86	91	868
Total Followers	**63**	**80**	**238**	**371**	**530**	**595**	**645**	**702**	**733**	**745**	**831**	**922**	**922**
LinkedIn													
Existing Followers	458	465	493	526	570	590	599	613	624	637	642	653	458
New Followers	7	28	33	44	20	9	14	11	13	5	11	16	211
Total Followers	**465**	**493**	**526**	**570**	**590**	**599**	**613**	**624**	**637**	**642**	**653**	**669**	**669**

December Highlights

- December introduced a new regular source of work: Client L. They pay $0.35 per word, which has equated to about $550 per assignment thus far. My point-of-contact said he'll have an assignment for me every two weeks or so, which bolsters my income stability going forward.
- Thanks to the addition of Client L, I closed the year on a high note. While $3,148 might not seem like much, I only eclipsed $3,000 four times in 2020, so that's a win in my book.

2020 Highlights

- My inner financial analyst loves digging into data, so here are some interesting stats:
    - 96% of my total income was recurring. In other words, one-time opportunities (e.g. Client C in January) only represented 4% of my income ($1,481).
    - 89% of my income came from six sources: five clients and Medium.
    - Only 13% of my total assignments were copywriting projects; however, these projects accounted for 27% of my income.
- It was my first full year writing for Medium, so I don't have a point of comparison, but I'm thrilled with my final numbers. I published 41 posts. I had 93,705 views and 40,514 reads, equating to a 43% read ratio. I also gained 868 new followers, bringing me to 922 — just short of my 1,000 follower goal for 2020.
- While I didn't prioritize it as much, my LinkedIn following grew by 46% in 2020.

Lastly, as promised, here's an overview of my implied hourly work rate in December:

Client	Project	Completed	Payment	Hours	Implied Hourly Rate
Client B	Edits	12/3/2020	79.17	1.58	50.00
Client L	Blog Post	12/4/2020	584.85	9.07	64.51
Client A	Blog Post	12/10/2020	160.00	2.35	68.09
Client A	Blog Post	12/10/2020	160.00	1.82	88.07
Client M	Blog Post	12/11/2020	116.00	4.25	23.53
Client A	Blog Post	12/16/2020	160.00	2.23	71.64
Client L	Blog Post	12/17/2020	523.60	4.47	117.22
Client E	Blog Post	12/24/2020	450.00	4.10	109.76
Client E	Blog Post	12/24/2020	450.00	5.15	87.38
Client B	Edits	12/31/2020	60.83	1.50	40.56
			$2,744.45	36.52	$75.16

AFTERWORD

Want to know how this whole thing started?

"Write a blurb once a day for a year. Covers the emotional journey, day-to-day ops, thought process of a business, etc."

That's what I scribbled down when I first thought of writing this book.

The idea was simple: provide transparent insights into the life of a freelance writer. By supplying comprehensive and honest accounts of my day-to-day journey, I wanted to help aspiring writers answer a life-changing question:

"Is freelance writing for me?"

I've sought my own answer to this question over the last year, and I can emphatically and wholeheartedly say, "Yes."

Before we part ways, I'd like to thank you. A writer is nothing without a reader.

And I hope you enjoyed the ride.

If you want to stay in touch or you have more questions, you're welcome to join the Facebook community: 365 Days of Freelance Writing. If you're having trouble finding it, feel free to email me at carter@carterkilmann.com.

CITATIONS

1. Steingold, David. "How to Form a Single-Member LLC." *Www.Nolo.Com*, 9 July 2020, www.nolo.com/legal-encyclopedia/forming-single-member-llc-important-tasks.html.
2. *Medium*. medium.com.
3. "Getting Started with the Medium Partner Program." *Medium*, help.medium.com/hc/en-us/articles/115011694187-Getting-started-with-the-Medium-Partner-Program.
4. Kilmann, Carter. "Bacon Bits." *Medium*, medium.com/bacon-bits.
5. *ClearVoice*. www.clearvoice.com.
6. *Write Jobs*. www.writejobs.info.
7. *FreelanceWriting*. www.freelancewriting.com/newsletters/morning-coffee-jobs-newsletter.
8. *Freedom With Writing Magazine*. www.freedomwithwriting.com.
9. Ebert, Manuel. "The Most Dangerous Writing App." *MDWA*, www.squibler.io/dangerous-writing-prompt-app.
10. Klettke, Joel. "Sales Trainings." *Business Casual Copywriting*, businesscasualcopywriting.com/sales-trainings/?fbclid=IwAR1rEypUn6hEppBzx_7iSbWuU6PSx4w-zcbItRxRmsgyv1wTYtfBOZCId3o.

11. Campbell, Meg. "Prune Juice & Diarrhea." livestrong.com, 9 Nov. 2018, www.livestrong.com/article/462356-prune-juice-diarrhea.
12. *Work Notes.* worknotes.co.uk.
13. Wu, Jun. "Top Writer Status On - Jun Wu Blog." *Medium*, 15 May 2019, medium.com/jun-wu-blog/top-writer-status-on-medium-162ad0e1a3c1.
14. Kilmann, Carter. "How I Cut My Monthly Expenses by 32% - Bacon Bits." *Medium*, 4 Mar. 2020, medium.com/bacon-bits/how-i-cut-my-monthly-expenses-by-32-5bb76bcff4ae.
15. "Write Better Headlines: Headline Analyzer." *CoSchedule*, coschedule.com/headline-analyzer.
16. Enubuje, Matthew. "Getting 30,000 Views in 1 Year Explained in 7 Minutes | Better Marketing." *Medium*, 23 Mar. 2020, bettermarketing.pub/how-i-got-30-000-views-in-my-first-year-on-medium-77c3cf5bffc8.
17. Crowley, Richie. "The Strategy I Used to Write My First $6,000 Story - Better Marketing." *Medium*, 16 Jan. 2020, bettermarketing.pub/the-strategy-i-used-to-write-my-first-6-000-story-69bf209c9d9e.
18. Kilmann, Carter. "The Sexiest 15-Minute Budget - Bacon Bits." *Medium*, 20 Dec. 2019, medium.com/bacon-bits/the-sexiest-15-minute-budget-f14e46434f6f.
19. *I Just Realized Something.* Ijustrealizedsomething.com.
20. *Canva.* www.canva.com.
21. Cain, Elna. "WriteTo1k - Write Your Way to Your First $1k – Freelance Writing Course." *Write Your Way to 1k*, writeto1k.com/?tb_affcode=109377_vr8zccwu.
22. Kilmann, Carter. "How to Invest When You Know Nothing About Investing." *Medium*, 8 Apr. 2020, medium.com/bacon-bits/how-to-invest-when-you-know-nothing-about-investing-a9d510240c71.
23. *Killer Cold Emailing.* www.killercoldemailing.com.
24. "Writing Revolters." *Facebook*, www.facebook.com/groups/writing-revolters-556133661229336.

25. Kilmann, Carter. "How to Take Advantage of the Down Market Before It Rebounds." *Medium*, 10 Apr. 2020, medium.com/bacon-bits/how-to-take-advantage-of-the-down-market-before-it-rebounds-b1df19495754.
26. "Medium's Distribution Standards: What Writers and Publications Need to Know." *Medium*, help.medium.com/hc/en-us/articles/360006362473-Medium-s-Distribution-Standards-What-Writers-and-Publications-Need-to-Know.
27. *Monday.com*. Monday.com
28. *Veem*. www.veem.com.
29. Kilmann, Carter. "4 Financial Tasks You Need to Prioritize as a Freelancer." *Medium*, 13 Feb. 2020, https://medium.com/bacon-bits/4-financial-tasks-you-need-to-prioritize-as-a-freelancer-8a7dfea7b291.
30. Kilmann, Carter. "'Tell Me About a Time You Failed' - The Startup." *Medium*, 28 Jan. 2020, medium.com/swlh/tell-me-about-a-time-you-failed-498235cc368d.
31. Kilmann, Carter. "365 Days of Freelance Writing." *Medium*, https://medium.com/365-days-of-freelancing.
32. Kilmann, Carter. "How I Think I Earned $1,250+ With One Post - 365 Days of Freelance Writing." *Medium*, 27 Apr. 2020, medium.com/365-days-of-freelancing/how-i-think-i-earned-1-250-with-one-post-bb50d4dd27f6.
33. Kilmann, Carter. "My Peace of Mind Cracked Today - Curiosity Never Killed the Writer." *Medium*, 3 May 2020, curiosityneverkilledthewriter.com/my-peace-of-mind-cracked-today-c2fb04bdcc67.
34. Kilmann, Carter. "How I Landed 3 Clients in My First Week of Self-Employment." *Medium*, 6 May 2020, bettermarketing.pub/how-i-landed-3-clients-in-my-first-week-of-self-employment-14cd080baad.
35. *Writing Revolt*. www.writingrevolt.com.
36. Kilmann, Carter. "Monopoly: Board Game or Our Current Reality? - Bacon Bits." *Medium*, 8 May 2020, medium.com/bacon-bits/monopoly-board-game-or-our-current-reality-1bcce58327ae.

37. "[SERIOUS] How to Teach Yourself Copywriting." Reddit, www.reddit.com/r/copywriting/comments/feazdp/serious_how_to_teach_yourself_copywriting.
38. Medium Creators. "Finding New Routines - 3 Min Read." *Medium*, 11 May 2020, blog.medium.com/finding-new-routines-f8ec1c159583.
39. *Substack*. substack.com.
40. Kilmann, Carter. "The 90% Economy: Indefinitely Temporary? - The Startup." *Medium*, 26 May 2020, medium.com/swlh/the-90-economy-indefinitely-temporary-53046140ec3d.
41. Kilmann, Carter "What's Going On With the Stock Market? - Bacon Bits." *Medium*, 8 June 2020, medium.com/bacon-bits/whats-going-on-with-the-stock-market-f7c0d0c22b29.
42. Medium Creators. "Showing up: Learning, Writing, and Taking Action - 3 Min Read." *Medium*, 12 June 2020, blog.medium.com/showing-up-learning-writing-and-taking-action-434d36f51dfb.
43. Denning, Tim. "The Blueprint I Gave My Friend Who Wants to Be a Writer." *Medium*, 16 June 2020, bettermarketing.pub/the-blueprint-i-gave-my-friend-who-wants-to-be-a-writer-30ebd95b8138.
44. *Rev.* www.rev.com/freelancers.
45. Campaign Monitor. "What Are the Average Click and Read Rates For Email Campaigns?" *Campaign Monitor*, www.campaignmonitor.com/resources/knowledge-base/what-are-the-average-click-and-read-rates-for-email-campaigns.
46. Kilmann, Carter. "How to Save an Extra $4,187 in the Next 6 Months - Bacon Bits." *Medium*, 1 Jul. 2020, medium.com/bacon-bits/how-to-save-an-extra-4-187-in-the-next-6-months-3138865be291.
47. Kilmann, Carter. "How to Charge More Based on Urgency - Better Marketing." *Medium*, 2 July 2020, bettermarketing.pub/how-to-charge-more-based-on-urgency-12fa0debf061.
48. Owen, Laura Hazard. "The Long, Complicated, and Extremely Frustrating History of Medium, 2012–Present."

Nieman Lab, 25 Mar. 2019, www.niemanlab.org/2019/03/the-long-complicated-and-extremely-frustrating-history-of-medium-2012-present.
49. Gaon, Jared. "How I Grew a Twitter Account to 40,000 Followers in 2 Days." *Medium*, 8 July 2020, bettermarketing.pub/how-i-broke-the-internet-with-some-help-from-michael-jordan-e14fefed6983.
50. Denning, Tim. "How I Write 20,000 Words in a Single Day - Better Marketing." *Medium*, 13 July 2020, bettermarketing.pub/how-i-write-20-000-words-in-a-single-day-c65cf525e02d.
51. Kahneman, D., and A. Deaton. "High Income Improves Evaluation of Life but Not Emotional Well-Being." *Proceedings of the National Academy of Sciences*, vol. 107, no. 38, 2010, pp. 16489–93. Crossref, doi:10.1073/pnas.1011492107.
52. Jebb, A.T., Tay, L., Diener, E. et al. Happiness, income satiation and turning points around the world. *Nat Hum Behav* 2, 33–38 (2018). https://doi.org/10.1038/s41562-017-0277-0
53. Parmar, Amardeep. "A Statistical Breakdown of $4,345 in 6 Months On." *Medium*, 23 July 2021, bettermarketing.pub/a-statistical-breakdown-of-4-345-in-6-months-on-medium-9a8811baf579.
54. A Purple Life. "$500,000 at 30: I Hit My FIRE Number!" *A Purple Life*, 23 July 2020, apurplelife.com/2020/07/23/500000-at-30-i-hit-my-fire-number.
55. Kilmann, Carter. "Freelance Finances: The Ultimate Guide to Managing Money!" *Writing Revolt*, 3 Aug. 2020, www.writingrevolt.com/freelance-finances.
56. Kilmann, Carter. "How to Protect Your Investments With Stop Losses - Bacon Bits." *Medium*, 6 Aug. 2020, medium.com/bacon-bits/how-to-protect-your-investments-with-stop-losses-bbfcbff4ed72.
57. *Upwork*. www.upwork.com.
58. Okona, Nneka. "Two Exes Wasted My Time. So I Sent Them Invoices. - ZORA." *Medium*, 7 Aug. 2020, zora.medium.com/two-exes-wasted-my-time-so-i-sent-them-invoices-ec6d2cc6a272.

59. *Hunter.* Hunter.io.
60. Powers, Bobby. "30 Things I've Figured Out About How Medium Works (and 5 Questions I Still Have)." *Medium*, 13 Mar. 2020, bettermarketing.pub/30-things-ive-figured-out-about-how-medium-works-and-5-questions-i-still-have-6829de3b1076.
61. Denning, Tim. "Be Aware of the Quiet Ones like Keanu Reeves — They Are the Ones That Actually Make You Think." *Medium*, 2 June 2021, medium.com/mind-cafe/be-aware-of-the-quiet-ones-like-keanu-reeves-they-are-the-ones-that-actually-make-you-think-de7c8f814d04.
62. Denning, Tim. "Reverse Engineer Your Life to Work for You - Ascent Publication." *Medium*, 19 Aug. 2020, medium.com/the-ascent/reverse-engineer-your-life-to-work-for-you-e62ba6f6ae91.
63. Wikipedia contributors. "Julian Calendar." *Simple English Wikipedia, the Free Encyclopedia*, simple.wikipedia.org/wiki/Julian_calendar.
64. *Ludwig.* ludwig.guru.
65. Lake, Rebecca. "California Assembly Bill 5 (AB5) Definition." Investopedia, www.investopedia.com/california-assembly-bill-5-ab5-4773201.
66. Rane, Zulie. "Two Years, $30k, and 507 Articles on Medium. Here's What I've Learned." *Medium*, 15 Sept. 2020, bettermarketing.pub/two-years-30k-and-507-articles-on-medium-heres-what-i-ve-learned-24f3b8ef689f?source=linkShare-8a4d5f49d78b-1600434698.
67. Kuegler, Tom. "I 'Wasted' 3 Years Hustling Like Gary Vee — Was It Worth It?" *Medium*, 7 Aug. 2020, medium.com/the-post-grad-survival-guide/i-wasted-3-years-hustling-like-gary-vee-was-it-worth-it-10c52f54eafd.
68. Black, Sarah N. "Sarah Noel Block | Content Marketing Strategist + Copywriter." *Medium*, 10 July 2018, medium.com/sarah-noel-block-content-marketing-strategist.
69. Lopez, Itxy. "A Breakdown of My Earnings From the Past 14 Months - Better Marketing." *Medium*, 6 Oct. 2020,

bettermarketing.pub/a-breakdown-of-my-earnings-from-the-past-14-months-9d686a0a5422.
70. *Swipe-Worthy*. Swiped.co
71. Kilmann, Carter. "How Quickly Can You Make $1,000,000 by Investing? - Bacon Bits." *Medium*, 10 Nov. 2020, medium.com/bacon-bits/how-quickly-can-you-make-1-000-000-by-investing-7bc3731a8111.
72. "HubSpot Academy - Certifications." *Hubspot*, academy.hubspot.com/certification-overview.
73. Rane, Zulie. "4 Lessons From My Full-Time Freelance Writing Income Report | The Post-Grad Survival Guide." *Medium*, 4 Dec. 2020, medium.com/the-post-grad-survival-guide/4-lessons-i-learned-from-my-fulltime-freelance-writing-income-report-929982304173.
74. "SEP Contribution Limits (Including Grandfathered SARSEPs) | Internal Revenue Service." *IRS*, www.irs.gov/retirement-plans/plan-participant-employee/sep-contribution-limits-including-grandfathered-sarseps.
75. Grimes, Shaunta. "How to Overcome Perfectionism and Just Write the Thing." *Medium*, 7 Oct. 2020, medium.com/the-write-brain/how-to-overcome-perfectionism-and-just-write-the-thing-a45636570643.
76. Kuegler, Tom. "Your Blog Posts Don't Always Need To Be That Long, Okay?" *Medium*, 16 Dec. 2020, medium.com/finding-tom/your-blog-posts-dont-always-need-to-be-that-long-okay-3155845c9d5f.
77. *Buy Me a Stock*. www.buymeastock.com.

INDEX

Unlike a traditional index, the following terms and concepts are organized by **day**. For example, I explained "Canva" on Day 97. I've also tried to make this index less cluttered by only referencing days that share valuable insights about the corresponding term. For example, I referenced Medium throughout this book, but I've limited the below references to entries that contain applicable lessons and guidance.

Advertorial – 335

Amardeep Parmar – 206

Bobby Powers – 233

Book publishing – 339, 358

Bookmarks – 236

Business tips – 19, 214, 259, 268, 274

Canva – 97

ClearVoice – 24, 81, 171

Client acquisition – 1, 3, 6, 27, 33, 37, 39, 40, 41, 49, 154, 196, 214, 227, 230, 234, 275, 329

Client calls – 39

Client issues – 7, 10, 35, 76, 87, 91, 93, 96, 168, 213, 238, 240, 280, 293, 295, 302, 316, 328, 334, 336

Coffee – 32, 36, 58, 79, 127, 357

Cold pitching – 48, 99, 112, 113, 125, 128, 140, 294

Copyediting – 150

Copywriting – 114, 131, 132, 236, 253, 286, 289

Cornelius Schmeckleman – 96

Coworking – 22

Ebook – 212

Elna Cain – 98

Email list building – 79

Firing a client – 35
Following up – 33
Gaming Nexus – 139
Gig economy – 252
Goal setting – 69, 133, 148, 205, 211, 304, 306, 365
Graphic design – 97
Guest posts – 8, 128, 165
Happiness – 205
Headlines – 84, 307, 337
Health insurance – 38, 313, 317
HubSpot – 332
Hunter.io – 227
Imposter syndrome – 33, 56, 59
Inbound marketing – 39
Itxy Lopez – 281
Joel Klettke – 39
Jorden Makelle – 99, 216, 274
Killer Cold Emailing – 99
LinkedIn – 70, 83, 88, 125, 203, 217, 315, 324
Losing a client – 91, 96
Ludwig – 248
Mailchimp – 138, 149, 158
Matthew Berry – 264
Medium guidelines – 101
Medium publications – 115, 165, 169
Medium tags – 330
Medium tips – 2, 68, 90, 101, 115, 141, 168, 170, 183, 203, 206, 209, 232, 233, 261, 303, 320, 322, 323, 330, 335, 363

Monday.com – 103, 110
Money – 7, 87, 93, 122, 124, 156, 175, 193, 247, 260, 261, 288, 289, 298, 300, 302, 341, 355
Negative criticism – 145, 162, 164, 323
Networking – 14, 15, 29, 37, 65
Outlines – 64, 191, 193
Outsourcing – 173, 348, 349
Overloading – 10, 66
Patreon – 94, 116, 138, 158, 159
PayPal – 355
Perfectionism – 59, 178, 191, 352
Personal finance – 156
Pitching – 93, 214
Portfolio – 24, 127, 211, 273, 332
Post length – 183
Productivity playlists – 9, 105
Productivity tips – 9, 45, 47, 179
Psychological obstacles – 11, 22, 33, 56, 124, 246, 247, 257, 267, 271, 284, 287, 309
Publishing – 162
Quora – 307
Radio silence – 185, 328, 334
Rates – 7, 24, 41, 49, 78, 102, 142, 147, 163, 168, 260, 289, 298, 303, 329, 340, 346
Reading time – 183
Red flags – 35, 48, 49
Reddit – 132
Rejection – 111, 166, 185, 231, 350
Repurposing content – 203, 212

INDEX

Rev.com – 175

Runway – 156

Self-doubt – 162, 186, 187, 220

Self-publishing – 115, 118, 123, 135, 140, 141, 147, 152

Service agreements – 46

Shaunta Grimes – 352

Squibler – 28, 249

Substack – 138, 158, 159, 161, 179, 189, 219

Swipe-Worthy – 286

Tim Denning – 108, 196, 203, 233

Time management – 4, 6, 16, 21, 43, 45, 54, 55, 80, 103, 163, 171, 190, 191, 196

Time off – 155

Time tracking – 342, 343, 346, 351, 359

Tom Kuegler – 268, 352

Twitter – 65

Upwork – 222, 225

Vacation – 250, 254

Veem – 107, 355

Warm pitching – 129

Website – 273, 274

White papers – 102

Writeto1k – 98

Writing gig newsletters – 27, 166

Writing gigs – 154

Writing resources – 28, 97, 98, 99, 103, 248

Writing tips – 12, 64, 98, 104, 107, 157, 184, 190, 191, 192, 196, 202, 230, 259, 260, 352

YouTube scripts – 281, 289

Zulie Rane – 261, 340

Printed in Great Britain
by Amazon